T0195886

FREEDOM IS NOT FREE

REFLECTIONS ON MORAL AND
INTELLECTUAL GROWTH IN A FREE SOCIETY

ALEX ADAMS

authorHOUSE®

AuthorHouse™
1663 Liberty Drive
Bloomington, IN 47403
www.authorhouse.com
Phone: 833-262-8899

Published by AuthorHouse 10/11/2021

ISBN: 978-1-6655-4021-6 (sc)
ISBN: 978-1-6655-4020-9 (hc)
ISBN: 978-1-6655-4032-2 (e)

Library of Congress Control Number: 2021920423

For Marion, Marky, Lois, and Frances

PREFACE

To laugh often and love much; to win the respect of intelligent
persons and the affection of children; to earn the approbation of
honest citizens and endure the betrayal of false friends; to appreciate
beauty; to find the best in others; to give of one's self; to leave
the world a bit better, whether by a healthy child, a garden patch
or a redeemed social condition; to have played and laughed with
enthusiasm and sung with exultation; to know even one life has
breathed easier because you have lived—this is to have succeeded.
                                              —Ralph Waldo Emerson

For all of my adult life, I have kept this quote in mind. I have always
aspired to live a successful life—a life I can look back on with pride and
a sense of having done my little part to make the world a better place.
This quote does as good a job of describing such a life as I have seen
anywhere. I write this memoir as a chronicle of my attempts to live a
successful life—as a career scientist and engineer and as a participant in
the remedying of injustices. I relate what drove me to make the choices
I made and what actions I took to make my career, my volunteer work,
and my political activities as consonant as possible with this aspiration.
But it is an aspiration only—a work in progress forever unfinished, never
an achievement to admire.

Though I did not originally choose my career paths with a view to
improving mankind's lot or aiding my own betterment, nevertheless,
my careers played a role in these endeavors. But these considerations
were significant in my choices of political causes and volunteer efforts. I
believe some of the adventures and missteps accompanying my pursuits
will resonate with many people, particularly my fellow scientists and

engineers. They might recognize themselves in various parts of the story, or they might see alternate ways to deal with the problems they encounter in their lives. I hope they may get ideas about how our country is faring and how to prosper in their careers in this turbulent twenty-first century. Some entertainment may even appear here and there!

The commentary on the American and world scenes illustrates my own evolution, whose highlights I would like to share. My intent here is to analyze and discuss the good, the bad, and the ugly aspects of human behavior and to come to conclusions about how our country arrived at its present state, where it is likely to head, what made me who I am, and how I should order my life. Many warnings appear about how disorderly and excruciating human life can become in the absence of freedom and human dignity when people are enslaved or allowed to revert to their precivilization ways.

This journey would have been difficult without national liberty; it would have been impossible without liberty within myself. Some sort of liberty is vital for any moral or intellectual maturation. I emphasize this point repeatedly throughout the narrative because I have seen many illustrations of the deleterious effect that lack of liberty has on human character and human conditions. Recognizing that many people have difficulty in managing freedom, I nevertheless caution everyone against authoritarian government in all forms everywhere, because it stunts the growth of individuals who have the capacity to evolve and because its limited ability to adapt in a dynamic environment inevitably corrupts and incapacitates it over time.

Being my first attempt at writing for publication, this exercise accorded me invaluable lessons and practice in organization of my thoughts and materials, precision in word choice, precise thinking about my topics, and fact-checking of my statements. In this process, I discovered many issues about which I have strong feelings, but expression of those feelings would be inappropriate in this book. Either my language is too intemperate for the audience, or the issue itself is not germane to anything in my story; thus, the issue is better omitted. I have acquainted myself with the art of pruning my prose; too many words can slow down the narrative more than they add to the presentation. Had I progressed far enough in graduate school to write a dissertation, I would have undergone this training in writing tracts for others to read much earlier in life. But I am grateful for this opportunity now.

The conclusions I set forth are certainly debatable, and some may even be refutable. But they are my own, and I cite numerous sources to lend them weight. I invite input from all parties; all I ask is honest and evidence-based debate.

ACKNOWLEDGMENTS

I would like to thank my partner, Frances Pratt, for her tireless efforts and helpful suggestions in reorganizing my narrative and cleaning out excess words. She also located the AuthorHouse publishing concern to polish and market my product.

INTRODUCTION

This memoir is partly a narrative of attempted character development and partly a panegyric to liberty. I have been fortunate to live in a free society all my life, and I have developed a profound devotion to my own liberty and to societies and nations that provide it. Such nations contain people who lead happier, healthier, and more productive lives than the inhabitants of authoritarian nations. National liberty and personal liberty form the most fortunate combination for any individual.

By *personal liberty* in an individual, I mean the independence, initiative, and intellectual energy to develop self-awareness; the capacity for honest and competent assessment of one's society; respect for facts and truth; and the willingness to take charge of one's own life and to find a way to play a fulfilling and meaningful role within society. Personal liberty includes an awareness that one has, or should have, rights and liberties provided by society, along with a resolve to exercise those rights and liberties, and a concept of rule of law, through which one voluntarily disciplines oneself to observe the laws and social rules and accept the responsibilities that stabilize law-governed societies. Also important is tolerance for differences in outlook, character, and origin of all people and all circumstances compatible with a law-based society. This tolerance is especially important in large, diverse countries, such as the United States, whose many ethnic and religious groups provide wide opportunity for intolerant people to foment civil conflict and lawlessness and threaten the destruction of national liberty itself. Most importantly, personal liberty entails the capacity and willingness to recognize and resist authoritarianism in any and all of its guises. This resistance must never degenerate into anarchy, nihilism, or alternate forms of authoritarianism.

I believe that people who lack personal liberty are psychologically bound to a passive role, whatever their external environment. Such people will never lead significant or even interesting lives. Seeking the dull, vacuous safety of a life closely supervised by a strong master—whether a dictatorial political leader, a religious cult leader, an angry and thin-skinned God, a domineering spouse, or a strictly defined political or religious creed—these individuals accept or even crave an overlord who makes all of their rules for them. Lacking the initiative to take charge of their lives or even to be major actors in their lives, they reject opportunities for leaving their haven in order to live and achieve. The life of any person who lacks personal liberty can be comprehensively described in a short biography: "He was alive. He is dead."

It is possible to possess personal liberty in a free, law-based society or in a lawless or slave society. In a free society, the individual with personal liberty will feel comfortable, as he is compatible with his surroundings. In a nonfree society, this individual will have a hard time of it, as he will be persecuted and reviled by his fellows and often punished severely by his government. Those who maintain their personal liberty under these circumstances are to be most admired, since they love liberty enough to suffer adversity for it.

It is also possible to lack personal liberty in a free or a nonfree society. In a nonfree society, such individuals feel comfortable, as they are in their natural environment, with a strong leader shepherding them closely. They will attribute any maltreatment or persecution by their government to their own misbehavior or to an inscrutable fate. In a free society, these people will live in external freedom but in a state of psychological unease. Removal of their shackles and cages benefits them not at all since they have no idea how to navigate after being liberated. They may passively, and often apprehensively, await direction and guidance, never able to decide which way to turn until a more independent individual points out the path for them. Alternatively, they may dash about anarchically in total disregard of other people, disrupting their surroundings, until forced into acceptable behavior. In either case, they eventually construct an authoritarian setting for themselves, finding peace and calm as the fetters are applied.[1]

Closely allied with personal liberty, though not identical to it, is good character. I have compiled a list of traits I believe adequately describe good character. These traits are the four cardinal virtues (moderation, good judgment, a keen sense of justice, and courage); the golden rule ("Do unto others as you would have them do unto you"); consideration and empathy for the feelings, outlook, autonomy, equality, and humanity of all other people, whatever their race, nation, religion, or sexual identity, and the recognition that they all have an equal entitlement to life, liberty, and the opportunity for fulfillment; and the many biblical verses exhorting one to avoid violence, malice, gossip, envy, one-upmanship, and deceit and to embrace tolerance, love, kindness, patience, and forgiveness and get along with everybody to the extent that this is in one's own power.[2] These rules are absolute and context-independent; they must be applied to everyone with whom one comes into contact—strangers, family, and friends alike. There are no exclusions based on defining personal characteristics, such as age, economic status, race, religion, national origin, handicapped status, gender, or sexual orientation.

Some humility about one's own fallibility is essential to good character; one must always be open to changing one's mind or to learning new truths about any issue upon the introduction of new data or well-reasoned argument—not from political calculation but from facts relevant to the issue. The ability to admit and correct mistakes is essential; one must be able to fail and recover as well as succeed and prosper, seeing each scenario as instructive in finding the way forward.

The effect of good and bad fortune on a person's behavior can serve as a broad indicator of the quality of his character. A person of high character rejoices in other people's good fortune. He is empathetic to other people's ordeals, and his own good fortune makes him generous. His suffering sensitizes him to the suffering of others and motivates in him a desire to try to ameliorate their conditions. Suffering teaches him about himself and about the world. His ordeals can become occasions to improve his character.

A person of low character lives for himself alone. Other people's good fortune may sometimes elicit envy or vengefulness; their misfortunes do not impinge at all. He regards his own good fortune as no more than his just due; he is indifferent to how his acquisitiveness affects other people. He regards his grievances as the worst in the world, eclipsing the misfortunes of everybody else at all times and places. His triumphs and trials change and teach him nothing.

The descriptive traits of personal liberty and good character are obviously interwoven. That is why I have come to understand that personal liberty and character development go together—they are joined at the hip, so to speak. It is not possible to have only good character without personal liberty or vice versa. A deficiency in one virtue neutralizes the other virtue. For instance, personal liberty with deficient character is defiant and self-absorbed. An example is the antimask "freedom fighters" of the COVID-19 era, who regarded the wearing of contagion-inhibiting masks as an infringement on their liberty. Their refusal to consider the peril that their actions inflicted on others marked them as low in character—and lacking in personal liberty, since they failed to use their liberties responsibly. Good character with deficient personal liberty is passive and ineffectual, like many of the Russian dissidents of the Soviet era. They sincerely wanted to be good to other people and build a better society, but because of their timidity and reluctance to be active players, they never got around to taking the necessary risks and steps, and they ended by not benefiting anyone. The traits defining each virtue overlap massively, with some of the component traits belonging rather more appropriately to one virtue than the other. Personal liberty traits mainly provide guides for physical and economic interaction with one's circumstances, and good character traits mainly provide guides for social and psychological interaction with other people.

A vital component of free societies is a generous contingent of citizens with good character and personal liberty. These people stabilize the society by behaving with justice, honesty, courtesy, and consideration toward all their fellow humans. They challenge and fend off authoritarians who would impose their personal rule. They do not shrink from telling the truth, regardless of what others want to hear. They are willing to sacrifice their own advancement and even well-being to advance liberty and justice. Perhaps most importantly, they serve as role models to whom others can point and say, "There goes a good person! Try to behave that way!"

Conversely, people who lack character and personal liberty are vital to any tyranny. Clearly, personal liberty is anathema to a despot since people possessing this quality would be continually resisting him and calling him to account. The despot himself has no personal liberty because he can't comprehend the rule of law and limited authority. But dictatorships also inevitably erode the character of the dictator and those living under him. A dictator must encourage low character in all with whom he relates, thus confirming his own domination over those he rules. A dictator requires strife and suspicion, along with greed, envy, and untrustworthiness, among his subjects since he may thereby induce people to serve him at the expense of those they dislike and distrust. People who are at war with each other will never combine in order to harm or oust him. A dictator relies heavily on people whose life goals are material awards and titles; by having control over those resources, he can control those who dedicate their lives to attaining these baubles.[3] A dictator benefits from those who reject absolutes in knowledge and virtue and imagine they can choose for themselves what is true and what is good. By intimidating such people or gaining their fond allegiance, the dictator can control them by imposing upon them his own outlook and behavior as epitomes of truth and righteousness.[4] His degraded subjects, paid handsomely by him, carry out his dirty work industriously and resourcefully. They keep their leader apprised of all subversive activity, and they willingly act as his enforcers.

I have observed many dismal dramas played out after the attempted forcing of freedom on people who have never acquired good character or personal liberty. Freedom and rule of law cannot long endure without understanding and appreciation of these two virtues by the majority of the public. A large mass of people who are deficient in these virtues can easily drive a free country into despotism, particularly if the institutions that uphold the country's freedoms, such as a free press, a sturdy independent judiciary, and separation of powers within the government, are weakly rooted.[5]

The United States has always had a contingent of people who are thus deficient. They have formed political or religious cults on innumerable occasions. Indeed, they have occasionally been successful in establishing dictatorial systems within the United States, most notably in the slaveholding and segregationist southeastern corner of the country before the passage of voting rights laws in the 1960s. They have occasionally directly threatened the institutions of freedom in this country, particularly during the ascendancy of Donald Trump. But so far, they have never attained sufficient critical mass to force dictatorship at the national level, and hopefully that will always be so.

So how did personal liberty and good character become a large part of the human story? I believe that both nature and nurture play a role in the formation of each individual. A book by Rick Shenkman[6] argues from an anthropological standpoint that the traits described for personal liberty and good character are evolutions resulting from humans abandoning the Pleistocene hunter-gatherer nomad life some thousands of years ago and settling down into cities.

A more historical view is promulgated by Joseph Henrich[7] and by an article in *Science* magazine,[8] wherein the authors argue that the influence of the early medieval Catholic church in Western Europe inculcated what is called WEIRD psychology (Western, educated, industrialized, rich, and democratic)—characteristic of Western Europeans and North Americans who had extensive contact with the Western Christian civilization and religions. These sources contrast WEIRD psychology (independence, self-reliance, skepticism of authority, physical and economic mobility, and cooperation with strangers) with kinship-based psychology (obedience and conformity, strong ties to family, dependence, static lifestyle, and hostility to strangers). Henrich argues that political and economic freedom, representative and accountable government, and technological innovation were all outgrowths of the emergence of WEIRD psychology. Among the aspects of WEIRD behavior are concepts of individual liberty, personal responsibility and initiative, and personal property rights; judgment of individuals by their character rather than by their relationships with other members of their tribe; cooperation and trust toward anonymous strangers, such as bank managers and government officials; rule of law rather than of tribal elders; and a sense of civic duty to a large, anonymous body politic. WEIRD psychology, in short, appears to encompass personal liberty and good character.

However this human psychological evolution came about (and

it probably arose from combinations of these and other factors), the concepts of good character traits and good morals are most likely very recent in the scope of the entire human story. Since we were hunter-gatherers for the first 99 percent of our million-year sojourn on Earth, we remain heavily Pleistocene. We retain and pass down to our descendants, through genetic predispositions and childhood training, many of our Pleistocene behavioral patterns. Kinship-based behaviors, such as tribal loyalties, racism, limited empathy for strangers, and so forth, were well suited to maintain the stability of small, autonomous, nomadic bands of hunter-gatherers competing with other bands for resources. But these traits are maladaptive in modern societies, which consist of large, dynamic, heterogeneous aggregates of independent-minded and self-starting individuals.

I have dwelled at length on the definitions and ramifications of personal liberty and good character because they play a central role in the recounting of my journey. They are cited in many episodes, and they can be inferred from many others. Without these virtues, intellectual and moral growth and a successful life are impossible. Without these virtues, a free and just society is impossible.

As my life progressed, I underwent many experiences that I believe aided me in my moral and intellectual growth. I stumbled in many places—in ways that illustrated my need for further improvement. My evolution received substantial assistance from many people along the way, particularly the significant women in my life.

The first part of this narrative is a description of a massive tragedy that struck me in my midfifties: the loss of two of my significant women. That decade of turmoil and grief marked the first time I was really tested for the content of my own personal liberty and character. I struggled in those moments to define who I really was and what kind of life I was leading.

Following that drama is a discussion of my origins and formative years. I give my thoughts as to how I started becoming myself and acquired my own quota of personal liberty and character. I move on into an account of my education, wherein I describe the evolution of my concept of who I was and what role I proposed to play in society. Next, I relate my careers and the encounters with my significant women.

The parts played by personal liberty and character in these facets of my life can be gleaned from the story. I relate my perceptions of the social milieu in which I moved during that time. The next part of the narrative deals with my political activities on behalf of justice and with my historical research on the events leading up to the Holocaust, performed as a service for the United States Holocaust Memorial Museum in Washington, DC. I then give an account of impressions gathered during my world travels. These chapters describe the way personal liberty and character affect human history in the United States and in various parts of the world, and I emphasize the vital role that freedom and justice play in the formation and function of well-ordered nations and societies. Finally, I end the discourse with my activities and impressions during the Trump administration and my hopes and warnings regarding the future of our country.

As I constructed this story, I noted denunciations of racism and sexism inserting themselves. This is natural since these vices are polar opposites to both personal liberty and good character. Racism and sexism formed the backbone of the caste-based despotism that oppressed everyone in the United States and desecrated our country for centuries.[9] Racism motivated the two original American sins—slavery and the slaughter of Native Americans—and it lies at the heart of the chief threat to American liberty and justice today. Racism drives many of the follies and calamities I explore in various parts of the world. Sexism damaged many of the women who crossed my path, particularly during my early life. A good future for our country entails the total banishment of these twin plagues.

Though I expatiate throughout the narrative on freedom and tyranny, this story is not confined to the benefits of liberty and justice; it is also an autobiography. Everywhere are anecdotes and asides that I hope will address a wide audience. Most of them are not reinforcers of my central message but are human-interest tales that touch on other issues facing our world. My life has been replete with adventures that I believe can be instructive, such as my aborted teaching career, the rebuff I received from an eminent scientist, the psychological stimulation attending computer software development, the mark I made as a lab chemist, geology lessons in Iceland, and episodes indicative of the workings of other countries.

Some of the discursive notes contain essays I feel should be part of my message about liberty and justice but could not reside in the mainstream of the narrative because they would have broken the flow of the story or rendered it excessively verbose. Other discursive notes discuss events or terms in detail that is not vital to the understanding of the overall story but might be interesting to a few readers. Still others add heft to points made in the main story. I do not cite well-known works of classical literature, such as Mark Twain's *The Adventures of Huckleberry Finn*, because they are well known and because I have no idea what edition or publisher pertains to famous books I read decades ago.

Throughout this narrative, I refer to World War I as the Great War. I feel this evocative European construct is more appropriate, as it more effectively conveys the breathtaking horror on the battlefields everywhere, the inadequacy of people and institutions to deal with the exigencies of the war, the massive upheavals and the extinction of idealism and decency that came in its wake, and the sheer purposelessness of the entire conflict.

This is a panorama I have enjoyed constructing; may the reader enjoy traversing it.

CHAPTER 1

RITE OF PASSAGE

October 13, 1998. Returning to New Jersey from a visit to see my parents in Montana, my longtime lady friend Marky Poindexter and I had just boarded a plane heading from Minneapolis to Philadelphia after a half-mile fast walk across the Minneapolis airport to make a flight connection. We had settled into our seats, when I noticed that Marky had a fixed look. She seemed to be talking vaguely, but I let it slide as a momentary glitch. My mind was on getting back home to Marlton, New Jersey, and resting in preparation for resumption of my duties as a computer software engineer for Computer Sciences Corporation and the US Navy.

As the flight progressed, Marky often grabbed her forehead as if in great pain. She had a history of migraines, so I assumed she was having a particularly severe episode but would soon recover. After trying to no avail to communicate with her, I alerted the flight crew.

When we touched down in Philadelphia, Marky was immobile and not speaking. We waited for everyone else to deplane while the crew hovered anxiously around us. By that time, I was so agitated that events went by in a whirl. I vaguely remember Marky being carried off the plane on a gurney, crying incoherently. I stumbled through the process of deplaning and getting a cab to take me home and then to the hospital where Marky was being attended.

I have just a few disjointed memories of the remainder of that evening. I remember being told by one of the neurologists that she had had a massive hemorrhagic stroke, which had destroyed half of her left frontal lobe. The neurologist hastened to assure me—multiple times, I believe—that I was not to blame myself for Marky's situation. Marky had been a massive stroke waiting to happen, he said, and if we had not dashed across the Minneapolis airport, something else would have provoked the crisis. She had been taking aspirin to guard against an ischemic stroke (caused by a blood clot blocking the blood supply). Unfortunately, aspirin, by thinning the blood, exacerbates a hemorrhagic stroke. Unfortunate choice! But there we were, and we had to go forward from there. In any case, at the time, I was too unstrung by the crisis to ponder blame.

After my hospital visit, the cab driver drove me home again. Hanging around the hospital would not have helped Marky, and I needed to get some rest. The cab driver was sympathetic, but I remember nothing of our conversation. Upon reaching my home in Marlton, I found a phone message from my father, who had called about the time we should have arrived home. He wondered if anything had happened and asked me to call as soon as I arrived. When I returned the call and relayed the news, my parents were saddened and supportive. My mother, being a nurse, felt that Marky would never again be the same person.

The next several weeks are a blur in my memory since I was processing that new catastrophe to the detriment of all my other mental tasks. The events recounted here are not necessarily in chronological order.

Marky spent a couple of weeks in a hospital bed with no signs of consciousness. At the same time, I had to take over her business affairs. To clear those up, I had to get a power of attorney so I could manage her assets. I also had to look after my own affairs and the everyday chores we had performed together, plus holding a demanding job as a software engineer. All of that was made more difficult by the fact that I was mentally processing the sudden catastrophe. I could not concentrate properly on any of my tasks, though I somehow managed to get through the situation, more or less. It was a constant breathless runaround with no rest stops and no end.

In all of the whirligig, I was alone; none of our relatives or original friends lived within 1,500 miles of New Jersey. The friends we had in New Jersey were not close and personal enough for me to feel comfortable in asking them for help. That meant I ran the myriad rounds unsupported. Later on, as I pondered my own situation and observed other people in circumstances similar to mine, I came to the conclusion there was an upside to my aloneness: there were no near and dear persons pressuring me or second-guessing my decisions regarding Marky's care. I have never been good at politicking; dealing with a thicket of relatives might have made my burdens intolerable when I was trying to learn the caregiving ropes for myself.

The first thing I learned was that Marky's disaster was not so sudden after all. My parents and Marky's friends and relatives all agreed she had been losing her sharpness for some time before the stroke. She had become absentminded, whereas she had previously been famous for being completely on top of all situations, with nothing escaping her eagle eye. As time went on, I reluctantly remembered similar deficits. The previous June, we had taken a cruise up the inside passage from Vancouver, British Columbia, to Anchorage, Alaska, followed by a train ride to Fairbanks. Two months later, we had visited Winston Churchill's Chartwell estate in Britain. When I casually had mentioned our Alaska train ride, I had discovered that she had dropped that entire trip into a hole; not one memory of it remained. On another occasion, she had recently placed tuna casserole in a plastic dish and set the dish in the oven to warm up. I'd gotten there in time to save the stove but not the dish. At that time, I'd refused to allow the warnings to register with me.

But even after the stroke, it wasn't that bad, was it? Life would go on as before, right? I would have my companion for another many years, wouldn't I? Over the next couple of months, every uptick in performance, from her first awakening in the hospital to the many times I saw the old Marky shine through, and every upbeat piece of news sent me into ecstasies. Every sign of deterioration and every dour report sent me crashing. During the lows, I would blubber out the story of Marky to anyone who would listen—often coworkers who barely knew me. That might have been annoying to them, but for me, it was vital catharsis. Talking through a loss like that was a necessary part of working through my grief. The alternative is physical illness or mental breakdown. Thankfully, some of my coworkers provided the necessary support.

Shortly before her stroke, I had talked Marky for the first time into traveling to continental Europe—Norway, to be specific, land of my ancestors. That was a first; Marky had always been reluctant to travel overseas, with the exception of a few trips to the British Isles. Our Norway trip was coming up the following June, and I had to be sure her rehabilitation proceeded apace so we could make the trip together. Through the following two months of rehab, I scrutinized every aspect of her recovery to reassure myself that she would be ready to make the journey. I pestered every nurse associated with her care: "She's improving, right? Right? Huh?" But nobody could predict the course or extent of her recovery—only that it would be slow and uncertain.

After two weeks in the hospital and six weeks in a rehabilitation center I had somehow located, Marky was declared to be plateaued, meaning that further improvement was not in the cards, and there was nothing further that a rehab operation could do. According to the report at the end of that period, Marky had multi-infarct dementia and would require supervision for twenty-four hours per day, seven days per week. The caregivers unsentimentally turned her over to me. My emotional off-road-vehicle ride was over, and my vehicle was overturned in a sand patch. Depression set in, and it was punctuated by screaming sessions and suicidal ideation in the privacy of my home. Pain at this level is both unbearable and unabating; often, it caused me to feel slightly asphyxiated. Pain like this gives rise to just one desire: to make it stop. And one is not finicky about how!

I needed to vent to my coworkers and an analyst. My employer, Computer Sciences Corporation, pointed me to one, and he provided additional lifelines. Reluctantly, I canceled Marky from our trip to Norway, though I left myself on the list; it was obvious to me then that I would eventually need a getaway.

The first thing I learned about caregiving was that it is impossible for one caregiver to manage the life of a dementia patient. Upon taking Marky home, I learned the hard way that 24-7 supervision means just that, and no one person can remain on the alert constantly. After a few days, I was ready for an alternative.

The social workers with whom I interfaced were not a lot of help; they tended to point me to piles of pamphlets and assure me I was welcome to look over all the facilities I needed to inspect. There were a few pointers on what to look for in an inspection, but I had no experience in checking out nursing facilities, nor had I imagined I would be doing anything like that. I was too unstrung and busy at work to dedicate much effort to inspecting an array of care facilities anyway. But I found a day-care facility near where I worked. They accepted Marky as a resident; I would have her at home nights, and they would look after her during the daytime. Now everything was settled, right? Well …

The facility cared for Marky through the day all right, but they closed at 1700 sharp, and I had to be there at that moment to take her home. They would immediately shut down if any snowflakes fell in the vicinity—liability issues with transporting the residents over slippery roads, I was told. As it was wintertime in New Jersey and climate change had not yet taken hold in a major way, snow emergencies recurred frequently; I was continually leaving work to dash to the facility to pick up Marky in time for their closing hour or upon receipt of a warning phone call.

I informed the staff at Marky's day-care facility about my work situation, but I got no relief. I was bound to be at their beck and call while working an eight-hour-a-day job with frequent additional night software testing sessions. Clearly, that was not a sustainable regimen for me; I had to rearrange my program again. One of the staff at Marky's day-care center pointed me to an assisted-living facility nearby. I was too overwrought to go through the formally required motions of looking the place over and taking charge of the paperwork. I just bundled Marky into the place and allowed the staff there to fill out the paperwork per my oral directions. It broke my heart to see Marky's name on the door to a room in a nursing facility after all those years of indispensable companionship. But at least she had a private room, all meals, and frequent entertainment available.

Finally, in the middle of January 1999, three months after Marky's stroke, I was able to slow down a bit and tend to my job. Even though I could take her home on weekends, I missed her terribly. She still had enough functionality to be a companion, though not the companion she had been in the good old days. Whenever I was not on a trip, I visited her every day at the facility. I took her home each weekend as well; I trust that made her happier than if she had spent all her time at the facility.

All through the ordeal, I was responsible for holding up my end at my full-time job as a software engineer. I used up much of my sick time during that period in caring for her. My coworkers kept management apprised of what was happening to me. Unfortunately, management was not so understanding; I missed out on some crucial test sessions and software development efforts. The following spring, I got the poorest work evaluation of my entire computer engineering career, and I did not get a pay raise that year.

I became socially isolated upon Marky's incarceration. Marky had chosen our friends, and I had been content to follow along; now I was tasked with finding friends of my own. I soon found out who were really friends and who were not. I acquired new friends, interestingly, among the residents of Marky's facility, who were impaired to varying degrees by dementia from Alzheimer's disease. To a lesser extent, the facility staff provided conversation and comfort. I also started attending an evangelical Baptist church at which one of my coworkers was a deacon. While I could never become a conventional religious believer, I appreciated the sympathy and companionship the people there provided.

It behooved me to acquaint myself quickly with elder law. Both the day-care facility and the nursing facility were private-pay for-profit operations—that is, they did not accept Medicaid. Marky and I were expected to furnish payment from our own pockets. Because of the equity I had acquired from Marky as a result of taking title to our house, at least two years had to elapse in order for Medicaid to become legally available to us. Fortunately, my salary was sufficient to enable me to contribute substantial sums to aid in paying for Marky's stay.

I settled down into a new routine after placing Marky in the assisted-living facility. My depression gradually lifted over the next few years. The nights alone in the house, screaming in pain, grew fewer and farther between. I slowly gained back the twenty-five pounds I had involuntarily dropped during the first few months after Marky's stroke. I drew comfort from my new companions, but being a loner, I needed space for myself as well. Reading about earth and cosmic science, history, and literature relaxed me and salved my anguish. These topics helped me to put my situation into perspective by reminding me that my predicament has been repeated millions of times over immense time spans, and we all are just small specks in the universe, spatially and temporally. Perhaps removing my mind from brooding over my loss helped to steady me.

I started to travel overseas in earnest during that period. Since Marky never had been an enthusiast for globe-trotting, it was an activity I could pursue without her accompaniment—an adjustment I had to make, as I now could be with her for only a small and diminishing fraction of my time. Diminishing because as time wore on, Marky got progressively more confused, and I got progressively less depressed and dependent on her. Toward the end of 2001, she became so confused that I could no longer take her home on weekends. She presented too much of a risk of losing items I needed. Time and effort were required to get her dressed and prepared for the day each morning, and the transitions between home and facility became too much for her to manage mentally.

Eventually, Marky had to leave the facility. The facility lined us up with a Medicaid facility that belonged to their parent company. The new place turned out to be awful for several reasons. It was a half-hour drive from where I lived. They placed Marky in a crowded room with two other residents, one of whom was hearing-impaired and needed the TV on at full volume. I often arrived at the facility as late as 1100 to find Marky still not dressed and still in bed or cowering in a corner somewhere. I sometimes had to chase down the attendant and push her into tending to Marky. On two occasions, I reported the facility to the state. The hassle of dealing with me and the state inspectors finally induced the facility to locate a Medicaid-accepting nursing home for Marky that would admit her at the time we needed it.

The new facility specialized in residents with behavioral problems. That turned out to be ideal for Marky; she was often bossy, territorial, and belligerent—which no doubt had added to the headaches we'd presented to the previous Medicaid facility. The new place had plenty of employees and plenty of space and quiet. Marky got a room with one other resident. She spent three years there, and my daily visits never uncovered any deficits in her care. She declined progressively over that time, but occasionally, she would break my heart by shining through.

She remarked upon entering the new facility, "This is a dismal ending." One evening, she said, "Wouldn't it be nice if I could get myself put together again?" I still get a tear-jerk when I recall moments like these. Her observations demonstrated that she was suffering. Unlike most dementia patients, she retained all along the self-awareness to realize she was failing and dying after being hypercompetent all her life and to recognize the toll her illness was taking on me.

Eventually, Marky declined to a point of docility where they couldn't justify her staying in that behavioral unit. I located a nursing home that was just starting up and needed residents, and Marky was admitted immediately as a Medicaid resident. She spent her last three years at that facility. They took good care of her there, but on days when the staff were short-handed, I could find her still in bed at 1100. Informed that all feeders—those who needed to be fed—were to be left in bed, I replied, "Not if her name is Marky," and I allowed the staff to dress her and put her in a wheelchair. I wheeled her around the vicinity of the building every day when the weather permitted; I fed her many of her meals and often accompanied her to the entertainment sessions at the facility.

Marky finally succumbed on June 15, 2009—ten years, eight months, and two days after her stroke. By then, I had already gone through the grief and pain attending her stroke. Besides, another catastrophe had intervened during my decade of tending to Marky, sending me into a second tailspin.

As 2001 was drawing to a close, I started to feel the yen for female companionship. By that time, Marky was confused much of the time, and she could no longer visit me at home. People often seek companionship when they have a spouse or lover with dementia, particularly when the dementia is advanced. I started a lackadaisical online search, and after a few months, I met an African American woman called Lois Fleenor. Lois was a sunny, gentle person with a syrupy voice, and it was love at first sight. She was living in an apartment with her brother in northeast Philadelphia, supporting him and working as a computer system manager for the State of New Jersey in Trenton. I was pleased I could provide her with a more comfortable home. She said she wanted to be there for me as I struggled with Marky's upkeep. She was sincere in that desire, though she was also conflicted. Being a woman, she felt uncomfortable with my having contact with any other woman, whether that other woman was whole or not. Nevertheless, she did her level best to provide me with the aid and comfort I so obviously needed. Unlike Marky, she was enthusiastic about the prospect of globe-trotting with me, and I looked forward to a happy and fulfilling life. I insisted on my obligation to maintain Marky with daily visits and monitoring, which she accepted since she appreciated that I would do the same for her should the need arise. How soon that need would arise startled us both!

Things were amiss with Lois from the start. Before we met, she was a dynamic and resourceful woman. She had been writing stories, and I came across an interesting and original story she had written called "Money," an account of the adventures of a sheaf of currency as it made its way through various owners in a drug-infested ghetto. She had also started up a couple of businesses. By the time we met, she was no longer pursuing any activities of that sort. She was having trouble keeping her blood pressure down to acceptable levels. She had sloughed off the tip of one of her index fingers. Crusty spots decorated her scalp, and she had an intractable cough that often flared up in paroxysms.

She had been taking blood pressure medications, but they ceased to be effective about the time we got together. Her blood pressure continued to be erratic, and she switched regimens continually in an effort to quell the spikes. She let me look at her medical records, and I noted "idiopathic pulmonary fibrosis." Looking up the term in a medical reference guide, I saw that it meant lung tissue degenerating into fibrous, nonfunctional mass—cause unknown. The comment that caught my eye was a note that people with the condition often lived for as long as seven years. *Preposterous!* I was not about to face losing her after so short a time, and I neither queried Lois nor pondered the observation any further. My inclination to go into denial, strong enough already, was intensified by Lois's extremely private nature and obvious reluctance to discuss matters like that. My nonconfrontational ways confirmed my resolve to avoid reality. I was so ecstatic at having a woman in my life that I didn't desire close examination of the woman—or the situation—and we decided to get married.

Shortly before our marriage, Lois woke up one morning complaining of chest pains. I rushed her to the nearest hospital and awaited the outcome. What came out was a diagnosis of scleroderma—a vicious autoimmune disorder featuring collagen (a protein that holds the skin and other organs together and gives scars and scabs their hardness) being produced in excess and accumulating in her skin and internal organs, hardening their tissue and eventually rendering them nonfunctional. A few days later, her primary physician called me at work and told me the details of her condition. Our conversation then took a turn.

I said, "It sounds like her immune system is a mess."

The doctor said, "That's a true statement. Her immune system is a mess. You're going to marry her, right?"

"Yes."

"Well, you're in a tight spot. You might have her for as long as three years."

After our conversation, I collapsed in my chair, weeping.

I had no idea how clued in she actually was as to her illness. The thought of abandoning her because of her condition would never have occurred to me had I not received unwelcome suggestions to that effect from people with whom I was associated. As repugnant as the idea was, I gave the authors the benefit of the doubt and attributed their suggestions to mere naivete rather than to monumental insensitivity. Still, I know there are people who behave that way. Soon I mentally set aside my conversation with her doctor, and we went forward with our wedding plans.

We lived together in my home for two years before our marriage. During that period, we went on two overseas trips: one to Britain and one to Bermuda. Domestically, we visited my family's ranch in Montana, where I introduced her to my siblings. We arranged to get her to Trenton for her job every day, and I went to mine every day, along with watching Marky. We cooked dinners together and attended movies and other entertainment.

We got married in a big ceremony on September 20, 2003. Our wedding was a great party and a great success. Coworkers, friends, and relatives from both sides attended, and we had an elaborate ceremony at the Catholic Saint Joan of Arc parish in Marlton. My sisters, Nina and Emily, came in from the West Coast, and my brother, Richard, served as best man. A bash at our Marlton house followed, and everybody wished us a long and happy marriage. In a well-managed world, I would have been on my way to full recovery.

Returning home one evening, I found Lois weeping in the garage. She had just been informed that she would have to go onto kidney dialysis. Her blood pressure problems were now explained: her kidneys were calling it a day after years under attack by the scleroderma. That garage scene causes a tear-jerk in me to this day.

A nephrologist took over as her primary physician, and we had to decide whether Lois would go on hemodialysis (which would involve Lois sitting for four hours three times a week at a machine that would wash her blood) or peritoneal dialysis (which would use Lois's peritoneum, the membrane surrounding the internal organs, as a membrane through which to purify the blood). Lois opted for peritoneal dialysis, which purifies the blood every day. Her body chemistry would be more up to date than with hemodialysis, which cleans the blood only every few days.

We got a peritoneal dialysis machine and a garage full of plastic bottles of peritoneal dialysis fluids. Kidney dialysis is a greatly degraded way of keeping the body chemistry up to specifications; the kidneys, after all, continuously monitor and adjust the levels of various chemicals in the body, whereas the machine just dialyzes according to its settings and parameters, which are adjusted manually according to the patient's condition. Furthermore, the dialysis is not active all the time, and the body's chemistry gets progressively more out of balance during the times when the patient is disconnected from the machine. For the rest of her life, rarely did Lois enjoy the proper balance of body chemicals. Her sunny disposition darkened considerably.

The strict session schedule on the peritoneal dialysis machine—twelve hours' dwell time each night, seven days a week—was frustrating and inconvenient. Travel was especially difficult since we had to transport a bulky dialysis machine and ship bottles of dialysis fluid to our destination. Airport security personnel were always fascinated by the machine. In that fashion, we traveled to New Orleans, Princeton, and the Shenandoah Valley.

Other inconveniences attended the dialysis adventure. Lois's diet had to be carefully controlled. At night, she would often roll over in bed onto the plastic tube connecting her to the machine, blocking the tube, setting off an alarm at any hour of our sleep and often requiring my calling a twenty-four-hour-a-day service desk technician to get the machine up and rolling again. A more significant problem was peritoneal infection. Since we lacked both adequately sterile conditions in my house and adequate instruction as to how to maintain sterility, Lois frequently got peritoneal infections, which needed to be tended to immediately. The infections, which caused excruciating pain, sometimes compelled me to call an ambulance to rush her to the hospital. Fortunately, no infections marred our trips.

One day Lois asked me point-blank if I would provide her with a kidney. The request presented me with an awkward situation. I would have donated one of my kidneys to Lois in a trice but for the ominous descriptions the doctors had issued to me concerning the works and ways of scleroderma when it has invaded the internal organs: it attacks all the organs, including any donated ones, and leads inevitably to death from general organ failure. I could hardly be honest and say, "I can't give you a kidney, because the doctors say you will not last long," so I hemmed and hawed. After a few minutes, intense love won the contest, and I agreed to donate a kidney. The idea was to save her the years of waiting that would have attended the receipt of a kidney from the donor list. I filled sixteen vials with my blood for the compatibility test, and a few weeks later, I got delightful news: Lois and I were compatible. She would not reject my kidney. That gave me some hope; trading the doctors' dire warnings for a happy state of denial, I looked forward to a long, happy, healthy marriage after Lois received my kidney. Thoughts of the coming paradise kept up my morale over the next year.

As we were going through the hoops in preparation for our kidney donation procedure, obstacles kept intervening to prevent the happy ending. Peritoneal infections and other complications forced postponement after postponement. Lois developed Raynaud's syndrome in her hands (intractably cold fingers). Her general condition deteriorated as time went on, forcing her to cancel her plan to accompany me on an overseas trip we had planned. Needing a pause in caregiving, I reluctantly went by myself to the Scandinavian capitals. But Lois's absence largely spoiled the trip.

Finally, one evening, as we were returning home from a movie theater, Lois sighed my name and passed out in the car. I immediately rushed her to a hospital and stood around ineffectually while she was examined. She had returned to consciousness before we arrived at the hospital and could help to tell her story to the doctors. The doctors transferred her to a premier hospital in the area, Cooper Hospital in Camden. When they had stabilized her, one of the doctors pulled me to one side and gave me the brutal word. There was to be no kidney transplant; Lois was at the end of her life.

I was stunned and numb upon hearing the announcement. I found no relief at that point; self-contained and independent as she was, Lois hated to be fussed over, and she would not let me mourn in her presence, discuss her condition, or allow me to attempt to comfort her psychologically. It might have softened the blow for me had we been able to talk at length about our circumstances, but again, maybe not. I assume that at some level, she was aware of her approaching death. She was a strong and intelligent woman who would most likely have picked up signals from people around her. But after her emphatic rejection of my first tearful display, I didn't dare to bring up the subject in her presence. Was she in fact in total denial? I have no way of knowing. It is even conceivable that she was fully aware of her prognosis during our entire three and a half years together. She could hardly have missed the loss of her index fingertip; the spots on her scalp; the declining stamina, which had terminated her enterprising ways; and the large weight loss that had occurred just before I met her. Did she consult with anyone over those things? Did she ponder them? All of these questions are forever unanswerable.

I visited her every day, often spending hours rubbing her feet and hands, which were horribly painful from the circulation being cut off to those parts of her body. Usually, merciful sleep eventually intervened to relieve her agony. I talked to her as soothingly as I knew how, and she apologized to me for getting into that condition and ruining our life together. I said that was OK. What else was there to say? She had no need to apologize for a situation for which neither of us had bargained. The scleroderma proceeded apace, chewing up her blood vessels; I watched her bedsores bloom to a size that would have enclosed a pack of cigarettes. As her toes turned black and crumbly like charcoal briquettes, I felt the old familiar suffocating sensation from sheer frustration and helplessness. As the weeks went by, she was conscious less and less of the time. As before with Marky, I appreciated that I was able to perform my duties without interference, and conceivably, I rendered her some benefit.

When visiting Lois at the hospital on the evening of April 4, 2005, I noticed that her voice had a gargling sound. In denial as I was, I thought, *Just one more of her many crises*, so I went to a church service, intending to see her the next day. At 0530 on April 5, 2005, the numbness left me abruptly. A call from Cooper Hospital informed me that Lois had passed. Would I please come to the hospital to verify her identity? The proximate cause of her death was pulmonary failure; her lungs had finally surrendered to the siege by scleroderma and to the attack by inhaled food. Inability to swallow was another feature of her disease. I was told two things. First, kidney care was now so effective that scleroderma patients no longer died primarily of renal failure, as in the past; pulmonary failure was now the most common killer. Second, the pulmonary fibrosis from scleroderma was closely akin to idiopathic pulmonary fibrosis—previously diagnosed in Lois. Probably they were one and the same. The autopsy report added congestive heart failure to the abominable mix. According to one doctor, the scleroderma had invaded her entire body. Scleroderma is a vicious disease indeed!

Emotions returned in a rush. Back came the screaming alone in the house at night. Back came the suicidal ideation. Off came the twenty-five pounds. This episode of grief was even more severe than that which had accompanied Marky's stroke. Added to the usual litany of pains was an intense rage at the cosmic-scale injustice of what had happened to Lois. Marky had been seventy-six when she had her stroke, after a long, fulfilling relationship and a long, meaningful life, and she'd lived on until the age of eighty-seven. Since she'd been nearly the age of my parents, I had always held in the back of my mind the likelihood that she would predecease me, though I never had let that thought linger in my conscious mind during Marky's salad days. Lois, on the other hand, had been full of energy, initiative, and imagination cut short damnably by her illness, and she was too young to die. She died at age sixty-seven after only three and a half years with me. We had never really gotten acquainted; we had never learned to complement each other in our relationship, and we had had only a few trips and other adventures together. Her illness had dominated our entire relationship, particularly during the last half of its duration. It was monumentally unfair!

My rage added to the overload on my brain and caused compromises in my cognition. When I drove, I often turned street corners before the street corners arrived, endangering my wheel balance and alignment. I could not balance checkbooks. I would dial a telephone number and immediately forget whom I was calling and why. My memories of the funeral; a visit from my brother, Richard; taking over power of attorney and executing her will; the trip to the Montana ranch to bury her; and even the trip to New Zealand we had arranged, from which I'd had to cancel her, all exist only as disjointed scraps. Unpleasant scenes arose at work when I erupted all over someone about some little thing—scenes for which I had to apologize and explain after I had regained some poise. I totaled the car that Lois and I had bought together because I rear-ended a car that I didn't see in the road directly in front of me, but I have forgotten large segments even of the story of that accident.

Reading provided no succor that time around, as I could not concentrate, and I had no interest in the subject matter anyway. I even went catatonic at times, sitting and staring at the backs of my hands for as long as an hour. My behaviors sounded to me like the symptoms of dementia I had learned while caring for Marky. Clearly, I needed to find some new direction to take. Antidepressants were a first step; they shook me out of the catatonia and probably dulled my rage as well. These drugs may well have saved me my job.

I attended therapy group sessions sponsored by several widows' groups, and the gatherings helped somewhat. I learned there were others with suicidal ideation who were as urgently in need of emotional rescue as I. We could be cheerful if we got into conversations about topics other than our loss, and we often played games and filled out questionnaires provided by the session managers. I remember one attendee particularly fondly because she was clearly concerned about me and my health. She advised me to hide my scholarly proclivities to better broaden my search field for new women. I mumbled thanks, and I really did cherish her for her attempt to help me find solutions to my grief, but the suggestion was impracticable; I was much too grief-stricken to search for a woman. More importantly, I have never believed in deception; were I to follow her advice, the truth about any incompatibility of interests and pastimes would inevitably come out. Any relationship thus begun would founder without fail. I dwell on this detail because I now sense a strong likelihood that some of the more intelligent women I dated in school were masking themselves from me in this way for this reason (see chapter 5 for my reaction to this ploy).

Eventually, I recovered enough psychologically that I no longer needed the therapy groups, and my attendance tapered off. As in the first round of grief, I obtained support from some of my coworkers. This time, somehow, I did not lose favor with management at work by failing to perform. I also threw myself with renewed vigor into the activities of my evangelical Baptist church.

After Lois's passing, I adopted her daughter, Gwen, as my own. She acquired a new family and established herself as an employee of the State of New Jersey.

Lois had been very religious, and she often had voiced her belief that the Lord had brought us together. Maybe he had; she certainly had brought comfort and joy to my life for a time. Devout as she'd been, she had frequently expressed concern about my spiritual state. I'd loved her more deeply for feeling that way, even given my chronic skepticism about religious dogmas in general and Christian doctrine in particular. I started thinking seriously about religion, and I read the entire Bible as an activity for a class put on by the church. Was there any meaning to my suffering? The magnificent human tapestry of love, drama, conflict, and admirable qualities could not be merely a giant cosmic joke, could it? Just eternities of nothingness bookending our struggles, sufferings, hopes, fears, joys, loves, sacrifices, and human relationships? A stolidly apathetic universe confronting the most sublime and the most abominable people alike?

I pondered the destiny of my existence frequently during the several years' mourning for Lois and Marky. I often wished I could have derived comfort from an absolute conviction that a better life for me and all my significant women awaited us after we crossed the great divide. Unfortunately, my scientific mind always demanded empirical proof of such an afterlife before it would accept this solace, even during my darkest hours—proof I was never able to discern anywhere.

I had problems with what the evangelicals were attempting to teach me. They hold that salvation based on good works is impossible since it is obviously impossible to behave perfectly, as required by the Bible. Their solution is simply that belief in Jesus's efficacy in paying off our moral debts leads us to God's favor. But how does a requirement to believe differ qualitatively from a requirement to act? Muslims check off boxes on the way to salvation: pray five times per day, give alms to the poor, accept Muhammad as the Prophet, and more. Is not belief in salvation through Jesus's crucifixion merely an analogous checkbox for evangelical Christians? Does this not render evangelical Christianity into yet another salvation-by-works philosophy—in this case, psychological works?

But more importantly, the evangelical God, who rewards or punishes people solely according to their beliefs, repelled me instead of comforting me. Shouldn't God reward character? Shouldn't he take note of people's attempts—even failed attempts—to behave the way Jesus did? After all, does not the Bible exhort one to feed the hungry, clothe the naked, and house the homeless[1]—empathetic and generous acts that mark good character? The evangelical God appears to me to lead toward moral laziness. Why strive to be a good person if such efforts make no difference to God? Why worry about biblical exhortations at all? Why not just coast through life; believe the proper doctrine; do whatever one wishes, such as violate the Commandments, ignore the Beatitudes, and boost such antibiblical characters as Donald Trump; and passively await the heaven that greets the faithful after death? If I ever figure out all these conundrums to my satisfaction, it will be according to my own reasoning and research, not the words of a teacher who, after all, is a mere mortal like me.

Nevertheless, I am eternally grateful to the coworkers, fellow bereaved, and church members who provided me with whatever balm they could find. With their help, I gradually recovered my health, weight, and equanimity for a second time. It took me an unusually long time—five years—to recover from Marky's stroke in 1998 and from Lois's death in 2005. My analyst told me that my recovery was complicated by a tendency to depression—a trait I inherited from my father. If my father and I are depressive, we are in illustrious company; Abraham Lincoln, Winston Churchill, and Franklin Roosevelt were all so afflicted, and they all had their ways of coping with it.

I continued to visit Marky daily until her passing on June 15, 2009. At that time, I didn't ruminate on religious issues. Marky was militantly irreligious, and it was repugnant to me that after the great life she'd lived, she was supposedly lost and forever damned because of her so-called lack of faith. Though I now accept that what lies over the great divide is unknowable, I say emphatically that if afterlife rewards exist, they are not confined to any religious sect manufactured and maintained by humans.

Today Marky and Lois rest together in boxes of ashes buried under granite gravestones on top of Aber Hill at the ranch in Montana (see chapter 3 for more on Aber Hill).

I had borne full and sole responsibility for the welfare of two desperately ill women whom I loved and who I know loved me. The agony of watching these women deteriorate and die slowly, suffering horribly along the way, and the knowledge that all I could do was attempt to palliate their pain hollowed me out physically, mentally, and economically. This trial suggested the biblical widow's gift of "all that she had."[2] Most importantly, there was a choice involved here. No coercion attended my behavior; no sanctions would have come my way if I had done with Marky what I observed many others do with their incapacitated loved ones: dump them into a nursing home, contribute minimally to their upkeep, let the nursing home assume the entire burden, and forget their loved ones' existence for months at a time, arriving only to attend to emergencies or death. I could have run away from Lois upon hearing her grim diagnosis, leaving her to cope God knows how in her apartment. But those thoughts never entered my mind unless suggested by a crass bystander. I so profoundly loved these unfortunate women that I had no choice after all. Though I failed to save them, I gave all I had to make their last years as bearable as possible, not because I had to but because I *had to*. I hope I shielded them from worse eventualities at least.

I struggled with myself for a long while afterward, but eventually, I came to accept that my inability to make these women whole again did not mean I was an abject failure as a human being. Lack of success in a worthy cause does not diminish the value of the effort. I find encouragement and inspiration in the story of the valiant White Rose Society,[3] whose revolt against Nazi Germany was doomed at the outset. They failed utterly to remedy Hitler's injustices and lead Germany out of darkness. In the end, they were guillotined by Nazi goons, but they fought the good fight for a great cause. Likewise, Sergei Magnitsky[4] died failing to bring his huge, lumbering Russian homeland out of its endless night, but he is no less a hero. These giant people are now esteemed by every individual whose esteem is worth having.

I feel I have had a trial by fire, and when I look into the mirror, if I don't see the faces of authentic heroes, such as Hans and Sophie Scholl,[3] Sergei Magnitsky,[4] and Senator John McCain,[5] at least I don't see little wretches like Donald Trump or his good friend Vladimir Putin[6] leering back at me.

So how did this ordeal affect me? The temper that had plagued me all my life lost most of its sharp edges, though occasionally, a few still appear. Patience and magnanimity improved, but those both still can use some work even now. Having stared Death in the face for more than a decade, I found that my fear of him almost completely vanished, and now, close to the end of my journey, I can contemplate my inevitable fate with equanimity.

My self-esteem notably improved. I had long felt that my life had been too cosseted as compared to previous generations: I'd faced no major wars, depressions, or other calamities to compel me to grow up. The war that dominated my generation's early adulthood, the Vietnam War, was barred to me by my bad eyes (see chapters 2 and 7). That war, moreover, did not bring average people in our country face-to-face with their own character in the manner of the Great Depression and the Second World War. However, I felt then, and I feel now, that in tending to and losing Marky and Lois, I underwent and passed some kind of test—a rite of passage—that made an adult of me at last.

Finally, I discovered that the fierce individualism I had always prized did not always apply. No matter how robust and self-sufficient one believes one is, there are situations that compel one to reach out to others for support. Being forced to change one's outlook constitutes part of a rite of passage. Not only did I get support from friends and church members during my trial by fire, but also, it dawned on me that ever since 1971, when I connected with Marion, up to the present day, my significant women had been helping me to sustain myself all along in spite of my vanity about my self-management capabilities. My true loves were always subtle enough about their support that I never became aware of, or resentful of, the vital role they played in keeping my balance. But vital they were, and they played a huge part in making my story a reasonably successful one.

CHAPTER 2

ANTECEDENTS AND BEGINNINGS

I was born in Portland, Oregon, on March 31, 1944, during the Second World War. I will describe my forebears at some length, because they played a major role in both the nature part of my formation (genes) and the nurture part (upbringing methods).

I am a believer in national, or regional, psychological characteristics. These features have nothing to do with any innate processes; they result from habits acquired by generations of living exclusively among people of one group. These characteristics do not affect everyone to the same degree in the country in question, but they appeared obvious to me in many of the national populations as a whole that I observed.

The races that dominate my ancestral palette are rather aloof, especially compared to Mediterranean and Middle Eastern peoples. My forebears also come from the most freedom-loving parts of Europe. During the last couple of centuries, they have been among the first and most effective implementers of law-based libertarian societies. This heritage is doubtless a major contributor to my individualism and my craving for liberty. My DNA, a test of which I obtained a few years back, indicates I am about 98 percent northwestern European, comprising 32 percent Scandinavian, 29 percent from the British Isles, 7 percent French and German, and 30 percent "broadly northwestern European," probably including Dutch and Belgian. Southern European,

East Asian, and Native American genes make up the 2 percent balance, which obviously would not contribute greatly to my makeup.

None of my DNA results came as a surprise to me, given what I know about my forebears. I will briefly discuss my knowledge of them. I am leaving out a great deal that I don't know, since ancestral branches double with each generation backward. But the DNA results contain nothing that deviates from the origins of my known ancestors. Any information about my ancestors other than what I present would have only minor effects on my conclusions about their effect on my nature.

My paternal grandfather, Ed Adams (Grandpa Ed), was a grandson of William Adams, who arrived in the United States from Ireland in 1841. William farmed in western Pennsylvania until after the Civil War. Sometime in the 1860s, he moved to eastern Iowa to farm there until the end of his days. His oldest son, Alexander, fought in the Civil War (100th Pennsylvania Regiment). After that experience, he settled in Shelby, Iowa, where he started his family. Upon his death, his widow and her children, including my grandfather, moved to Columbus, Montana. Grandpa Ed fell in love with Montana and worked as a cowboy there for a while in the early twentieth century. He eventually moved back there to ranch after a career in the stockbrokerage business in Spokane, Washington, and Portland, Oregon. During his stockbrokerage days, he made a fortune and used much of it to purchase land in Montana north of Big Timber in Sweetgrass County. That was where my family ranch originated.

My paternal grandmother, Elizabeth Covert (Grandma Beth), was descended from Theuniss Janssen Covert, who came over from Holland during the seventeenth century. Grandma Beth was the middle of three children born to John Covert and Anna Jane McCarty, a.k.a. Mam, in North Dakota. John died of pneumonia in 1894, leaving his widow with three children, ages six, four (Grandma Beth), and one, to raise in the cold, wild country of 1890s North Dakota. Somehow, Mam and her family ended up in Billings, Montana, where Grandma Beth became a schoolteacher and met Grandpa Ed.

My maternal grandfather, Alex Johnson (Grandpa Alex), arrived from Oslo, Norway, around 1902 at the age of ten years. He worked as a pipefitter and later hired on with Union Oil Company, where he was a successful executive until he retired.

My maternal grandmother, Petrine Larson, a.k.a. Mimi, was born and raised in the Lofoten Islands in northern Norway. A fantastic artist in cooking and sewing, she arrived in the United States around 1912 at the age of twenty-two years. My maternal grandparents met and married in Thunder Bay, Ontario, Canada, where they had settled after entering North America. Subsequently, they moved to Duluth, Minnesota.

My mother was Alice Muriel Johnson, born in Duluth. She obtained a nursing certificate at the Mayo Clinic in Rochester, Minnesota, and then worked as a stewardess. Later, she worked as a nurse for Grandpa Ed's physician, through whom she met my father.

My father, John Alexander Adams, named after his two grandfathers, John Covert and Alexander Adams, was born in Billings, Montana, but went to school in Spokane, Washington, and Portland, Oregon, following his father as Grandpa Ed pursued his stockbroker career. My father got a civil engineering degree from Oregon State University in Corvallis. After his service in the war, he settled on his father's land in Montana to run a ranch. I was named after my father; thus, I am John Alexander Adams Jr.

All four of my grandparents spent their formative years in unforgiving parts of the world. An inhospitable environment may inculcate self-reliance as a way to cope. Certainly, both of my grandfathers believed in individual self-sufficiency, and both of my parents imbibed this independence and spirit of doing for themselves from their parents. I inherited this tendency—an important component of personal liberty—from my parents through their genes, and they also taught it to me from birth. I have always been and still remain jealous of my independence and freedom of action.

In addition to my ancestry, my individualistic evolution probably derived from extreme myopia from birth, coupled with, or leading to, a possible Asperger's score.[1] Certainly, I had some of the characteristics that have been reported for Asperger's syndrome, such as slow development of interaction with other people, but most listed symptoms were absent. The Asperger anomaly is controversial in the scientific community—it is supposedly a mild form of autism. Hans Asperger, after whom the condition is named, studied allegedly autistic children in Germany during the twentieth century. His work was hardly scientific as we would know the word today; psychiatry and neuroscience were too immature during his time to sustain rigorous, repeatable scientific research. But Asperger himself was hobbled by major personal shortcomings. He was highly sexist, and his bias heavily compromised his research, confining him to male subjects for study. He was also a participant in the Nazi child euthanasia program, which killed children deemed not worthy of life—that is, disabled in some way. He was not a major actor in that drama, but he did play a part. The tendencies of his studies swayed with the ideological winds surrounding him throughout his career— pre-Nazi, Nazi, and post-Nazi. As a result, some authorities dismiss Asperger's syndrome as merely not fitting in socially, clearly a highly context-dependent diagnosis. As will be seen, this latter evaluation did fit me all my life.

There was nothing controversial about my myopia. I could see to an extent, but everything more than a few feet away was fuzzy. I have vague memories of blurred images of lights and of indistinct faces. This myopia was not known and not corrected until I was six years old. If one can't see, one can't interpret the emotions shown in other people's faces, including one's parents. One thus does not interact as efficiently with people and with the world as others might, and I must have retreated into my inner mind as a result. It was not until the age of seventy-six, when I had cataracts replaced with lenses appropriate for my eyes using state-of-the-art technology, that I really learned to see.

I retain a few disconnected, episodic memories from that period of my life. Almost all of them are positive; a few are neutral, and none are negative. I remember being spoon-fed by my mother, and I recall my parents winking at me and embracing each other while holding me up beside them. One of my aunts rubbed noses with me after my afternoon nap, while I was standing in the crib. She and my mother's brother beamed at me in our house in Portland. My first memory of Grandpa Ed was his approaching me with lots of smiles and loving words, though I didn't understand the words at the time. His face was visually indistinct to me, but the voice was unmistakably Grandpa

Ed's. Mam and Grandpa Alex playfully mimicked my babyish working around of my lips.

In short, the great majority of my memories from our time in Portland are of being fussed over by adult relatives. It helped, no doubt, to be among the first of a new generation in the clan. At that point, there were few children to fuss over, and the adults were not yet jaded by interacting with many babies. My mother must have been exceedingly conscientious about her diet, exercise, and healthy living habits during her pregnancy with me, since I observed that she dealt that way with her later pregnancies. Any problems introduced by myopia or Asperger's syndrome were probably counteracted by the copious affection from adults, along with my mother's generous solicitude for me during gestation.

Some experts[2] claim the first thousand days after conception are critical for the proper development of the person. For me, this would be the period approximately from my conception up to our moving out to the Montana ranch in 1946. If one is afflicted with uncorrected myopia during this period, one can be socially and intellectually crippled all of one's life. Expert researchers are not always 100 percent correct in all cases, and they add that plentiful adult interaction and affection during these thousand days can neutralize the effects of the foregoing pathologies.[3] These adult interactions I certainly had in abundance; while my eyesight probably postponed my childhood social development by several years, I don't believe my intellectual development was affected.

Two more causes of my individualism were isolation from people my own age, especially after we moved to our Montana ranch and before I moved on to high school, and a curiosity about many things and a general love of learning, experimentation, and exploration, which I have had as long as I can remember. Obviously, individualism can easily arise from social isolation, probably augmented in my case by my status as a firstborn. But my learning passion reinforced my individualism by compelling me to forgo the companionship of those who were not interested in acquiring lots of information and insights—a large percentage of the people among whom I moved later in life. On a few occasions, I have received warnings about the limitations that my bookishness imposes on my social life. I have always shrugged off this advice because I am convinced that a forced closeness with people who don't share my interest in things mental is worse than no closeness at all. Being introverted, I have always been satisfied with having fewer but more profound friendships than an extrovert would prefer, and I have never felt I had too few friends.

One interesting inheritance deserves to be discussed among the psychological attributes obtained from my ancestors: my attitude toward race and differences among people generally. My paternal grandparents, being fully American all their lives, absorbed American virtues and vices from infancy. Being from the midwestern plains, they knew few or no blacks personally, nor did they carry the bitter memory of defeat in the American Civil War, so they lacked the fiery hatred that one still finds in the southeastern corner of the United States. Nevertheless, antiblack sentiment was present to varying degrees all over the country when they were young, and they could not help absorbing some sort of mild, or not so mild, prejudice, doubtless hearing it from their parents and others. My maternal grandparents, having arrived in the United States after they were partially formed, had not imbibed American prejudices from their caretakers during their critical development years. As a result, they had no problem with African Americans after they arrived in the United States. This is not to say these grandparents were saints; my mother once remarked that her mother did not like the Sami, the Finno-Ugric people inhabiting northern Scandinavia. This would have been something she absorbed during her critical infancy period, probably from her elders on the Lofoten Islands.

I believe racism is woven into all of us to some degree for a couple of reasons. First, it seems to me that hostility to outsiders would have been a valid survival mechanism in a Pleistocene world populated by independent roving bands of hunter-gatherers; a stranger who looked or acted differently from us was perhaps a scout from another band scoping out our resources for later extortion. Second, the disorder called racism is remarkably widespread and resistant to retraining in our species. The black-white conflict in the United States is but one facet of a many-faceted problem. There are the many tribal conflicts in Europe, such as the Russian-Polish enmity, the French-German discord, the various Balkan and Middle Eastern tribal rivalries, and so on. There are the Hutu-Tutsi conflict plaguing Rwanda and Burundi in Africa, Vietnamese-Chinese hostility, Native American wars, and myriads of other antipathies. Local historical context and events can generate specific tribal hatreds (e.g., European anti-Semitism stemming from medieval conditions, and African tribal wars over resources and prestige), but I submit that the tendency to adopt these hatreds of the other from our elders during childhood is, to a degree, an innate hangover from our Pleistocene days. The particular groups toward which we hold prejudice are determined largely by the teachings of our caretakers in infancy.

Another inherited characteristic of mine is well illustrated in Norwegian playwright Henrik Ibsen's works. Ibsen was relentlessly satirical about his Norwegian compatriots. In *The Wild Duck*, he defines "rectitudinal fever," which he calls a Norwegian "national disease."⁴ This characteristic consists of an earnest desire to set things right, be on the side of the angels in all cases, be neat and orderly, and follow the rules (i.e., a pronounced moral and physical fastidiousness). All members of our family inherited a generous portion of this characteristic, and examples of its action will appear in this narrative. Taken in a healthy small dose and coupled with an open, curious, flexible, and resourceful mind, rectitudinal fever can make a sturdy contribution to good character. Associated with a closed, rigid mind, rectitudinal fever makes a person dogmatic, self-righteous, un-self-aware, and likely to persecute, just like many of Ibsen's characters.

Both of my parents had a strong sense of right and wrong. They were highly moral without being overly moralistic. I am grateful to them for inculcating this sense of right and wrong in me, as well as passing it to me through their genes. Being only human, I stumbled on many occasions in this regard. Nevertheless, I feel this need to do the right thing (rectitudinal fever) helped me to be successful on many occasions in life.

From both parents and both grandfathers, I inherited a short temper accompanied by a low tolerance for frustration. The temper has cooled off over the decades, particularly during my rite of passage described in chapter 1. But the impatience has stuck with me, alleviated to some extent by the rite of passage but still cropping up in traffic and other situations at times. In later chapters, I will describe how these characteristics closed off a couple of options for a profession.

I am told I was a difficult child. I remember being disciplined a lot, both verbally and physically, during the first few years at the ranch. This probably arose from my short temper, my low frustration threshold, a willfulness deriving from the fierce independence previously mentioned, and the curiosity that drove me to tamper with things. I hated to be ordered to do anything I did not want to do, and I occasionally damaged property by experimenting to see what would happen if I pushed a button, turned a handle, or tested the strength of some material object.

I was often forced to abort explorations and experimentation. On one occasion, I decided I wanted to explore a bare, grassy butte visible from our ranch house to the northeast. I set out toward that butte, but Dad came and retrieved me when I had progressed about fifty yards. I protested that I wanted to see "that hill," as I called it, but he took me back to the house—lovingly but firmly. It's probably a good thing he stopped me; it is approximately a three-mile walk each way from the ranch house to "that hill"—a strenuous effort for a child about three years old.

One of my passions at the time was pipes and plumbing. Grandpa Alex had given me a set of pipes, and I developed a fascination with connecting pipes into a network and running some sort of liquid through them. One day I hooked an assemblage of pipes to the spigot on the oil tank that supplied our house heating, and I turned on the oil to run through my pipes. The oil got all over my sister Nina and all over the grass near the tank. That was an occasion for physical punishment, and the grass near the oil tank took years to recover (Nina was quicker to recover). Several other experiments with pipes were much more benign.

My father's aunt gave me a hollow plastic toy bird one time when I was four or five years old. I had observed birds (and people) eating, so for my biological science training, I decided to watch the toy bird "eat." Over a couple of weeks, I picked holly berries from a tree in my grandmother Mimi's backyard and stuffed them into a crack in the bird—a few each day. I assumed that the bird would somehow use up the berries it had "eaten," just as people use food, and that I could continue to feed the bird indefinitely. To my disappointment, the bird soon became overstuffed with holly berries, and nothing more happened.

None of my experiments lasted long, as I lacked the patience and love of hand work to spend weeks or months in a single effort to create an elaborate and smooth-running apparatus. This deficiency will be recounted extensively in later chapters; it was central to my career decisions.

Hyperactivity appears to have been a problem at times as well. Old home movies of me bear this out. I remember being spanked for being overactive once or twice. Hyperactivity caused problems in relating to some of my contemporaries during my grade-school years. Few people knew about hyperactivity as a psychological issue in those days. I worked my way out of mine as years passed, and I successfully socialized with peers. I doubt that physical discipline played any role in my recovery.

In fact, I believe physical discipline is probably largely counterproductive since it sends a message to the child that violence is a good answer to conflict and behavioral problems. Since my childhood, I have known, or known of, several individuals who I believe were beaten excessively during their upbringing, and it was obvious to me that their excessive imbibing of violence as a tool in relationships crippled them socially and economically. There is undoubtedly a primordial instinct for clouting people during disagreements, and spanking and slapping only reinforce that instinct. In my opinion, exiling me to my bedroom for a time-out and compelling me to spend hours at a boring chore were much better approaches to my behavioral infractions than physical discipline.

Another issue I had was a tendency to worry about ailments in such a way that any ache or scrape became a perceived new normal in my mind. My first memory of this psychology was an occasion when I bumped my forehead, and my father said I was going to have a black eye. I envisioned a hideous black spot surrounded by concentric black circles where my eye used to be—a condition that would obviously last for the balance of my life and turn me into a pariah. I bawled for a long time—until my mother reassured me that my eye would merely turn red for a short time. This small neurosis dogs me to this day; I tend to see the onset of any ache or pain of old age as the beginning of a lifetime plague, even though they have all (so far) diminished or disappeared after a while.

My parents encouraged me in my learning, and they had lots of books around the house for me to leaf through. Mom even took Nina and me through a brief kindergarten, during which we colored pictures, made paper figures, and sang from a song book. I don't remember whether we were taught letters and numbers at the sessions, but I do remember having some literacy and numeracy before I entered the first grade. Dad read to us many evenings—mostly comics early on, and later, we perused Oz books by L. Frank Baum and other literature. There is no doubt in my mind that these reading sessions helped me greatly in becoming literate later on. It is well known that children benefit from this sort of parental participation.

I had an early fondness for music, which has stayed with me through life. We had an old upright piano in the ranch house, on which my mother, a good pianist, frequently entertained the family and visitors. I loved for her to go through a book of songs we owned and play each one on the piano. I'm told I knew the entire sequence of songs in the book, and she could not skip one without a protest from me. My parents had platters (both 33 1/3 and 78 rpm) that I liked to listen to on a little phonograph. I could spend hours thus occupied, and I developed a strong taste for string solo and chamber orchestra pieces with piano accompaniment. To this day, this is my favorite musical arrangement. Unfortunately, the records were composed of plastic or hard rubber, I was myopic, and I had the manual dexterity of a typical less-than-six-year-old. This led to several broken records, but we still have many of these platters out at the ranch. My mother tried to get me into piano lessons, but lacking the patience and perseverance for such a long haul, I rejected those overtures. Facility with my hands was a chronic problem; even so, I wish now that I had gone through and become a competent pianist. Nowadays I can work out melodies and harmonies by ear on a keyboard, and sometimes, with practice at a particular song, I can even sound as if I know what I am doing. But there is no substitute for rigorous training, and this omission is one of my big regrets.

My parents always had my back when I needed it, and I never doubted their love for me. In spite of all the cross-purposes, I feel that

I had a stable, healthy home, especially in light of counterexamples I encountered firsthand or read about later in life. Scott Rozelle[5] claims that a lack of loving contact and intellectual stimulation from parents in early life results in inability to take advantage of economic and social opportunity later on, a deficit that he says lasts for a lifetime. This conclusion comes out starkly in J. D. Vance's work *Hillbilly Elegy*,[6] his memoir about Appalachian children deprived of even minimal parenting. Reflecting on these works and on examples I have personally observed, I am grateful to my parents for my siblings' and my early intellectual stimulation and love. Like all parents, they made mistakes, but I shudder to contemplate what might have been!

We moved out to the Montana ranch in 1946, just after the birth of my sister Nina on August 11. Nina became my boon companion during our first years at the ranch. Since children were few and far between in that part of the country, Nina probably prevented me from becoming a complete hermit. Ranch work was strenuous and incessant for all adults, and the roads were execrable in the 1940s, especially in winter and spring. Social gatherings were much less frequent than they would have been in an urban or small-town environment.

We were real pioneers at first. Electricity came from a fuel-powered generator; rural electrification did not arrive at our ranch until 1949. Heating consisted of an oil-burning floor furnace and an oil-burning stove connected to an oil tank west of the ranch house. I remember fruit-box crates as kitchen and bathroom cabinets before my father had time to construct real cabinets. After several years, we installed a telephone, which was an apparatus connected by wires run between houses; this was our vocal communication with the rest of the world. None of our communications equipment was owned by Bell Telephone; my parents could not afford that luxury. Water was pumped by an electric pump from a well under the house, and sewage was disposed of through a septic tank north of the house. My father built all of this over a period of years after we moved out to Montana. He constructed the ranch house itself on the site of a ranch house that had previously burned to the ground. The ruins of many buildings from the previous ranch operation surrounded our living quarters.

My sister Nina was my main playmate during my preschool years at the ranch. We would play games of imagination, such as conjuring spirits that were responsible for good and bad fortune. I sometimes accepted input from Nina during the games, but usually, I wanted to direct things. Naturally, that could lead to conflict; Nina had a will of her own. If my temper and frustration came to a boil, I would sometimes hit her, savage little beast that I was. But more often, upon encountering differences with Nina in our games, I would patiently repeat the instructions several times, concluding from her deviations that she was simply too dense to absorb the material I was trying to teach her. As a rule, these differences just dissolved spontaneously.

Sometimes Nina and I would cooperate in an experiment. We had a pet housecat called Calico. One day Nina and I decided to see what would happen if we caked Calico with mud we manufactured. What happened was that we both got our hands slapped with a ruler.

On another occasion, we put a few pieces of modeling clay onto the hot grille of a floor furnace in the living room of our ranch house. We wanted to see what would happen to modeling clay under such circumstances. As the clay melted and flowed through the grille onto the top of the furnace proper, Nina and I agreed it looked just like butter. Mom overheard us, ran out into the living room, snatched up the clay, and cleaned up the furnace, breaking up our experiment. The punishment that time was the confiscation of all our modeling clay.

The experiments tapered off over time during my school years; my mental energy was absorbed enough in learning the scholastic material and reading for outside pleasure that I had neither need nor opportunity for that type of exploration. My appetite for those actions probably decreased as well because as I matured, I could surmise the results of pushing buttons, bending panels, and engaging in other activities from past experience. Knowing the results in advance, I no longer felt compelled to experiment with family property.

My brother Richard arrived in 1949, and my sister Emily arrived in 1951. They were playing companions for me, but when they were around me, my school days and the accompanying socialization with schoolmates meant my younger siblings were never the sole fence between me and solitude that Nina had been. School started in 1950, and I reached a new stage in my life.

The bare-bones living style we enjoyed during the first several years at the ranch would probably appear too austere for most people today. But it carried one distinct benefit: it made me less demanding of creature comforts than I might otherwise have been. I have always been content with good-enough living quarters, good-enough transportation, good-enough eating, and good-enough entertainment. The unavailability of diverting pastimes, such as television and game parks, forced me to rely on my own resourcefulness to discover fulfilling occupations. Thus my personal liberty grew.

I concede that genetics may have played a part here: none of my grandparents or parents believed in sybaritic splurges. We all managed our finances prudently. The result, whatever the combination of causes, was a boon to me over my lifetime. Never feeling the urge to purchase luxuries I did not need and could not afford, I found it easy to live within my means all my life, whatever those means happened to be at any time; to trim spending whenever necessary; and to save up a good retirement fund, which today provides me with a good-enough income.

CHAPTER 3

SCHOOL DAYS 1: GRADE SCHOOL IN RURAL MONTANA

In the fall of 1950, I entered the first grade in a proverbial one-room schoolhouse about half a mile northwest of the ranch house: Pine Hills School. At that time, we were in an old-fashioned rural setting. Sweetgrass County, Montana, contained twenty-six small country schools in addition to Big Timber city grade school. Some, like mine, had one classroom, plus a room to house the teacher. Others had two or three classrooms. At my school, we had neither sewers nor running water; our toilets were outdoor privies, and our drinking and wash water came in buckets drawn from a spring about a hundred feet down a hill from the schoolhouse. Heat in the classroom came from a large stove fueled by an oil tank outside the building. Our modern luxury consisted of real electricity for the lights; the power lines had been run out to that area just before I started school. Any nineteenth-century American novelist would have readily recognized the setting of my grade-school experience.

Pine Hills School was where I started getting significant socialization outside my nuclear family. Over those years, the Pine Hills School student body size ranged from two to six; neighborhood kids and the teacher's offspring attended the school alongside my siblings and me. The small student body made the schooling process less a school in the known sense and more a tutoring exercise.

During the first grade, my myopia was discovered, and I was presented with thick eyeglasses. I could now see better, but I frequently complained about seeing "shines" around everything—the result of fog settling on the lenses during humid days. But I believe those two factors—classmates and eyesight—allowed the commencement of the social growth that had been somewhat retarded previously.

The teachers I had during my grade-school period were a variegated lot, judged not by the techniques they used or the effect they had on the students in general but on my assessment of their effect upon my learning process. Most of them did a good job. I was fortunate in that; given the work conditions and pay we were compelled to offer, we could have ended up with a series of comedies and tragedies! With the exception of my fifth and sixth grades, which were taught by one person, none of my teachers stayed for more than one school year. Who could blame them? The conditions described above would have tried anybody, particularly on a -20 degree Fahrenheit Montana winter's day.

My first-grade teacher, Ednah Clairemont, was the middle-aged wife of a retired ship's cook and the mother of two grown children. I was fortunate to start out with her, as she was a good teacher who inspired me to want to learn, and she partially overcame my native obstinacy and aversion to being directed. A poor teacher at that point could have damaged my learning process and social development for years to come. My second-grade teacher was a nineteen-year-old girl called Fran Stall, and she continued the good practices of Mrs. Clairemont. She pushed me to learn, particularly in geography and history.

Another good teacher, Frances Carlson, was able to get us to learn copiously and well. She had two sons, one a year ahead of me and one a year ahead of my sister Nina.

A girl in her early twenties, Marilyn Srigley, was one of my most memorable teachers. Alone among my teachers, she lasted more than one school year in that austere rural setting. She was an excellent teacher who encouraged me to exercise my intellectual powers above and beyond the requirements.

Miss Srigley encouraged us all to read. We were put into a reading contest to see how many books each of us could read by the end of the school year. I came in a poor fourth; the girls all beat me by about two to one: about fifty books to my twenty-five. I don't believe my intellectual growth was stunted by that performance, because Miss Srigley set me to reading real literature. The example I remember best was "The Legend of Sleepy Hollow" by Washington Irving. Since he wrote flowery eighteenth-century prose, I had to look up many words in the dictionary. It always took a long time for me to look up a word, because I found many other interesting words along the way, and I would absorb those definitions as well. Poems by Eugene Field were another area of study. These were more children's literature than was Irving, but Miss Srigley had me put together a book containing Field poems I had memorized and add pictures illustrating the concepts that appeared in those poems. Miss Srigley was highly knowledgeable on the ins and outs of English grammar, and she inspired me to learn all about types of functions played by words in sentences and about grammar constructs, such as clauses, participles, prepositional phrases. I was moved to learn some of that material outside of classroom assignments, and I entertained myself with the recondite art of sentence diagramming. I remember Miss Srigley with gratitude and affection for contributing mightily to my love of learning.

Like almost everybody else, I learned massively during grade school. Although I brought a minimal literacy (knowledge of the alphabet and the ability to read some words) and some numeracy to the table upon entering first grade, I remember two facets of my early education: I was ecstatic at becoming able to read and write more fluently, and I developed a fascination with numbers.

All through grade school, I read for school assignments, along with extra reading for pleasure. Though I was in a rural community, I was lucky that I had books at my disposal and people who actively encouraged my interaction with them. During the latter part of second grade, my extracurricular reading included a good paperback primer astronomy book, through which I got to know a little about stars, planets, and constellations. The usual boys' literature attracted me for pleasure reading: *The Mercer Boys in the Ghost Patrol*[1] early on and, later, science books, such as *All about Dinosaurs*[2] and *All about Volcanoes and Earthquakes*.[3] Dinosaurs were presented to me as sluggish, dull-witted lizards since nobody then knew about their complex birdlike behaviors and their biological relation to birds. The explanations for volcanoes and earthquakes were not much more than a lick and a promise; much has been discovered about these geological phenomena since that time. Throughout my grade-school period, an old 1920ish edition of the *Book of Knowledge* encyclopedia provided me with much satisfaction as I plowed through it for information on natural sciences.

Late in grade school, I moved on to literature such as *Captains Courageous* and other works by Rudyard Kipling and *The Jinx Ship*.[4] I tried science fiction for a while, but I soon got bored with the same space travel, same humanoid (or Earth-taxa-like) organisms encountered, same time travel, and so on.

My literary growth was undoubtedly enhanced by the practice, performed by most of my grade-school teachers, of reading to the student body for the first fifteen minutes after each lunch hour. That may have been a local school requirement, but we went through many an interesting book in that manner.

During the second grade, I even wrote a couple of books. One of my history assignments was a biography of Abraham Lincoln. The pages were shaped like a log cabin, and the front cover was drawn and colored like a log cabin. I felt mournful at the tragedy of Lincoln's assassination. The book was a childlike effort, but as a result of that literary excursion, I pondered Lincoln at length, and history as a concept began to take shape.

My other writing effort, also during the second grade, was not part of schoolwork. It was a biography of an animated clock, called *The Runaway Clock*. That effort was derived from a fascination with Holland I had acquired while reading, or having read to me, *The Dutch Twins Primer*[5] a few years earlier. Since then, I had been fantasizing about having the Dutch twins as playmates. The protagonist clock, colored brown and fashioned like a small mechanical alarm clock with an alarm bell on top, lived with his mother and sister. One day they ran off to Holland. I remember nothing about what they did there, but I assume they met the Dutch twins. I remember they crossed the Atlantic Ocean in an oared ship. This and other aspects of the story were illustrated in pictures that occupied the top half of each page. The clock hid under the bedcovers when he was frightened, painted himself purple, and more. I have heard that the mark of a successful man of letters is that he discards the first million words he writes. In any case, my attempts at producing literature fell away at that time and did not return for some decades.

At the end of the fourth grade, I came to prominence in the county by winning a countywide spelling bee. Dixie, the runner-up, lost out to me by spelling *servant* as *servent*. I would have spelled that one properly had they asked me, but I was declared the winner forthwith. Dixie recalled that incident to me many years later at our fiftieth high school reunion; obviously, it stuck with her all that time.

Late in grade school, my literacy level came to the notice of school officials, which led to my being drafted into a couple of efforts to underline and reinforce my alleged precocity. During my sixth grade, Miss Srigley pushed me into a countywide spelling bee normally reserved for seventh and eighth graders. Miss Srigley drilled me endlessly for the contest. I came in fourth; I missed *happiness* because the woman giving the words pronounced it "hap'-un-us." I had no idea what *happenis* meant, and it didn't occur to me to ask for a meaning. My sister Nina took a long time to forgive the spelling bee MC for mispronouncing the word, and I have appreciated Nina's concern for my success ever since.

The second instance was less noble; my social immaturity became evident. Mrs. Margaret Deegan, the county school superintendent, asked that I read and review a serious novel called *Thaddeus of Warsaw*.[6] The novel was a story about Poles seeking British help against foreign occupiers of Poland after the Third Partition of Poland in the 1790s. Mrs. Deegan had great respect for my scholastic proclivities, and she thought I should reach upward from the usual seventh-grade repertoire. I could follow the storyline, and I remember a few episodes from the book, but my interest in history and geography had not yet truly blossomed. That provinciality, while understandable given my age and background, did not come close to excusing the playful, trashing review I wrote after reading the book. Mrs. Deegan was hurt and upset by my shameful behavior, and my mother emphatically relayed those feelings to me. My teacher at the time should have stepped on the so-called review before it left my desk; still, the primary culpability was mine. I partially atoned by reading a book provided by Mrs. Deegan about the life of a boy in Kashmir, north of India. This time, I wrote a reasoned and sensible review. Unfortunately, I don't remember the title of the book or much about its content. Perhaps the sport of writing a trashing review of *Thaddeus of Warsaw* focused my mind on that work sufficiently for me to form lasting memories of it. But I at least hope I acquired a small amount of character as a result of being called down for lack of it.

My fascination with numbers manifested itself in a habit of counting, a habit that lasted through the first and second grades. I either counted items or just plain counted. During the second grade, I pondered the idea of counting forever—where would I end up? I knew that one could not count forever, because forever never arrives, so I developed the phrase "on and on," which meant "an infinite number." One practical consequence was that when I came to a curved surface while counting the sides of an object, I would give up because I thought of curved surfaces as having "on and on" unimaginably short straight sides—the beginnings of differential calculus. During the previous summer, Dad had taught me the names of huge numbers: *million, billion, trillion,* and so on, up to *decillion*. But "on and on" was much greater than any of those. Checking with my parents, I asked one day how many sides a round tin can had. The idea was to check out my proposition that the can had "on and on" miniscule sides. I believe the answer given was "One curved side," but I'm not sure since I didn't have the vocabulary to understand and absorb that answer fully, and I continued to have faith in my own analysis. Such was my mathematical profession in those days.

At another time during second grade, we studied something about Chinese culture, and somehow, I got the idea that China was nine thousand miles from where we were in Montana. The inch was the smallest unit of length I knew at the time, and I asked my teacher, Fran Stall, how many inches there were in nine thousand miles. She obligingly took out pencil and paper, did the long multiplication, and gave me the answer: 570,240,000.

Later on, I engineered further numerical adventures. As I was learning long division and fraction arithmetic, I created practice problems in those areas to sharpen my skills. I made up problems more difficult than those in the school books, such as adding 58/93 to another fraction of equal improbability. I would then beg my parents, all-wise as they were, to check my arithmetic. They would usually oblige, but Dad finally asked me why I was concerning myself with "absurd" fractions, such as 58/93. Eventually, I acquired faith in my own accuracy. A mathematical nerd I was becoming, and a mathematical nerd I remained!

I graduated from grade school with a good nodding acquaintance of other subjects, even though my interest in them had not yet evolved to the inspired level. I ended up with a rudimentary but reasonable understanding of the human body, and I knew the functions of most of the organs and how the body works generally. I could name most of the US states, and I had an idea of what economic activities characterized many states. My history lore lightly covered ancient Greece and Rome, along with fairly extensive introductions to Greek and Norwegian mythologies, which serve as basis for much of those nations' literature. We delved in some detail into the stories of the explorers of the fifteenth to seventeenth centuries but without looking at underlying issues, such as the Turkish takeover of the eastern Mediterranean in 1453. A good introduction to US history included the story of the first North American settlements and of the colonial period—topics I have unfortunately neglected since. My history was mostly presented as isolated stories; there was no discussion of interconnections among events, such as the Puritan New England settlements' origin in the English Civil War or how the American participation in the Seven Years' War led up to the American Revolution. I got some dreck in the process, such as Parson Weems's myth about George Washington chopping down his father's cherry tree, the so-called martyrdom of Julius Caesar, the Spartan boy who supposedly let a fox eat into his insides and kill him, Christopher Columbus's so-called discovery of the Americas, and the might-have-been if Abraham Lincoln had lived out his second presidential term. All these were standard-issue schoolboy study material at the time. I will discuss the deficiencies in my early history education in more detail—and with more emotional heat—in chapter 10. I didn't recognize this material as such then; my more recent studies have made me aware of the problems here. Fortunately, my parents were able to straighten me out to some extent. My father pointed out that Julius Caesar was a dictator and that his killers, Brutus and Cassius, were trying to save the free constitutional Roman republic. My father also got me to question the Adam and Eve myth I had been taught about human origins, stating his belief that humans evolved from lower animals over a long period of time.

During this present era, which features the flooding of news outlets and social media with disinformation, I am grateful for having had such a thorough grounding in many subjects during my impressionable grade-school years. This subject matter—omitting the myths—plus the love of learning inculcated in me by that school system, left me with an information base that largely inoculated me against the bad actors who polluted our lives later on. But I wonder how many people today accept the official lies because they failed to obtain adequate correctives early in life.

We kept up on national and international news via a publication called *My Weekly Reader.* For my last couple of years, it was *Current Events.* Doubtless we covered much history that way, but the only events I remember internalizing were the election of Dwight Eisenhower as president in 1952, the Soviet military intervention in Hungary in 1956, and the beginnings of the space race in 1957–1958.

The launching of the Russian *Sputnik* satellite in 1957 really caught my attention; all of us were shaken badly. The success of *Sputnik* and a second Russian satellite convinced everyone that the Russians were about to get a stranglehold on us, using weapons from space. I was appalled, particularly over several news articles describing American rockets lifting off a few feet and then tipping over ignominiously, in contrast to images of awe-inspiring, picture-perfect Russian rocket launches thoughtfully provided to us by the Soviets. I pored over magazine articles and listened to radio broadcasts bemoaning our complacency and incompetence and the superhuman Russians, whose schools were much better than ours, whose scientists were much more dedicated and gifted, whose students were much more motivated, and whose system was much better. Notable in my reading was an article in *Life* magazine that compared a serious, frowning Russian student called Alexei Kutzkov to a frivolous, smiling American student called Stephen Lapekas.[7] I remember the relief we all felt when the United States launched its first satellite the following January, and I ceased to fret about our failing educational system. I educated myself a little about the Van Allen radiation belts discovered by this satellite—particles from the sun that are trapped by Earth's magnetic field. There was a good outcome from that shocking episode: as a country, we got up the energy to upgrade and reward scientific, engineering, and technological education. For a while, that was the place for a student to be.

During my grade-school time, I discovered a definite limitation to my potential as a discoverer and intellectual. While worrying at problems with my brain never ceased to be enjoyable, use of my hands to create apparatuses turned out to be less than thrilling and fulfilling. Except for a model train engine built from a wooden barrel, a wooden box, wheels, and a frame, my products were slapdash, if they were finished at all. I built a small wooden wagon, but it wouldn't stand on its own wheels, since the wheel supports were too rickety. My plan was to attach a winch to the side of the wagon and tie the ends of a length of rope to the winch and to a stake in the ground several meters from the wagon. The rope would wrap around the winch as I sat in the wagon and turned the winch, pulling me toward the stake. Unfortunately, the wooden winch was not nearly strong enough for that purpose. A gravel filterer consisting of a box with a screen bottom, mounted at the top of an inclined wooden platform, was another creation. That apparatus stood up by itself, but the angle of the platform's slope was too shallow for the purpose of filling a box at the bottom of the platform with filtered sand; the filtered sand gathered under the screen instead of sliding down the platform. A magpie trap—boards constructed into a rectangular cage covered with chicken wire, with a hole in the top to admit the entrance of magpies—was too fragile to withstand the pressures of our pet dog, Timmy, as he went after the meat bait in the trap. Those failures caused me discouragement rather than a desire to correct and improve my product, and I dropped the efforts. My most public relative success in manual construction was a robot I built using instructions in a *Boys' Life* magazine from late 1956.[8] My dad's guidance and aid were essential to finishing the project. My robot won prizes at a Livingston exposition and at the Big Timber county fair in the summer of 1957. The robot got a lot of attention, but I believe the prizes would have been larger had I spent more time and effort on good workmanship.

All of this is of a piece with my experience with gifts I received for holidays and birthdays over my grade-school period. One of my teachers, Mrs. Carlson, gave me a chemistry set for my birthday during the fourth grade, and my parents gave me a microscope set about the same time. I spent many hours playing scientist with those gifts, burning spices and making soap and looking at blood cells and a dead amoeba through the microscope. I was too juvenile to learn general principles from the experiments, but they accorded me much pleasure nonetheless.

During my seventh grade, my parents and I bought me a kit for building a three-inch reflecting telescope on a wooden tripod. My dad did most of the assembly since I was not handy with my hands. But I spent many a long evening gazing at stars, the moon, and planets. I familiarized myself with some of the constellations. Not much was gained by looking at the stars, since much more magnification than I had available is required to see them as more than points of light. But I did see the Galilean moons of Jupiter and the rings of Saturn, along with its moon Titan. Venus and Mars appeared as merely larger versions of their naked-eye selves. Earth's moon was always spectacular, even when it was not full; I loved exploring the maria and the mountains.

On other occasions, I received a couple of erector sets and a model airplane to assemble. The erector sets occupied my interest for only a matter of days, and the model airplane I produced was hasty and slipshod. It is possible my ineptness with my hands made piano lessons unacceptably difficult and limited my facility with musical instruments generally.

Despite my manual clumsiness, I received instruction from my father in the use of tools, and I retained enough of this skill to be able, in a pinch, to mount pictures on a wall, replace rotten lath, paint surfaces, and fix leaky faucets and toilets. But I still prefer to pay a professional to perform these tasks.

My pastimes during grade school were largely solitary: building the above-mentioned contraptions, riding my bicycle around the area, fishing for trout in the brook that ran by our ranch house, hiking in the hills surrounding our ranch house, and finding other ways to use time.

Starting in the summer after my sixth year, I worked as a ranch hand, helping to get rid of weeds, maintain fences, and stack hay for feeding cattle in the winter. I was competent enough in most of those jobs, but I never took pleasure in horseback riding to move cattle, nor did I ever get a knack for maintaining and running machinery. Ranch life would not have been my calling!

My social interactions during that period were necessarily sparse in our rural environment. They were mainly interfaces with a handful of schoolmates—teachers' children and neighbors—and siblings. The interactions consisted of childhood games and fantasies, which I seldom allowed to interfere with my alone time. My siblings and I constructed a sort of fairyland near the ranch house. I attached the name Aber Hill to a small fir- and pine-covered knoll at the foot of the butte east of the ranch house. Its trees made me think of Abraham Lincoln's chin—a leftover from my biography of Lincoln written during my literary period. We explored the knoll and attached names and mythical significance to each of the features there: a rock ledge, a bare windswept area, and the large pine tree on top of the knoll.

Together we siblings produced several plays to entertain the adults at family parties. We wrote the plays ourselves, and the adults applauded politely at appropriate times during the performances. Shakespeare we were not, but at least we acquired acting experience for whatever purpose that could serve.

Several times a year, I would have short-term (less than one day) social contact with local children at country square dances, Sunday school, church, and 4-H meetings. I was terribly bashful at the gatherings, and I needed time to adjust to the presence of more than a few peers. With practice, I largely overcame my bashfulness by the end of my grade-school experience. Looking back, I suspect my peers were actually as uptight as I was. We all had to acquire social grace and confidence, though the awkwardness of others wasn't apparent to me at the time.

My real opportunities for sustained social contact with many of my peers arose in two ways: biannual trips to Portland, Oregon, taken by the family and Bible camps late in my grade-school tenure.

Every two years from 1948 to 1954, Mom and her children would spend a month in early summer visiting her relatives in Portland. Mom needed to get away from the rural Montana ranch setting once in a while, and contact with her family was a necessity. Dad would show up in Portland briefly during the visits, but he spent most of his time at the ranch, as June was a busy time there. We stayed at her mother's place, and I roamed the neighborhood when permitted. Since I was just as socially awkward in Portland as I was in Montana, I had to get over some hurdles in relating to the many peers I met there. Still, I believe those Portland excursions were a major opportunity for me to grow socially in the early part of grade school. I ended up making many friends. We played children's games and put on plays to entertain the adults. There were city amenities not available in Sweetgrass County, Montana, such as zoos, amusement parks, and fancy restaurants. I remember our Portland trips with great pleasure.

During my 1950 visit, I developed a crush on a neighborhood girl called Katherine, who was one year older than I. I neglected to inform her of my feelings, and the affair soon died out. My first real romance was with another neighborhood girl, Karen, whom I met during my 1952 visit. Karen, also one year older than I, was a lovely girl with long, straight dark brown hair; ivory skin; a broad smile; and dark brown eyes. We played together several times during that visit, and we considered ourselves soul mates after that. She had a twin brother called Kevin and a circle of friends that included two boys called Tommy and Jim. Over the next couple of years, I imagined myself in many romantic scenarios and activities with Karen, and I talked to my family about marrying her. Dad reminded me that I had at least fifteen years to go before I could consider marrying anybody.

In the summer of 1953, after third grade, I went through a maturing experience. I traveled to Portland with Grandma Beth and no siblings. I was away from my nuclear family for an extended period for the first time. My grandmothers looked after me during the trip. That was when my romance with Karen really blossomed; I actually overcame my bashfulness and declared myself to her! Fortunately for my poise and self-esteem, she reciprocated. One evening during that visit, Karen and I sat on the steps in front of her house for an hour or so, looked into each other's eyes, and swore our love for each other. At that time of moonlight and roses, I was nine, and she was ten. Like almost all puppy loves, that one dissolved over the next year, but to this day, I occasionally wonder whatever became of Karen and her friends. Alas, the road not taken.

I attended Bible camps during the summers of 1957 and 1958, after seventh and eighth grade. The camps were held for a week in July at Luther Lodge in the mountains south of Big Timber, Montana. The activities consisted of Bible study in the mornings; sports, hiking, and free time in the afternoons; and sometimes lectures about miscellaneous topics in the evenings. I was not very good at the sports—baseball and volleyball—but I became known among the boys as a mental whiz because of my prowess at a word rummy card game called Snare. A good vocabulary was essential in playing the game. My interface with the girls consisted of schoolboy mockery and a date with one girl called Carla. I don't remember what the date was officially about, but I brought her a chocolate bar as a gift. She accepted the candy, but she didn't like the fact that the candy bar was broken into several pieces inside the wrapper. Our entire date, in fact, consisted of that candy exchange. On another occasion, I noted that it was cheap of some of the boys to shout repeatedly, "Tub of lard!" at one of the overweight girls during the sports games, but I never made my sentiments public; it would have been impolitic at that time and place. Ah, the joys of youth!

I will dwell on one grade-school experience for a while because it introduced me to a decidedly unsavory ethic: a stand-your-ground mindset that brooks no "disrespect" and always throws the last punch. A schoolmate repeatedly beat up on me while he was in Montana. My family and associates continually urged me to bully this schoolmate in retaliation for his confrontations with me. It was stressed to me that I alone was responsible for putting him in his place; social networks and legal frameworks had no business in injecting themselves into that test of my manhood. This ethic was amplified by the cultural messaging of the time: song lyrics, television shows, books, and movies, particularly those of the Wild West genre, defined the measure of a man as the desire to stand up for himself against all challengers with no support from anyone else in a lawless or semilawless society. Brute physical blows probably would have gotten my schoolmate off my back, but I believe that in general, especially in the twenty-first century, this is a poor approach to human relationships and a poor message for parents to send to their children. Physical violence is the method by which lower animals—and penitentiary inmates—establish their place in hierarchical groups. But in a modern, fluid, heterogeneous society, such behavior is disruptive in situations wherein many people must work together in complex ways, and it demoralizes the entire group. Furthermore, physical attacks often lead to revenge attacks and counter-revenge, possibly spiraling into harmful or fatal outcomes. For these reasons, I believe firmly in calling in the authorities—police or company management—whenever anyone attempts a physical confrontation. This is what the authorities are for: to pour cold water on hot contests that may lead to catastrophe and to prevent violence from becoming established as a norm.

At the time, my failure to adapt that approach to personal differences stemmed less from pondering its ramifications and more from my reluctance to enter into fights; however, I now count myself fortunate that I never attained either enthusiasm or skill in pugilistic encounters. These attributes would have served me very ill in my career; toward antics like these, all of my employers had a strict zero-tolerance policy— painfully acquired by losing lawsuits brought by employees hurt on the job in that way. In my workplaces, striking anyone would lead not only to summary termination but also to likely civil and criminal legal sanctions. I never challenged, and if challenged, I alerted the proper authorities. While this is not the way to make a good impression on old-fashioned red-blooded men (and what person of character would wish to impress such specimens?), it did preserve me from bodily injury and career difficulties.

Like most early teenage boys, I started getting erotic feelings in the sixth grade or so. Twilla, one of the daughters of Grandpa Ed's hired hand, had a pretty face and figure. I developed a small crush on her, as did many of the local boys. I would demonstrate my affection to Twilla by pulling her hair, kneeing her in the behind, teasing her about the fact that she was in my grade but nearly a year older than I, and engaging in other such twelve-year-old stunts. My crush burned out after a few months, and we settled comfortably into a type of mutually antagonistic relationship commonly found among sixth and seventh graders.

There were not many companions out on the ranch in Montana

from which to choose and from which to draw conclusions about human nature and relationships in general. As a result, I was vulnerable to distortions emanating from the popular culture at the time. Those distortions did not perturb my male-to-male social development, as popular culture did not distort that aspect of human interaction much. That side of my social being developed satisfactorily over my high school and college years. But my relationships with women were significantly retarded by the emphasis placed on girlish immaturity—no doubt due in part to the sexism and sexual repression of the time and place.

Like a lot of boys in their early teens, I listened to hit-parade songs extensively. The lyrics were written from the standpoint of adolescents, who drove popular culture at the time. Characteristic of that mindset, the lyrics were commonly about a brokenhearted boy or girl whose so-called true love had suddenly walked out without warning or apparent cause. Others were about boys lamenting that their girlfriends had left them because they dated around when they were supposed to be steady in the relationship. Then there were songs about one of the mates being too poor, too low class, or not sufficiently entertaining to be acceptable to the other mate. Teenagers telling their parents to butt out—because teenagers are mature and know all about love—constituted another theme. Magazine short stories laid out the same narrative. Breakups, makeups, and emotional dramas have always been part and parcel of teenage boy-girl interactions, but more nuanced portrayals were not readily available for me to peruse. One day my dad referred to all of this as "bad propaganda." He had no idea how accurate he was!

Also taught was the notion of women as the so-called weaker sex. They were portrayed as slightly incompetent and needing help in sitting down to the table, ordering from a restaurant menu, opening doors, putting on coats, and more. They were fit for housekeeping and child nurturing but not for public office or running a business. The *Saturday Evening Post* had a column called "You Be the Judge," in which the reader was supposed to study the story of a real legal case and then decide for himself how the verdict should go before peeking at the judge's actual ruling. A case relevant to women's issues at the time concerned a man accidentally hitting a woman with his car.[9] The woman ended up with scars on her face. The man agreed to pay for her medical care, plastic surgery, and lost wages, but the woman demanded more on the argument that no man would marry her because of her scars. The man rejected the additional payouts, so the case came before an Ohio judge in 1951. The judge ordered him to pay her the further damages. The *Saturday Evening Post* reproduced the wording of the judge's ruling, and I transcribe those words here in order to demonstrate how this case epitomized the absurdities and injustices faced by women at that time: "Injury to marriage prospects may blast the money value of a woman's whole life. It is open to every woman, however poor or humble, to obtain a secure and independent position in the community by marriage and, in that matter, which is said to be the chief end of her existence, personal appearance—comeliness—is a consideration of comparative importance for every daughter of Eve." Since those were the dark pre–women's liberation days, the misogynistic nature of the ruling didn't register with me at that time. At the tender age of thirteen, I agreed with the man because I saw the award as unwarranted compensation for vanity. Today that ruling is repugnant to me for a different reason—the orthodoxy that the entire purpose of half our species is to catch a husband and have babies! The prospect of being a single woman was alleged to be incomparably worse than the prospect of spending a lifetime with a man of such deficient character that he would ditch a woman because of her facial scars![10] The idea of women as lovely but burdensome and frivolous beings in need of protection came through clearly to me as a result of all that training, which accorded with the superior male ethos of the era.

Real-life examples of the feminine stereotype were plentiful then; the adult women I observed during grade school were mainly praised as good wives, mothers, and housekeepers—never as good human beings. The narrow purpose of women was clear, but that was never the entire panorama. To get a more fully rounded conception, I would have had to observe more counterexamples personally, and the human material in our Montana neighborhood was simply too sparse and too biased to benefit me in that regard. That deficiency was exacerbated by my natural preference for aloneness. As a result, I carried with me for many years a wariness about women combined with a gross naivete.

Counterbalancing all the solitude and suspicion was my parents'

49

relationship, which was a solid, loving marriage illustrating better possibilities than the adolescent melodramas I witnessed vicariously. Since I was carefully shielded from the infidelities and pathologies elsewhere in my family tree until much later in my life, those problems did not impinge on my development. My father gave me lick-and-a promise talk on the facts of life as well—nothing to make me an expert but an introduction nevertheless.

My grade-school period ended in 1958, and so did Pine Hills School. During the autumn following my eighth-grade graduation, a new county school superintendent supervised the consolidation of our twenty-six country schools into four, and Pine Hills School was one of the casualties. The surviving schools all had several rooms and accommodations for many students. One-room country schooling in Sweetgrass County was no more. The Pine Hills School building still stands half a mile northwest of the ranch house. It is now a dilapidated hulk and an eyesore home to vermin, gutted of its furnishings, and letting in all kinds of weather. But it still calls forth many memories.

CHAPTER 4

SCHOOL DAYS 2: HIGH SCHOOL IN SMALL-TOWN MONTANA

I started high school at Sweetgrass County High School, Big Timber, Montana, in the fall of 1958. Big Timber has a population of just under two thousand. This move to a city was a major dislocation for me at first. A tranquil and isolated setting tends to prolong one's social youth, and I was no exception. Outside our Portland vacations and the two Bible camps, high school was the first time I had experienced sustained daily contact with dozens of my contemporaries. Country hobbledehoy that I was, my peers and, at times, certain members of the high school faculty kept me reminded of my lack of sophistication.

Inauspiciously, I missed the first week of high school as a result of a chicken pox bout. More importantly to my schoolmates, I missed out on high school initiation, a day of hazing by upperclassmen. That marked me as a shirker, and eventually, a group of seniors corrected that deficiency by abducting me one night and smearing lipstick all over me. I got into a couple of fistfights as a result of prankish challenges by certain schoolmates who exploited my naivete. Nobody understood the idea of getting the authorities to stop that sort of thing, and it is possible in those dark days that the authorities would have disowned any idea of intervening. I was frequently sent off on other wild-goose chases. My dad intervened with the high school principal and then took me aside for a discussion of my hayseed ways. After a few months, I finally learned to cope, and the hazing stopped. Fortunately, I had enough independence and inner strength that I was able to slough off the pranks. Whenever any peers had a laugh at my expense, I considered the source, as the saying goes, though at times, my temper would rise within me. But it never escalated to violence or even verbal retaliation, and I was never traumatized as far as I can tell. Possibly because of that hazing, I never felt the slightest desire to join any groups that hazed other students.

Bashful and solitary as I was, I never ran around with any schoolmates, nor did I join any cliques. The proximity of many girls brought forth in full flower the physical feelings I had previously felt briefly for Twilla and Carla. None of us knew what to do about those feelings. We were all awkward, even if I was more awkward than most. Some of us had been apprised of the facts of life, to degrees of sophistication that varied with each individual. But experimentation was strictly off-limits—not only because the necessary social graces were underdeveloped in us but also because we were still living in that dark era before contraception, before abortions, and before women's liberation. Having received a quick, broad-brush instruction on the facts of sex from my father several years before, I was able to discard the more outlandish tales and instructions from my peers. But obviously, my father, being a secondhand source, could not instruct me clearly on the emotional aspects of sex from the female standpoint, and it was a generous decade, and several missteps to be described later, before I got this issue somewhat straightened out in my mind.

My romantic life was limited by my social deficiencies. For a while, I carried schoolboy crushes on a couple of the girls, and a couple of other girls had quick crushes on me. Unfortunately, wary and countrified as I was, I didn't know how to handle those situations or how to build a relationship. I never had a long-term serious relationship with any woman until after I started my professional life well beyond university.

I was among the college-bound set from the beginning. We took Latin and biology during my freshman year, rather than shop (boys) or home economics (girls) and general science. From there on, our courses were geared toward higher education: four years of mathematics up to trigonometry; chemistry and physics during our upper-class years; two years of Latin; and four years of English and literature. I aced mathematics and science tests enough to overawe many of my classmates. Latin was interesting enough to get me to apply myself, as was English sometimes. History and civics bored me, and my grades there showed it. Internal fire for those topics was not yet born within me, and as mentioned before, I learned primarily what I wanted to learn. Unfortunately, since many of the teachers and much of the academic material were less than inspiring, my enthusiasms were strictly limited to fields of endeavor for which the inspiration was previously present. Branching out was to occur several years later.

I had terrible problems with making presentations in front of a class. That must have compromised my grades in biology, English, and history in at least a small way. Stage fright plagued me all the way through high school and college, and it did not wear off until I was into my professional life. Perhaps it was an outgrowth of the impostor syndrome from which I suffer—certainty that failure and exposure of my hollowness are inevitable. My stage fright in high school was not helped by the fact that adolescents like to pick on each other, particularly if the victim is a rural naïf or is perceived as different in any way from the run of the pack.

I quickly became known as the class brain as well as the class bumpkin. The brain part inspired enough respect among my schoolmates that I was never chronically persecuted, though I could become a sensation. During my sophomore year, I so impressed a couple of the girls by being able to recite the Greek alphabet that they made me go through it repeatedly, in front of several groups of their friends. I was an exhibit, but how and when I acquired the Greek alphabet is now a mystery to me.

I gained additional respect by doing homework assignments for my classmates when they deemed it necessary. This latter activity showed that my character was still underdeveloped. I had always wanted to help people who needed help, but I was doing no favors by doing the homework myself. Much better would have been to tutor them, using the homework assignment as a basis. Later on, in college, I aided students in doing their homework, but I never took the assignment to write out myself. By that time, I realized that homework was more than just a meaningless chore; the other students needed to learn the material as well as I.

Extracurricular reading for pleasure dropped off markedly upon my entry into high school, and it didn't recover until well into my graduate school studies. While I did a little recreational reading during those years, keeping up with the homework assignments and extracurricular-activity demands was enough to crowd out that activity. Another casualty was 4-H Club activity, which had partially occupied several summers during my grade-school period.

The teacher I had for biology and civics, Mr. Collins, was a no-nonsense type who radiated authority; nobody acted up in his classes. He presented the material adequately, and I had scientific inclination enough to ace biology tests. That was the first course in which I had to suffer a real laboratory experience. The microscope afforded interesting views of live microorganisms in action. We dissected a couple of small animals, but I just couldn't be enthusiastic about drawing what I saw. My drawings were hasty and slapdash; my lab partner did a much better job. Civics was a course I coasted through, doing adequate but not spectacular work. Mr. Collins engaged us with interesting questions to ponder. He presented us with a bar graph showing the percentage of voter turnout for various countries. He pronounced the graph "propaganda" and asked us why it was so. I answered that question properly: the bar graphs displayed not the real percentages but how far the percentages exceeded 50 percent. That made the 55 percent US turnout look like a small fraction of the 70 to 80 percent turnouts of other countries—clearly a distortion. Later, he teased us with the question of the difference between civil rights and civil liberties. None of us could get that one. Today I would postulate that civil rights are those activities specifically allowed to us by statute and not revocable except by due process of law. Civil liberties are those activities not specifically forbidden to us by the legal code. For example, we have the right to vote spelled out in laws, but we have the liberty to criticize the president. Unfortunately, since Mr. Collins is no longer with us, I cannot check this out with him.

For three years of English, I had Miss Conwell, who was decidedly an acquired taste. During my sophomore year, I had difficulty adjusting to her methods and requirements. The literature presented was largely uninspiring—thumbnail-sketch biographies of prominent people. I found it difficult to concentrate and remember such scattershot material. In that class, moreover, we were all required to talk in front of the class about books we had read. That petrified me, and my first few oral reports were fiascos. To ease the burden, I pulled a trick a couple of times that I'm sure many students pulled: reading the first half (or quarter) of a book, reporting on that part, and then assuring the class they wouldn't want me to spoil the story by giving away the ending. If Miss Conwell caught on, she didn't so indicate; she was a little obtuse in spotting cheaters. Each time I recall this trick, I kick myself mentally for having behaved so cheaply. I cheated myself of learning along with cheating in class. My gaming was hardly a mark of high character, but as time wore on, I became able to benefit from Miss Conwell's classes. The material we studied during my last two years greatly surpassed in quality the smatterings that characterized my sophomore year, and I developed a real appreciation for fine literature at that time. Perhaps being forced to present to the class so many times over the years even wore away some of my stage fright. I believe Miss Conwell and I got along reasonably well by the time graduation arrived.

For chemistry, physics, and one of the advanced mathematics courses, we had Mr. Schump. He had been teaching at Sweetgrass County High School since the early 1920s, and he had run his laps so many times that he could almost lecture in his sleep. He knew and presented the material in the high school textbooks well, and under his guidance, I prepared a couple of science projects for presentation at district and state fairs (more about this topic later). I started thinking about doing science as a career because Mr. Schump presented the material at his disposal so interestingly and well. But as you shall see later, facility in grasping scientific concepts is necessary but not sufficient for becoming an effective scientist.

Mr. Schump was an excellent laboratory instructor; he knew good technique and strove mightily to inculcate it in us. Unfortunately, I didn't absorb much lab technique, probably because of its emphasis on manual dexterity. The upshot was that my first chemistry lab notebook consisted of a sheaf of loose papers bearing scribbles. Mr. Schump did not give me a grade for that first attempt at a lab notebook, and he kept it for years afterward to show students how he did not want lab notebooks to be constructed. My later lab notebooks were improvements—enough to merit a C grade.

Mr. Schump's only weaknesses were his failure to keep up with the evolution of scientific knowledge after he started teaching and a tendency to punt when asked a question that stumped him. He flubbed a question I asked about atomic nuclei, which had been a controversial concept when he got started as a teacher in the 1920s, and about which little was known then. When I asked him how an atomic nucleus stayed together when the positively charged protons within the nucleus repelled each other, he replied rather tentatively that gravitational force among the protons maintained the integrity of the nucleus by overcoming the repulsive electrostatic forces. I accepted his answer with some discomfort; gravitational force seemed to me to be quite weak compared to electrostatic forces. The weight of a scrap of paper electrostatically attached to a balloon certainly did not detach the paper from the balloon, but maybe at intranuclear distances—what did I know? In the event, Mr. Schump's spectacularly wide-of-the-mark speculation was a disservice to his class and to Mr. Schump himself; he should have looked up the answer (strong nuclear force) and passed it along. Better yet, he should have already known about strong nuclear force, which was well-established science by the time I was in high school. Had Mr. Schump stretched to get us the correct answer, we all would have learned something that was not in the textbook, and Mr. Schump would have been jarred from his comfort box a little. I got the correct answer at university a few years later.

I took a world history course from Mr. Ollestad. He taught adequate material, and he pushed us by requiring oral history reports in front of the class on topics researched by us, not in the textbook. I gave several reports over the school year—with great trepidation, given my stage fright. But maybe those ordeals calmed my stage fright somewhat. The racism and ethnocentrism of the times was apparent in that course. It was tagged as "world history," but it was actually a history of the Greek and Roman empires and Western Europe, with a little of the Middle East and Latin America thrown in because of their interactions with

Europe. Not a trace of Chinese and East Asian, South Asian, or Pacific Island history was presented, and no African or Native American history was included in the course, except in brief accounts of European exploitation of those areas and peoples. In short, our so-called world history course was a history of the white man. I don't fault our teachers or the school; that was just the thinking and the availability of materials in those days. It would have been a challenge to include all of those topics in one school year's course without degeneration into a series of smatterings. Nevertheless, I believe it could have been accomplished with good organization and presentation of the history—pointing out interconnections but not bogging down in detail anywhere. I have often since reflected that I could have rendered myself and the course a great service by making my oral reports about those non-European areas—assuming that adequate source literature was available.

Our teacher for algebra, geometry, and trigonometry was Mr. Holmberg. He was the favorite of many of the students. His teaching was very effective because he had great interest in mathematics himself, and he knew how to present the material to high school students. Since my enthusiasm for numbers was already high, I did extremely well in his classes. Mr. Holmberg was more introverted than the other teachers, so our social interactions were weaker with him than with the others. He was there to teach, period, but he had no weaknesses I can recall.

About halfway through high school, I underwent a scholastic awakening. I had always assumed that some of my classmates were much smarter than I was, since their grades were better. But one day my mother said, "You are much smarter than they are!" To me, her statement was startling as well as slightly incredible, but I remembered it, obviously, and the statement had a lasting effect on my subsequent behavior. From then on, I got better grades than my classmates in math and science courses, as well as outscoring them on national tests. I suppose my mother's observation gave me a psychological boost that impelled me to give a damn about scholastic achievement. But I still don't care who boasts the most intellectual candlepower; I have never believed in spitting contests like this. The idea is to make the best possible use of whatever gifts one has, not to beg for what one does not have or waste time and energy in pointless one-upmanship.

My extracurricular activities in high school were many and varied. Those activities helped me to emerge from my social isolation and put me more at ease in interacting with other people.

I played drums in the school band for all four years. This was a nod to my musical tendencies, but I had my shortcomings in the endeavor. I learned to read rhythm from a musical score after a fashion, but since reading pitch from a score was not necessary for drum players, I never troubled myself to acquire that skill. I never got the hang of generating a good snare drum roll; my rolls were always ragged and hesitant. I moved to bass drum, which was much easier, during my succeeding years.

Our band teacher, Mr. Woolley, was not especially popular with the students, but I got along with him fine. He did a good job of getting us to perform musical pieces skillfully, as high school students go. We entertained the local people with concerts at Christmas and in the spring, and we were usually praised for our performances. We played at football and basketball games as well, hyping our team and cheering it on.

During the spring, our band attended district music festivals in Billings. The band as a whole would play a piece, and individuals and groups from the band would present performances. Judges rated our performances as 1 (superior), 2 (good), 3 (adequate), 4 (needs work), and 5 (not prepared). Those who got a superior rating were eligible to go to the state music festival in Missoula later in the spring to present their skills to tougher judges for ratings as described above. My first attempt at something outside the whole-band performance was as one of a drum and cymbal trio during my sophomore year. We got an adequate rating from the judges, which I thought was just; I was thankful to do that well. My stage fright was alive and well at the time; one of our teachers, Mr. Ollestad, who witnessed our production, commented to me about how terrified I looked during the performance.

For my junior year, a group of us presented an ultramodern new-age piece played on drums, cymbals, triangles, castanets, and other exotic instruments. We enjoyed the piece and performed splendidly, and we were looking forward to getting a superior rating and taking the piece to Missoula. Unfortunately, the judge gave us a mere good rating because he didn't like the piece, and we were all disgusted. My senior year saw me perform a bass drum solo with my sister Nina as a piano accompanist. This time, I got a superior rating at the district festival and finally got to go to the state music festival. At Missoula, I got another superior rating, which made everyone proud of me. To an extent, the accomplishment compensated for the injustice visited upon us the previous year at the district festival.

I believe our whole-band performances got good ratings at the district festivals each time I was there. During my junior year, we presented a difficult work: the prelude to act three of the opera *Lohengrin* by Richard Wagner. Mr. Woolley drilled us endlessly on it; he was determined that it would be our magnum opus. I remember with amusement the judge's comment on our performance. As he gave us the good rating, he said, "A gallant attempt, but I do believe this piece is a little beyond the reach of high school students." Having since heard this prelude performed professionally, I can see that judge's point!

My athletic career in high school is worth mentioning not because I was anything memorable but because I participated in all the major sports available at the time in our school: football (junior and senior years), basketball (all years), and track (all years). I lettered in football and basketball for my junior and senior years and in track for sophomore, junior, and senior years. I lettered in football and basketball because our coaches, Mr. Graham and Mr. Dunham, believed in giving credit for the many endless practices as well as actual playing time. I was a fair-to-mediocre participant in those sports, and my status as a team member resulted mainly in my having a ringside seat at all the games. At times, I would be put in during the last few minutes of games, but only when (1) Big Timber was ahead enough and the time left in the game was short enough that the coach was certain I couldn't blow Big Timber's lead, or (2) Big Timber was hopelessly behind, and the coach decided I would benefit from a little playing time and could not possibly make the situation any worse. Track and field was where I actually earned my spurs. I ran in the half-mile run at each track meet, but I placed only once in that event at a track meet. High jump and broad jump were my real events, and during the years when I earned sports letters, I placed in those events regularly.

My general attitude toward sports was probably too philosophical for me to become a great. I felt that sports were a way to keep in physical condition and perhaps train my body to be more dexterous. But the competitive bug never bit me, and I never felt that athletics were a gateway to success in later life; that was not why I was in school. Thus, when Big Timber won the divisional football championship during my senior year, after another game wherein my participation consisted of a ringside seat, I was pleased but not ecstatic, as the coaches and most of my teammates were. The basketball tournament games in Billings were interesting to watch, but I never got overwrought about wins or losses. The thrill of victory and the agony of defeat were just not in me.

As happens in all schools, we had superstars in the various sports, particularly in basketball, which was a long-standing Big Timber specialty. They were the heroes of the student body, naturally. But I never respected or envied athletic prowess as such, and I certainly never got up the motivation to emulate the great athletes. Upon completion of high school, some of these superstars had trouble finding remarkable college or professional careers. I sometimes think that for a while, they pined for the good old days of high school at the expense of pursuing meaningful activities after their athletic lamps dimmed. Much later in life, Marky and I plowed together through the Rabbit series of novels by John Updike.[1] These stories resonated with me, as they outlined the life of a high school basketball superstar who, during the next forty years, never regained anything like his former glory. I felt grateful that I had resources that could see me through life.

Those resources were developed via the rest of my extracurricular activities. I acted in plays presented by our high school thespian club. Acting in front of an audience helped further to dispel my stage fright, since I was complimented on my acting ability, especially in our junior class play. In that production, I was the harassed father in a somewhat dysfunctional family and was obsessed with my competition with a business rival, and my daughter was a college psychology major practicing her arts on our family. In another play, I was the husband half of a racist couple from Texas visiting a friend up north who had adopted children of all complexions from all over the world. It was important to remind the people of Big Timber that racism was a problem in our country, but at the time, I was not sophisticated enough to internalize the message of the play. My real racial awakening was to come decades later.

In late summer after my junior year, I was selected to go to Western Montana College at Dillon, along with four of my male classmates, for the annual Boys State convention. The purpose of the convention was to provide an opportunity for boys to practice active participation in municipal and state government. The attendees were divided into inhabitants of eight mock towns, where we elected town mayors and councils. Later, we elected officials to a mock state government. Campaigns, including speeches, slogans, and posters, accompanied the elections. That week proved to be educational for me, but it could have been much more educational had I been more interested in civics at the time. I did get a feel for local and state government structure and campaign techniques. Unfortunately, the details escaped me because I did not pay enough attention to the lessons and procedures. Needless to say, I didn't run for any offices, though it is more than likely that stage fright contributed as much to my lack of political ambition as did my low level of fascination with government. Attraction to that topic arrived much later in my life, and I will deal with it in later chapters.

One unattractive feature of the event was the fact that its organizers were extremely conservative Republicans who ran the show from that standpoint. Everybody was ferociously anti-Communist and probably equally anti–New Deal and anti–everything since 1930. Our daily schedules were rigorously regulated, and we were forbidden to leave the Western Montana College campus on pain of summary expulsion from the Boys State conference. Fraternization with women was heavily discouraged, and there were rumors of saltpeter in our food to keep us tame. I remember that my own sexual longings were attenuated during that week. Was it placebo effect or real saltpeter? The exception to all the prudery was a dance at the end of the week, but after the dance, all couples that had formed were broken up. At a fork in the path outside the dance hall stood a mean-looking policeman with a club pointed toward us as we exited the dance hall. "Boys this way! Girls that way!" he barked.

My Boys State experience introduced me not only to government as practiced but also to the political, social, and sexual darkness that characterized that age, especially in rural states, such as Montana. As if to underscore the reactionary, misogynistic culture of the time and place, the pictures of female college employees in the Boys State album were labeled with their husbands' names—both Christian names and surnames. "Mrs. Ken Johnson," "Mrs. Ray Hendricks," and several other similarly named women were pictured; these women had neither names nor identities except as adjuncts to Ken Johnson, Ray Hendricks, and the others. (I have changed the names to protect the guilty.) Thankfully, this pitiful practice has mostly disappeared from women's signatures nowadays. As is to be expected from the very conservative Boys State mentors, much ado was made about American freedom, but personal liberty was neither discussed nor encouraged. Good character was never a topic.

During my junior and senior years, I constructed a couple of science projects for exhibition at science fairs. Both projects were labeled in the chemistry category. Mr. Schump provided the ideas and inspiration for my projects, and he had a history of turning out winning science projects. I was able to continue in this vein, even overcoming my reluctance to work at producing well-done handmade exhibits. Mr. Schump insisted I take the time and effort to produce attractive illustrations of my work, in contrast to my usual slop. But I was inspired by building the projects; they enabled the learning of fascinating scientific material outside the routine school program, and there was no scholastic compulsion about completing them. Since those science displays were built of my own volition, I was inclined to do a good construction job. In that case, rectitudinal fever was able to overmatch sloth.

Great lab technician that he was, Mr. Schump insisted I record all data I observed. Other than that, he allowed me to collect data as I saw fit and interpret it as I saw fit. His was a strictly hands-off approach as to science exhibit content. He allowed me to make my own mistakes—a much better approach to getting students to learn than spoon-feeding and micromanaging.

My science projects were first displayed at a district science fair in Bozeman. Projects could get a superior rating (blue ribbon), a good rating (red ribbon), an adequate rating (white ribbon), or a fair rating (no ribbon). Projects awarded a blue ribbon were later exhibited at the state science fair in Missoula.

Both of my exhibits were set up as graphs and other displays mounted in a triptych of wooden panels. Details of the science involved and my triumphs and blunders are recounted in the notes; those with a scientific bent may go there.

For my junior year project, I measured the electrical resistances of water solutions of several electrolytes.[2] This exhibit got a superior rating at Bozeman, and I went on to display it at Missoula, where it was also considered a winner.

During my senior year, I illustrated the Hall effect in nonferrous metal strips, the anomalous Hall effect in iron strips, and the Hall effect in shallow strips of aqueous salt solution.[3] Despite the amateurishness of my effort in this admittedly esoteric topic, I got a superior rating for the exhibit at the district science fair in Bozeman. At the state competition in Missoula, I got an award for the best exhibit in the chemistry category. Given the inadequacies of my scientific analysis concerning the Hall effect for salt solutions,[3] I suspect the professors who evaluated my exhibit were somewhat less than knowledgeable about the ins and outs of the Hall effect and, thus, could not criticize my work adequately, particularly as to liquid strips of salt solution. Fine details of the Hall effect's mechanism are still being debated today, and they were much less well known in the 1960s.

A special evaluator arrived at my exhibit at the state fair in Missoula sometime after the main inspections had been completed. He quizzed me about the anomalous Hall effect in iron and what explanations I could offer for it. I could offer none since I had not pondered the *why* of the result—another sign that I was a long way from scientific maturity at the time. I was presenting data but not necessarily explaining it. I was later informed that he was probably evaluating me for a special award; if so, I missed out because I muffed his question. He most likely had only an elementary and inaccurate answer himself since a purportedly definitive mechanism, based on experiments and theories that evolved between 1970 and 2000, has only recently been proposed to explain the anomalous Hall effect.[4] Based on this observation, I conclude that he was evaluating me not for my extensive physics lore but for rigor and curiosity in my scientific thinking—certainly not adequately evolved when I was in high school!

Going over recent material on the Hall effect, especially the anomalous Hall effect, I have become impressed by just how complicated and controversial are the mechanisms relating to this phenomenon in various materials, even in the twenty-first century. Reflecting on that science project, I am amazed I received any awards at all, given the numerous holes in both my scientific knowledge and my scientific reasoning. I wonder if the previously noted remark by the judge of our musical band's production of the prelude to act three of *Lohengrin* ("A gallant attempt, but ...") applied as well to my effort to untangle the Hall effect.

During the summer after my senior year, just before going away to college, I managed to plow through *The Rise and Fall of the Third Reich*,[5] a lengthy but competent primer on the genesis and history of Nazi Germany. In that way, I made my first serious effort at educating myself in history and other nontechnical areas with no school-assignment compulsion. But the demands of college life prevented me from following up on such endeavors for several years afterward.

The end of high school marked the end of my life in Sweetgrass County. My high school experience had enhanced my self-confidence greatly in academic pursuits, if only slightly in social ones. I felt ready, and even eager at times, for the adventures coming up—leaving Big Timber and beginning a new life. I visited the ranch and even worked briefly there on occasions afterward, but from the autumn of 1962, I was running my day-to-day life according to my own judgment. High school graduation and leaving the area of my childhood and adolescence were significant benchmarks in my life.

I am thankful my formative years were spent in Sweetgrass County. I derived a distinct advantage in my quest for personal liberty and good character by observing the people around me. Counterexamples were few; I rarely encountered any of the broken people described by J. D. Vance,[6] whose characters now often come to mind when rural life is discussed. I attended the local Montana Lutheran churches with my family from an early age, in an era before many American churches had been morally compromised by participation in secular political life. The church, my parents, and the community at large all taught me the virtuous attributes of conservatism: honesty, a sense of justice, and the conviction that one must take control over one's own life and is free to make choices but is also obligated to accept all the consequences of those choices.

My early Montana and Oregon neighborhoods were uniformly Caucasian. That was inevitable at the time, since the introduction of non-Caucasians to any of those neighborhoods would likely have resulted in an epic upheaval and the public expulsion of the minorities. While that was a grand moral failing among Caucasians during my formative years, it benefited me during my vulnerable development period by depriving me of concrete examples of minority individuals whom my elders otherwise might possibly have pointed out to me as bad and undesirable companions. Our elders offered us a few tepid remarks on the subject, but nothing ever stuck. The fact that I never had vigorous, active indoctrination in race politics during my early years made it easy for me to work with a wide diversity of colleagues over my university and professional careers.

How an upbringing among truly committed racists can cripple one's moral development was made clear to me later in Oklahoma (see chapter 6) and to a smaller extent in Cuyamaca, California (see chapter 9), as well as in miscellaneous observations at work, during travel, and in reading. Anybody who, at the age of three years, started attending lynching parties; hearing vehement lectures on the evils of some local, visible ethnic or social group; or being beaten with switches for associating with children of that group is likely a heavily damaged human being. I have formed the impression that an individual who is born into a social injustice and imbibes it with his mother's milk will probably regard that injustice, however horrendous or massive, as part of the natural order; he can be weaned from it only with great difficulty, if at all. On the other hand, someone encountering an injustice after some years of development outside of it would be more receptive to the idea that it really is an injustice to be combated. Whether I would have had the free will to shake off allegiance to a race-based injustice that was part of my life from birth—in a community containing people handy for the persecuting—is forever an open question. I like to hope I'd have had such power, but it is most likely better that I did not begin my journey with those additional hobbles.

Also of great benefit for me was the positive attitude toward success among Sweetgrass County residents—contrasting with attitudes in stereotypical rural, small-town, and working-class communities. Books and music were everywhere in our ranch house, our parents and teachers read to us, and our curiosity about all topics was actively encouraged. I finished my twelve years of rural Montana school experience with as good a preparation for more advanced education as one gets anywhere. With a few notable exceptions (which I will not note here), all the adults in the area pushed their children to go as far in education as possible, and they were delighted to see their offspring collecting university degrees and scattering over the globe to pursue exotic careers.

This contrast was unremarkable to me when I lived there, but since moving around the country and living life, I have seen counterexamples. These incidents vividly illustrate the destructive effects of what I call "have-nots' revenge"—strong resentment of those who have prospered better in life, often leading to active measures against them.[7] During my professional career, two personal acquaintances recounted to me the resistance and resentment of their families and neighbors at the idea of their getting an education, leaving their village or urban blue-collar enclave, and making their mark in the world. Since then, I have read a fine book by Alfred Lubrano[8] detailing the tribulations of many who start out in peasant or working-class families and leave home to educate themselves and rise to white-collar careers. There is a feeling among certain peasant and working-class parents that their kids must never think they're better than their families or communities by striving for personal achievement. During my childhood and adolescent years in Montana, I never encountered this attitude, except in fiction—for example, in Huckleberry Finn's oafish father in the Mark Twain classic *The Adventures of Huckleberry Finn*. Pap orders Huck to "drop that school" and not "put on airs over his own father." But observing it in real life, I pitied and admired those people who had to swim upstream to lead fulfilling lives and, in so doing, left behind an embittered and estranged set of relatives and neighbors. I consider this attitude toward one's children's educations and careers to be despicable and tantamount to child abuse. For each escapee, how many fine minds and lives have been imprisoned forever unsung either because their peasant families successfully corralled them or because the idea of rising above one's origin never arose? This is a loss not only to the person but also to the country and to the world, especially as the twenty-first century wears on and the demand for weak minds and strong backs wanes.

Why Sweetgrass County residents, rural and somewhat provincial though many are, remain largely immune to "have-nots' revenge" is open to speculation. I posit that Sweetgrass County youngsters are encouraged to grow and diverge partly because many of the area's original settlers were not passive low-caste peasants and laborers but middle-class farmers and tradesmen who brought with them a respect for learning and diversity and an understanding and acceptance of the idea that one can and should take charge of one's own life. Having recently uprooted themselves to seek better lives, they understood social, economic, and physical mobility, and they lacked the caste mindset, which is an essential progenitor for "have-nots' revenge." They passed these salutary attributes down to succeeding generations. Another factor may be that Sweetgrass County has retained many vibrant social institutions—churches, clubs, libraries, and school functions—that allow people to mingle and not brood about their aloneness. They are thus spared the alienation, bitterness, and fatalism that commonly characterize people whose social interactions are minimal or nonexistent. Finally, Sweetgrass County is extremely homogeneous economically, ethnically, and politically.

Almost all business in Sweetgrass County is agricultural—raising of wheat and cattle primarily. Town businesses mostly cater to middle-class farmers and ranchers, with the addition of a few art-oriented businesses to allow for esthetic sensibilities and some hunting and fishing establishments for the sports-minded.

Few people whose ancestors do not hail from Northern and Western Europe are to be found. Thus, little testing of public racial tolerance arises; there are few "different" people around who would elicit bad behavior and expose low character.

Sweetgrass County was and is thoroughly conservative. Voting Republican was presented to me as holy order all throughout my early years by all my adult contacts, and justification was never seen as necessary. Voters in Sweetgrass County cast votes for Donald Trump by a three-to-one margin in both the 2016 and 2020 elections—in most cases, not because they were Trump cultists or white supremacists; the social resources and educational attainments of the majority of Sweetgrass County residents are too healthy for the development of those pathologies. They simply imagined that Trump was really a Republican and a conservative, and they were thoroughly habituated to voting straight-ticket Republican through generations of practice.

Lowering the potential for conflict, this multifarious homogeneity, coupled with the healthy social life, makes social bonding among the inhabitants of Sweetgrass County much easier than it might otherwise have been and prevents the emergence of a caste system, with all the friction and resentments that would result.

During my formative years, moral stature and intellectual vigor were prevalent in Sweetgrass County, and these virtues influenced me enough that I could make good choices throughout my career. If one had to start out in an isolated rural community before going out to be somebody in the world, Sweetgrass County was certainly one place of choice.

CHAPTER 5

SCHOOL DAYS 3: UNIVERSITY LIFE IN MONTANA AND OHIO

In college, I left the family nest to fly more or less on my own. I say "more or less" for several reasons. My father was paying my college bills for tuition, housing, and books. At that far-off time—the fall of 1962—state governments were providing substantial subsidies to their state universities, of which my alma mater, Montana State University in Bozeman, Montana, was one. That made it quite easy and comfortable for parents to pay for their children's university educations, relieving us all of the prospect of finishing college with the heavy student loan burden that plagues both present-day university graduates and the current US political and economic scene. The cost of attending Montana State University is now nearly three times the cost in the 1960s in real purchasing power.

I was still legally a child; in those days, twenty-one years of age was considered the threshold of legal adulthood for males in Montana. One could be drafted into the military, but one could not vote. Parental consent and parental responsibility were still governing principles concerning marriage, legal actions, and more.

I was still physically close to the family. Bozeman is sixty miles from Big Timber and less than a hundred miles from our ranch. My mother was concerned about the proximity because of possible sabotage of my college career with frequent trips home. She preferred I attend a university farther from my childhood grounds. But Mom's worries were groundless, as I threw myself into college life, and though I sometimes felt a little homesick, I was never tempted to go home at any time except for Christmas and Easter breaks between the academic quarters. Weekends turned out to be good times to do the massive amounts of homework that college studies entailed.

My major field was chemistry from the time I entered until the time I completed university studies, with mathematics as a minor. During my freshman year and the first part of my sophomore year, I was all technical student. I attacked my studies in mathematics and science with enthusiasm and did not pay a lot of attention to the outside world. My grades were slightly higher during that period than they had been in high school, and I felt proud in noticing that detail. I took a couple of philosophy courses and a series of English composition and literature courses in my freshman year and a literature course in my sophomore year. During my junior and senior years, I took German. I took a speech course to combat my eternal stage fright. Much of that nontechnical coursework was required for the chemistry curriculum; otherwise, I might have loaded up on technical courses to the exclusion of all else. I did well enough in those areas, but I preferred to loaf as much as possible. I never got fluent in German, and I regret that and other omissions. I have since supplied some of those deficiencies with pleasure reading but not until a much later part of my life.

Montana State University required all freshmen to live in dormitories. The dormitory experience was remarkable in a number of ways. There were several party animals on my floor, and the dormitory was not conducive to effective studying. The parties were celebrated partly in the dormitory and partly in downtown Bozeman. Officially, the dormitory rules forbade loud functions in the rooms, but the parties, pranks, and harassment forced me to repair to the university library to accomplish anything. The university was forgiving of such antics in that those students were allowed to stay for an entire academic year or more. They could switch majors as necessary to get around the requirement that they not flunk out of too many academic quarters in a row.

The fare in the dorm kitchen was the bargain-basement slop well known to college dormitory veterans everywhere. But this is an old thousand-times-told tale, and no further comment is necessary here.

Compounding the dormitory problem was the attention of a gay student on my floor who found me attractive. To get him to understand that I was not interested took several stern brushoffs. I formed no grudge against gays or hostility toward that individual, but whatever one's sexual orientation, I feel strongly that one rebuff should suffice to end all advances.

I endured the various negativities throughout my freshman year in the dormitories, and I left that distracting environment with great relief after one academic year. I lived in the Kappa Sigma fraternity house for the rest of my career at Montana State University.

I was starting to reach out socially at that time, and it was in college that I formed real human bonds that I had never before experienced. This blossoming was greatly aided by my membership in the Kappa Sigma social fraternity. That experience vanquished most of the hobbledehoy bashfulness that had impeded my relationships with others in the past. Though I have always been a loner, I was popular among the members once they got to know me, and I consider my fraternity experience to have been both pleasurable and supportive during my college stay.

Fraternity life involved the usual college-boy socializing, parties, and study. The fraternity house was better than the dormitory for getting assignments done, though I still found the library congenial at times. Food and board were part of the package, and nighttime was usually, but not always, for study and sleeping. Kappa Sigma was one of the most tolerant fraternities on campus. They had to be to accept an introvert like me! The other fraternities would not even give me a bid. Consequently, a wide variety of personalities populated our chapter, but there was one species invariably and instantly blackballed: loud, self-absorbed, mendacious braggarts never lasted in our fraternity. I remember three specific examples, all of whom, interestingly, call Donald Trump to mind (more of him in chapter 12).

That was still a dark period in some ways; none of the fraternities on campus allowed minority students into their ranks—not that there were hordes of minorities at Montana State. Several of our members could always be counted on to blackball any non-Caucasian student. We did admit one Jewish man during my junior year; we were not entirely reactionary. But I felt the fraternity's attitude toward minorities was generally unjust, though I was not confrontational or morally evolved enough at the time to protest. Our American society was not that far along the road to justice either; it was a different world from the present. The civil rights agitation and the attempts to open up the American South still lay some years in the future. Even so, I like to hope I would have spoken against the grain if I had taken a real liking to any minority students who tried our door.

I participated in intramural sports for the fraternity: volleyball, basketball, and track. As in high school, I was no star, and I completely lost interest in competitive sports of any kind by my junior year in college.

Another extracurricular college activity was the university band, for which I played bass, tenor, and snare drums. During my freshman year, I demonstrated a need for more maturity. Things went fine during the autumn quarter, but during the winter quarter, I had an English literature course that was exceptionally demanding of my time. I decided I needed to prioritize my tasks, so I worked hard at the English (I received an A and a commendation from the professor) and skipped out on most of the evening band practices. The band instructor, Mr. Sedivy, was such a softhearted man that he gave me an incomplete that quarter and allowed me to make it up the next quarter instead of flunking me, as he well might have. In college, the instructors do not consult each other to make sure they are not collectively overloading the students; it is up to the student to cope with whatever the professors decide to throw at him. Obviously, I needed to learn this lesson.

During my sophomore year, I did not participate in the band, but I reentered the activity during my junior and senior years, and I really enjoyed the experience. Since, as a sports band, we played at football and basketball games, we had ringside seats at all the games. The symphonic band was bused around the state to give concerts.

Among the people I ran with were two physics majors, Tony and John, with whom I shared many math and physics courses. I was able to talk Tony into joining my fraternity, but John was never interested in Greek life. We enjoyed our classes for the most part, and we often played cards for amusement. Another good friend was Tom, a member of my fraternity and my roommate during our sophomore and junior years. Since he was a chemical engineering major, we shared a lot of courses. My lab partner for many of my courses was a Vietnamese exchange student called Nguyen Vu Hien. His major was chemical engineering, and he was in the United States to get higher education in anticipation of going back to South Vietnam, as it was then called, to apply his expertise to advancing his country.

The female side of the social equation was not so well filled; I never formed bonds with any of the female students. I had cordial relationships with the wives and girlfriends of fraternity brothers and real friendships with one or two. But my liaisons with unattached women tended to die after one to three dates. Several schoolmates who lined me up with women expressed frustration and exasperation to me for giving their offerings such short shrift. Looking over my life's scene from decades away, I see several reasons for my reluctance to hook up. My wariness and social naivete rendered me reluctant to reach out to women. Reinforcing these deficiencies were the many bad actresses who crossed my stage during my college career: (1) women who would make a date, agree on a time and place to meet, and then not show up; (2) women who would make a date and then break it in order to go to the same function with a "better" man; and (3) women who would use me as a filler during the absences of their steady loves and announce their attachments after one or more dates. I cannot count the many such misadventures I endured, but all the universities I attended were rife with these pests. However, so imbued was I with the spirit of the feminine portraits presented to me during my earlier youth that my Adams temper was never piqued. I regarded that behavior as reflective of the way women were wired—as part of the natural order, like earthquakes: we don't like them, but we recognize they are inevitable, and the best we can do is to mitigate their impact.

I was chary of being pulled into a honey trap before I felt that my life had reached a stage appropriate for a permanent relationship. My father had promised to cut off my funds if I got married before finishing my education, but he needn't have worried; I had no desire to be caught up in a premature love. I honestly had no idea what I really wanted to do with my life, but like many youngsters, I knew I wanted to do something big and bold. I wanted to retain independence enough to choose any life path without the encumbrance of a serious relationship or a family. I never felt, and do not feel now, that college is the place to begin a decades-long commitment to a life partner. College is the place to get acquainted with oneself and to prepare for a career; my commitment in those days was to those endeavors. Many female students, on the other hand, were in college not to get an education but to get a husband; their goals were at cross-purposes with mine. I knew then that I was not prepared to support a wife; unfortunate indeed would have been the woman attached to me during my drifting-and-dreaming phase (see chapter 7).

The competition for women was fierce at Montana State—a result of the great preponderance of men—and I was always too noncompetitive to run in such a race. There was something demeaning to me about being part of an animal behavior study in a nature show—male birds clustering about a female and showing off their plumage and sometimes getting into fights. Those thoughts firmly deterred me from joining groups of men competing for a woman, particularly if she was pleased with herself about the situation. I would always back out of a social contact if I saw an eager billy goat making a beeline for my feminine conversation partner.

The women I met tended to be not very interesting. They exhibited no moral or intellectual standout qualities that would have attracted me to a relationship with them and by which they could have broadened and uplifted me. Whether they really were inspired by little beyond getting married and living in a suburban house with two and a half kids and a dog or whether they just wanted me to believe that of them made no difference; either approach led to the same end. A housewife as domesticated animal would have oppressed me, and I would have bored her, and I knew it then. I was also aware of an orthodoxy—no doubt the result of our training during that era—that a woman was never to appear to outshine her man in any respect; she was required to hide her gifts lest his demand for superiority induce him to run away from her. I had no respect for men who demanded that pretense of their partners, nor did I have any respect for women who hid their qualities in deference to that demand. Any partnership had to be based on honesty, respect, and equality.

Raised in the 1950s as I was, university women of my era had probably suffered such severe cramping of their outlooks from the training in dependency they had received (e.g., see the Ohio judge's 1951 ruling in chapter 3, and most of their parents probably did little to counteract him) that they could scarcely imagine strength and taking charge of their own lives. Most of them were as adept at forcing themselves to fit the roles prescribed for them as their chaste, hoop-skirt-and-corset-clad ancestors had been a century before. But hopefully, as women gain status in our society and acquire personal liberty and as higher education becomes more and more a gateway to good careers for women as well as for men, female college students such as these will become less prevalent.[1]

Around the time of the assassination of President John Kennedy in November 1963, two changes took place in my mental priorities. The first change was the onset of continuous monitoring of world and national news events to an extent unprecedented in my life. Previously, I had learned about current events after weeks or months—from magazine articles, not in real time. Never before had I studied world history in the making in a sustained or organized way. But the Kennedy assassination got my attention, and I watched the unfolding story with interest. I concluded from the evidence presented that Lee Harvey Oswald was a lone wolf, and I never subscribed to any of the conspiracy theories that eventually surrounded the tragedy.

From that beginning, over a few years' time, I evolved an interest in tracking world events generally as they occurred. This interest was enhanced by my membership in the international club during my senior year. The club was an association of Montana State University students from countries all over the world; US students were welcome also. Nguyen Vu Hien was a member, and I got to know several other interesting individuals. Hien taught me a few things about the Vietnamese language, and he demonstrated palm reading to me. Those experiences broadened me by making me aware of the world at large and piquing my interest in different cultures and histories. Through my participation in the club, I first developed an urge toward world travel, but that desire was not fulfilled for some decades. I also developed a passion for human diversity, which has never left me.

The second change in my outlook was an erosion of my interest in chemistry, my major field of study. This change started in the middle of my sophomore year, but I was not fully aware of my declining desire to study chemistry until well into my senior year at Montana State University. This decline manifested itself mainly in a struggle to stay focused on the material I needed to learn for my chemistry courses and an intermittent state of depression accompanied by a dread of tackling chemistry topics. I was conscious of the struggle to study and the dread and depression, but it took some time for me to detect the underlying cause: chemistry had lost most of its luster for me. My interest in mathematics never wavered, and indeed, the math courses served as an antidote to the anguish caused by my internal conflict over chemistry studies. Had I been able to diagnose this problem in good time, I could have switched over to mathematics as a major at the outset of my junior year without juggling courses and lengthening my college stay. But switching during my senior year would have added at least a year to my curriculum at Montana State University. I was becoming painfully aware by then that job openings in both mathematics and chemistry were getting scarce out in the real world. Besides, enough fascination with chemistry remained for me to visualize a career as a chemist through which I could earn a living and contribute something to society while enjoying life outside of work; I just didn't see myself as a superstar chemist adding in a major way to humanity's knowledge base. My industrial experience in the summer of 1965 (see chapter 6) made me aware that a PhD was not vital in chemistry unless I wanted an academic career. During my senior year, I formed a plan to acquire a MS degree only and pursue a career in private industry.

Still, a mathematics career would have been a natural outgrowth of my early childhood fascination with numbers. I could probably have retained enough internal fire to go all the way through to a PhD in the field. Even today, my interest in math remains intense, and I often use Google to search out mathematical solutions and proofs.

The summer after my sophomore year was germane to my maturation process. I spent the summer in Bozeman, doing lab research for one of the chemistry faculty members. The experience gave me an obvious reason why chemistry was not a good fit for me: I had neither inclination nor competence for designing experiments or constructing lab apparatuses. It was not a high school science project, and there was no Mr. Schump to work out technique and experimental design. I was required to rely on my own ingenuity to tinker and fuss! Any competent experimental scientist in any field must possess notable manual facility, which was not among my strengths. Such a scientist must sometimes throw out months' worth of work because a procedure or a lab apparatus was misdesigned or because the apparatus malfunctioned during data collection. My lack of patience would have made a start-over like that unendurable.

I fiddled all summer with a procedure to synthesize a chemical compound. It was essential to exclude air from the synthesis during all steps of the procedure; any oxygen present would instantly combine with the intermediate compounds and disrupt the entire experiment. I never did work out a way to keep air away from my chemicals; my lab technique was poor and would remain poor throughout my university career. My adviser in the effort was decidedly hands-off in supervising me, but I doubt that close guidance on his part would have cleaned up the fundamental problems just described. Forcing myself to continue retrying my synthesis without any measurable progress caused me to get progressively more frustrated and depressed over the summer. I would arrive later and later in the morning for my day's work at the lab, eventually not arriving until afternoon. At the end of the summer, I put together an attempt at a presentation of my experimental results. My attempt fooled no one; there were no real results, and it was obvious to everyone. My adviser had me take a speech course the following fall to enhance my presentation skills, but presentation technique was not the half of it. How do you present and interpret no data? Clearly, that summer's work accelerated the diminution of my enthusiasm for chemistry as a whole. The experience should have persuaded me to switch majors, but I was not yet self-analytical enough to realize that necessity.

One bright spot during that summer was acting a part in a production of *Paint Your Wagon*,[2] a play about the rise and fall of a gold-rush town in the American West in the middle of the nineteenth century. I played a minor role as the town storekeeper, and we practiced rigorously before putting on about a half dozen productions. That was my last attempt at acting, and it was educational in that it was a serious production with weeks of rehearsals, choreography, costumes, and news media photography.

That summer and fall, I followed the news of the Johnson-Goldwater contest of 1964. I was one of the few Goldwater supporters in Bozeman, and I was often needled by my fellow students as a result. I supported Goldwater mainly because family and Sweetgrass County tradition demanded I go Republican, but I was never passionate about that election. By that point, my hide had thickened to where I was not disturbed by my fellows' gibes, and I could see even then how that election was likely to end. Since I was too young to vote, I remained sidelined and watched the numerous Johnson supporters help Johnson to his landslide victory. For the Republican Party, the election was a disaster whose effects reverberate to this day.

During my senior year, the US involvement in Vietnam started to impinge on my thoughts. I didn't feel any pressure concerning the draft, since the military was not pursuing college students at the time. I started out supporting the war effort since it was a popular war at the time, particularly among my family; we were supposedly taking a stand against world Communism. My support was mild; I was aware of my own ignorance of the subject, and I was open to suggestion. To inform myself, I read newspaper articles and read a book by political scientist Bernard B. Fall.[3] Nguyen Vu Hien and I had many a conversation about that policy and his future. He had heavy reservations about the US policy in his country, telling me that the main motivation for the Viet Cong and North Vietnamese fighters was nationalism, not Communist ideology. As I observed what was going on there, I came to agree with his assessment. But when I asked him what he would do upon his graduation and return to Vietnam, he fatalistically accepted that he would join the South Vietnamese army. I thought that was a waste of his education money and efforts, but I could hardly offer advice. My talks with Hien and my readings turned me against the war effort over a year's time. I noted that many of my reading sources—notably Fall's book—were tendentious toward opposition to the US policy in Vietnam. Nevertheless, I gleaned from the sources that the South Vietnamese government was a corrupt dictatorship more interested in ripping off its US benefactors than in establishing a nation. We were supporting one despot against another despot. What *was* our business in Vietnam?

I was disgusted by the tactics of the supporters of US Vietnam policy, who seemed more inclined to shut down discussion than to find good solutions. One friend of mine who supported the war policy gleefully recounted a story to me: another student I knew had been sitting at a coffee table in the student union, declaiming against the war, when a thuggish war supporter had come up behind him and beaned him over the head with a pile of books. I didn't react externally to the tale, but internally, I was appalled at the thug's anti-American behavior. While that barbaric act did not result in any permanent damage to the victim, as it well might have, it was a reprehensible repudiation of all the principles on which our nation was founded, especially the free-speech First Amendment to the Constitution. But nonconfrontational as I was, I didn't see any benefit in buttonholing my friend about his attitude; I would not have converted him to a more enlightened view, and he certainly would not have converted me to his view. The appeal to violence by supporters of the war effort amounted to repressing freedom to defend freedom. Between the South Vietnamese dictatorship and the dictatorship in those people's hearts, what freedom could they possibly have been defending?

At the same time, as the war rolled on and peace movements flourished, I had no inclination to join their demonstrations. The demonstrations did not seem to be bringing about much change, except for a growth in public hostility to the demonstrators, especially early in the war, when the war was still popular. More importantly for me, too many of the peace activists professed admiration for such scrofulous actors as Cuba's Fidel Castro and China's Mao Zedong. Some of the activists threw rocks and firebrands while supposedly fighting for peace. The most prominent of the activists later ended up in vicious ideological wars against each other. I was not about to get mixed up with actors like those. While their demonstrations, and the police overreactions, undoubtedly contributed to the waning of war enthusiasm among the

American public generally, my preference was to use the means at my disposal for effecting change: voting and contributing money to political causes that shared my views.

I received my bachelor's degree in chemistry in the spring of 1966. I had been in what was called an honors program, wherein I was supposed to do research in labs during my junior and senior years. But my enthusiasm for lab science had ebbed to the point that I could not make myself do the research, and I graduated with a regular degree without the honors attachment. I went on to two years of graduate school at Ohio State University in Columbus, Ohio, still doggedly pursuing chemistry studies in spite of myself.

My stint at Ohio State University in Columbus, Ohio, from the fall of 1966 to the spring of 1968, was a rather melancholy operation. My experience with E. I. du Pont de Nemours in the summer just before I entered Ohio State University (see chapter 6) considerably dulled my enthusiasm for a private industry career, particularly in management. Though I was enchanted to be living in a new culture thousands of miles from home, I was fully aware that I was not PhD chemistry research material. I entered graduate school without enthusiasm and without real goals. The professors at both of my universities made it clear that *their* goal was to generate more professors, even as it was becoming obvious to all of us that there were several times more candidates for academic employment than there were open academic positions. The post-*Sputnik* boom in commitment to technical education by American institutions was long since extinct, and an academic career would have been improbable for me, even if I had been enthusiastic in my studies.

Despite my lackadaisical attitude, I did surprisingly well on the entrance exams; several of the professors were delighted at the prospect of having me as their student researcher. They were clearly not aware of my less-than-adequate enthusiasm at first, though my stated goal of stopping at a master's degree began the process of enlightening them, even as it consternated them. They may have started out with the impression that I had academic prospects, but I harbored dreams of finding a niche in *something* with a master's degree. I had no idea of the nature of that niche or of my general path in life.

My living quarters during my first year consisted of an attic room in a Victorian near the campus. The houses in the neighborhood had largely been carved up into small rentals for poverty-stricken students to use for shelter and study. My fare consisted of McDonald's junk, machine-dispensed sandwiches, and cheap groceries—typical graduate student fare. In the Victorian, I put out warfarin rodent traps to eliminate the competition for my groceries. My transportation was an old car inherited from Grandpa Ed. Sometimes I would take the car out for a one- or two-hour drive just to entertain myself and get away from my surroundings.

During my second year, I lived on the top floor of a house about a mile and a half from campus. It was a better neighborhood and a cleaner house than my living accommodations during my first year. No warfarin was required. Still, it was affordable housing, as we say today.

I stumbled through graduate-level chemistry courses for one year, pushing myself to study as hard as I was able, getting mediocre grades, and supporting myself with a teaching assistantship. My second year at Ohio State University was mostly sham as far as graduate school is concerned. I made a feeble attempt to do lab research on the effects of chemical reagents on chlorophyll. But I discovered anew my strong aversion to hands-on lab research, and that effort petered out after a couple of months. I made an equally feeble attempt to take courses, but that too came to nothing, as I could not concentrate on the material and soon dropped the courses. I continued supporting myself by teaching undergraduate laboratory.

I was beginning to branch out by listening to classical music on a stereo I owned, reading history and literature books I purchased at local stores, and following the news in newspapers. I got acquainted with Dante's *Divine Comedy* and a few Shakespeare plays, along with many biography and history books. My musical education consisted largely of Tchaikovsky and Rossini, with a little Richard Strauss and Richard Wagner thrown in. That period marked the beginning of a love affair with books, current events, and music that has lasted to this day and has proven to be one of my chief sources of relief during down periods of my life. Here is one of the major reasons for the failure of my Ohio State endeavor: mental broadening is definitely not characteristic of a successful graduate student. Graduate school is not for the education of a Renaissance man; it is for developing a specialized knowledge in one's field for the purpose of further research related to that knowledge.

I achieved my master's degree by gaming the system. The university chemistry department offered a master's degree via courses and a general chemistry test, with no thesis required, but the degree was supposed to be for those who were picking up their master's degree on the way to their PhD. My adviser was softhearted enough to sign off on my using my first year's course work, my small amount of research, and the test to get my master's degree without continuing in school toward a PhD. I am grateful to him for being so patient and forbearing with me, but I do not look back on that chapter of my life with pride.

I made a paltry attempt to hook up with women through a computer matching service, but I netted only a couple of relationships that lasted a few weeks before dissolving in our mutual incompatibility. The female graduate students were mostly already attached, and in any case, they were too busy gorging on chemistry to form any real new social bonds. I was too demoralized anyway to consider forming a romantic relationship, and that enterprise sank into the sand like all of my Ohio State efforts.

I avidly followed the news at that time, as did my fellow students. The Vietnam War, and the demonstrations against it, gathered fury, and we chemistry graduate students were all opposed to the US effort in Vietnam. We followed the Six-Day War between the Arabs and Israel in the spring of 1967, and we were all Israeli partisans. The Six-Day War established Israel as a permanent fixture of the Middle East. I was saddened and indignant about the assassination of Martin Luther King Jr., which seemed to me to be a triumph for the worst Fascist elements in our society. I knew little about African Americans at the time, but I could sense the monumental injustice of that barbarism. The assassination of Bobby Kennedy affected me less; I thought he had achieved prominence mainly by piggybacking on the efforts of Eugene McCarthy to get viable official opposition to the Vietnam War effort established. My reaction to the withdrawal of Lyndon Johnson from the presidential race was as cynical as some other people's: I wondered if he was just maneuvering for sympathy at the Democratic National Convention. I was inspired by the Prague Spring in Czechoslovakia in the spring of 1968, which brought hope that decency could triumph even in the Communist world.

An Egyptian graduate student called Sami provided me with invaluable companionship. We took several classes together and had many a chat over coffee. He and I discussed world politics, along with helping each other with coursework. He was a fierce critic of the then despot of his country, Gamal Abdul Nasser. I was one of the ones who comforted him during the Six-Day War; he was depressed about how his country was chewed up by Israel. He blamed Nasser for the catastrophe, but he knew how little he could do about it. He returned to Egypt about the time I left Ohio, and I often wonder how he fared as a returned expatriate.

During my second year, I formed a good friendship with an older woman who took kindly to me. She lived on the first floor of the house whose second floor I occupied at the time. Bertha was her name, and she was a Jehovah's Witness. She was an organist, and she owned an organ, which she allowed me to play. I got reasonably proficient in picking out tunes, though I never learned to read sheet music or play as skillfully as she did.

She liked me enough to be concerned about my spiritual welfare. At the time, the Jehovah's Witnesses had decided that the world as we knew it was about to end; by August 2, 1975, the new paradise on earth under the Lord, reserved for believers, was to commence. I was too scientifically literate to accept creationism, a young Earth, or anything like an imminent wiping clean of the world to make way for God's people. That worried Bertha. She warned me that the Lord's Day was coming on fast, and I had no chance for survival unless I rearranged my beliefs. She was so nice to me that I could never reject her pleadings outright. Besides, it was touching to me to have finally found someone so far from home who was genuinely emotionally engaged with my well-being. So I agreed to attend Witness services and allow some of them to witness to me in my apartment. I tried to see the virtues in what they were saying, but I never considered joining their church, nor could I have believed in anything that ran counter to science, such as creationism. I tried not to sound too skeptical, but I never gave them the impression that I was convertible. It was their companionship I needed, and I formed friendships with several of the congregants. While I could never accept their beliefs, I learned a lot about them. The psychological oppressiveness—the tiny, dark, overheated closet—of membership in a strict religious congregation repelled me. Even had I wished, I could never have fit myself into such a small box.

I sometimes think about those Witnesses, and I wonder how they coped with God's failure to put in an appearance in the summer of 1975. I am grateful to them, and to Sami, for helping me through a barren patch in my life.

Looking back upon my experience as a graduate student at Ohio State University, I believe my main takeaways were the final and firm realizations that I needed diversity in my studies and was not to be a research scientist. Aside from my impatience and lack of facility with my hands, there was yet another factor. Those who were most successful among my fellow students, and those who go on to great fame as scientists, are exceptionally capable and so driven that their science consumes all of their lives. This point has been driven home to me by many observations in my years since graduate school.

A good example of an exceptionally successful research scientist is Dr. Saba Valadkhan, an Iranian-born cell chemistry researcher. She came to my attention with an essay that won her a Young Scientist Award.[4] Her research preoccupies her constantly, and she has made great discoveries and achieved lots of prestige. Thank God for people like her! She saves lives and advances our medical care. But I am definitely not like her. I am too noncompetitive and too interested in multifarious studies to dedicate myself to such an extreme degree to one field of endeavor.

In the spring of 1968, I bade farewell to Ohio and drove back to the Adams ranch in Montana. I had several career irons in the fire by then, and my intention was to await results and, hopefully, land a job. But I still had no overall strategic objective for my life other than not an academic faculty position and not industrial management. My challenge was to discover what that objective was.

CHAPTER 6

CAREER 1: SUMMER INTERN CAREER BEGINNINGS

This chapter relates beginning a career and living on my own. I held three summer intern jobs, which were offered to me as a result of interviews with industrial recruiters. The jobs lasted between my junior and senior years at Montana State University, between my graduation from Montana State University and the beginning of graduate school at Ohio State University, and between my first and second years of graduate school at Ohio State University.

Shell Oil Company, Los Angeles, California, Summer 1965

My employment as a summer intern was a major evolution in my maturation process in several ways. It was my first time outside the northwestern corner of the United States. It was my first try at earning my living and running my own life independently of my family. It was my first attempt at navigating in a large city. It included my first encounters with African American experiences—encounters there were few opportunities for in the northwestern corner of the United States at that time.

I stayed in an efficiency apartment in Lomita, a suburb of Los Angeles. Small living units rented for reasonable rates in that part of the country. My food consisted of groceries purchased at a small nearby grocery store, plus local restaurant food and lunches from a catering truck at the Shell workplace in Torrance, another Los Angeles suburb. Not having a car for the adventure, I had to cadge rides to work with Shell employees. I was able to use taxis and occasionally rent a car for movies and other entertainment. It was difficult to find a car rental, since most of those outfits required the renter to be at least twenty-five years of age, and I was twenty-one. I found one company that would rent to me, though.

Work consisted of measuring the force needed to stretch and break strips of rubber manufactured by varying processes. The enterprise was a research effort into the best ways to concoct rubber. Since the entire operation was a company secret and I was a temporary summer intern, I was never apprised of the manufacturing processes or the chemistry of the rubber. My work was rather routine, but I enjoyed it nonetheless. Being my first professional work experience, it was fascinating just for that.

My work colleagues consisted of lab technicians—blue-collar people who had some college training but had dropped out before finishing their bachelor's degrees. They were friendly and easygoing, and I got along well with them. In fact, that internship was my first try at forming work-colleague bonds, the type of relationship one forms with coworkers. I liked these men because they were tolerant of one another's individual personae, were sincere in their dealings with one another, and seemed to be at peace with themselves and their prospects. Lunch hours were occupied by a card game called hearts, and I occasionally joined in the entertainment. My acquaintances with the white-collar management personnel were nodding but not close; the lab technicians were my real friends and confidants.

Starstruck as I was by the big city, I was not yet in a position to gauge the edification qualities of my off-hours occupations. In fact, I was quite naive in all ways of the world. I would have enjoyed meeting women, but I had no idea where there might be eligible ones. Evening entertainment consisted largely of brain-dead commercial TV shows in my efficiency apartment. Later in the summer, I purchased a stereo record player and a few classical music platters, which provided me with higher-brow diversion. Movies were the main destination of my evenings and weekends on the town, though I also visited Disneyland and Marineland of the Pacific. One weekend, I took a boat trip to Santa Catalina Island, where I hiked around and took a ride in a glass-bottomed boat. Since I had only a few dollars in my pocket, I couldn't afford any of the snazzy attractions—not that I missed anything edifying. That locale turned out to be a disappointing, crowded, commercialized tourist clip joint—a far cry from the "island of romance" described in the 1958 Four Preps song. Bumpkin from Montana I certainly was!

My personal experiences with racism began that summer. Prior to my stay in Los Angeles, I had never before observed or pondered a race problem, other than the occasional tepid racist lectures I had received from my forebears in Montana. I found time to buy and read *To Kill a Mockingbird* by Harper Lee.[1] A couple of years before, I had seen the movie starring Gregory Peck as Atticus Finch, but not much of the material had stuck with me. That was the summer of the Watts riots, which conflagrated neighborhoods about ten miles from where I worked and lived. I followed them vaguely in a daily newspaper I bought from a peddler each weekday evening, but I didn't delve deeply into the causes and results of the tragedy. The chief of my lab at work was an enlightened individual called Bill, with whom we discussed the riots. When the question came up as to why there were not riots in the Old Dixie heartland, where the situation of blacks was much worse than in Los Angeles, Bill pointed out that in Alabama and Mississippi in the 1960s, the blacks were so psychologically repressed that they could not contemplate a riot of despair. My subsequent readings and observations have confirmed Bill's assertion.

Fallout from the riots never got physically close to my living quarters and workplace, but I did accept and read a leaflet passed out by a black activist in the shopping mall close to my motel. At my workplace, I observed, for the first time with full appreciation as far as I can remember, an instance of institutional racism. Shell had a new African American employee called Ralph, who held a PhD in physical chemistry. That credential should have launched him on a stellar career with Shell. Instead, the company assigned him a routine job running a machine that tested the abrasion resistance of various rubber products.

It was a blue-collar lab job of a type normally handled by people without college degrees. Ralph was clearly not happy with his situation, and he deserved something with more challenge and more potential for career advancement. Though I never discussed his assignment in depth with him or anyone else—I didn't know how to approach the subject—I felt then and feel now that he was being treated shabbily. It seemed to me that he was employed more to benefit the company's image than to profit the company or to benefit Ralph. I suspect his salary was less than first class, and I could not conceive of Shell dealing thusly with any white man then or now. But such work assignments to minorities were perfectly normal back in 1965, before the real instabilities got started that resulted in some emancipation for blacks and other minorities. I sensed that Bill, the lab chief, was aware of Ralph's disgruntlement and of the waste of talent he represented. I hope Ralph eventually found fulfilling work in spite of the headwinds he faced.

At the end of the summer, I received high praise for my performance, and breaking up with that group to go back to school caused me grief. It was a positive work experience for me—so positive, in fact, that I decided then that my professional pursuit would be in chemical industry rather than in academe.

E. I. du Pont de Nemours, Wilmington, Delaware, Summer 1966

This assignment excited me because it was by far the farthest I had ever been from home. For the summer, I had a workable Chevrolet I had inherited from my recently deceased grandfather, Grandpa Ed. I drove from Big Timber, Montana, to Wilmington, Delaware, in three and a half days, covering about seven hundred miles each day. That impressed my parents, who were used to the three hundred to four hundred miles a day we'd covered during our summer Portland trips years before.

I was truly a stranger in a strange land; finding a place to live was at once a challenge and a priority. I thought to rent a motel efficiency apartment, as I had done in California the year before. But Delaware motel room prices were twice the price of the efficiency apartment prices in California, making motel efficiencies a nonstarter. I rented a motel room for one week while I searched out the area for permanent living quarters. Eventually, I found an affordable house bedroom for rent in a middle-class suburb of Wilmington called Ardencroft. There was to be no home cooking there; the house kitchen was for the family who owned the house, and I was to get my fare from local restaurants and from the cafeteria at the du Pont facility where I worked. My workplace was at the du Pont headquarters in Wilmington. Unlike the previous summer, I could drive to work without depending on other employees.

Du Pont had just discovered a powder of alumina called Baymal. My work for the summer consisted of exploring the feasibility of using a Baymal colloidal sol as a charge adjustor to facilitate the binding of clay fillers to paper substrates, creating a smooth surface for the paper. Permeating clay and Baymal slurries with an electrical field, I measured the charge of the clay articles suspended in various concentrations of Baymal sol. Having generated much data over the summer, I proposed a recipe for use of Baymal to make clay paper fillers useable: at least three parts of Baymal to one hundred parts of clay. Unfortunately, Baymal was too expensive for that to be a realizable industrial process. The alumina powder was not attractive for use in electronics and cosmetics—two of its other proposed uses—because of its vinegar odor. So the product never got off the ground as a seller for du Pont. Even so, it was interesting work, and I felt I was contributing, even if negatively, to the du Pont enterprise.

The cultural contrast with California may have been due in part to the gulf between famously nonconformist Southern California and the more buttoned-up East Coast. But my work colleagues were a decidedly different set from those of the summer before: white-collar college graduates. Some were fellow interns, which I hadn't seen in Los Angeles; the rest were du Pont employees. One, George, worked in the same lab as I and was a holder of a PhD and a brilliant chemist. His assistant was called Dino, and they were the two I interfaced with the most over the summer.

I was unable to form bonds with many of the people, except to a slight degree with George and Dino. That was because the group provided my first real introduction to the much-maligned species called organization man, as described by William H. Whyte in his 1950s book,[2] which I had read during my undergraduate years. The book painted a rather dismal picture of American white-collar industrial employees in that era: cheerful, foppish, vapid conformists who shunned contact with anything suggesting intellectuality or individualism, eschewed all strong opinions, and earnestly climbed over one another to rise on the management ladder while equally earnestly reassuring their fellows that they meant no harm. George had some intellectual interests, and Dino was blue collar like my California colleagues. With those two exceptions, almost everybody conformed to a greater or lesser degree to the organization-man model. I could not carry on sustained, stimulating conversations; their discussions of one another's foibles never caught on with me. Listening in and occasionally contributing to talk about the events in their everyday lives was all I could muster. The differences between me and them led me to aloneness. Even so, while there was no fellowship between me and my coworkers, they did present an opportunity to study in vivo laboratory animal samples of organization men.

To begin with, I was emphatically rebuked about my Montana garb—out-of-style slacks and shirts. Wondering why my clothing made a difference in a chemistry lab, I was told that in several years, I would be a department head representing the company to people who set great store by the snappy appearance of their interlocutors, and I needed the practice. So I sprang for one suit and tie, which I wore every day to work all summer (with dry cleaning at proper intervals). On occasion throughout the summer, I was teased and scolded for not being skilled at the vacuous small talk said to go down well with high-ranking company officials and customers (e.g., "How's tricks?" or "What do you know?" or "How's the little woman?" and so on). I was continually mocked for being interested in literature, music, and other life of the mind and not sufficiently interested in head games related to the organization. Despite all my education from my colleagues, I never acquired the slightest desire or competence to reign as a senior manager.

While my interest in chemistry had diminished over the last couple of years, it still greatly outweighed any interest in forgetting all about my scientific training and becoming a politician. At one point, I asked about the prospects for getting promotions on a technical, rather than a managerial, path. My question was met with embarrassed silence;

how could anybody ask that? I thought about George, who kept to his science and ignored the call of office politics. The scuttlebutt had it that there was some dissatisfaction with him for his reluctance to become a manager and trade his lab for an office, but his great scientific productivity kept him in good standing in spite of his individualistic ways. I felt then, and I still feel, that forcing all employees of all abilities and all preferences into a one-size-fits-all political career path was a criminal waste of human capital. Personal liberty was seldom noted or rewarded; more was the pity for the company as well as for its employees. An enterprise that wishes to be efficient and competitive must encourage initiative, individuality, and imagination and must utilize the gifts of all its employees in the best possible manner.

The consensus at work was that everybody liked me, but I was "different" and "too smart" for the others. Of course, no one is too smart for anyone without the consent of the latter. Nevertheless, the experience dimmed my previous summer's enthusiasm for a career as an industrial chemist, particularly in management.

Since no TV was allowed in my rented bedroom, I had no access to that entertainment, but I played classical music on my stereo and did a little reading. There was lots of extracurricular activity available on the East Coast, and my car made the sites available to me.

I spent one weekend in New York and one weekend in Washington, DC. In both places, I spent Saturday night at the local YMCA. I visited many of the tourist sites one is supposed to see in those cities: the Empire State Building and the Statue of Liberty in New York and the Washington Monument and a couple of the Smithsonian museums in Washington. Still dazzled by the big city, I was more enthusiastic than discriminating in my choice of destinations. Nevertheless, I consider those visits to have provided me with valuable education.

For the Fourth of July weekend, I drove all the way to Provincetown, Massachusetts, at the end of Cape Cod. Bumpkin that I was, I imagined myself getting a motel room on a walk-in basis. Naturally, everything was full to the brim, and I wound up sleeping away Saturday night curled up in the backseat of my car. One of my drivetrain U-joints had just gone out, and while the car was drivable, there was a shimmy and an instability. I parked for the night in a gas station on the promise that in the morning, they would repair my drivetrain there. In the morning, the personnel were so busy and short-handed that they could barely keep up with tourists wanting gas tank fill-ups. As there was to be no service for me there, I limped down the cape about ten miles until I located a service station that would fix me up. One of the roller bearings had rusted completely away, but a new U-joint had me back on the road. Later in the summer, I had to replace the clutch. My grandfather's idea of car maintenance had been keeping the gas tank full, and the consequences were visited on me.

The real Cape Cod was even noisier and more crowded than Santa Catalina Island the year before. The singer Patti Page, in her 1957 song "Old Cape Cod," was no better a tour guide for Cape Cod than were the Four Preps regarding Santa Catalina Island. I chalked the experience up to education—I was certainly in need of one!

My experience with women in Delaware mirrored my adventures with college women: slightly ridiculous two- or three-date affairs that dissolved in irrelevance. But the availability of so many exciting and educational places to visit more than compensated.

The African American issue never touched me during that experience, beyond my driving and walking through a few slums in East Coast cities. I had always been rather fleet-footed, and I counted on that to liberate me from any jams arising from people who wished to confront a white man. The summer riots in 1966 were mainly in the Midwest, especially in Chicago and Cleveland. None of my organization-man coworkers had the slightest interest in what was going on with African Americans.

At the end of the summer, I took a few days' driving trip through New England into French Canada, up to Rivière-du-Loup in Quebec Province. It was a scenic drive with only one tourist trap to attract me: Fort Ticonderoga in upstate New York. In Quebec, nobody understood English, or so they indicated to me. But since I had money to spend, they found ways to communicate with me. At the end of that trip, I descended southwest to Columbus, Ohio, to begin my stint as a graduate student.

Continental Oil Company, Ponca City, Oklahoma, Summer 1967

My last summer intern job landed me squarely in the middle of the Bible Belt. Ponca City, a small city in north-central Oklahoma with a population of about twenty-five thousand, served as headquarters for Continental Oil Company. Still in possession of my grandfather's Chevrolet, I drove down to Ponca City from Columbus, Ohio.

My professors at Ohio State were distressed at my taking off a summer to work. Their argument was that such a break would add at least a year to my PhD program. I didn't answer; the truth that I wasn't interested in a PhD anyway would have added nothing to the discussion. I went ahead with my plans despite the exhortations.

For living quarters in Ponca City, I located an old apartment building within the city. The apartment was one of those places that one endures in the knowledge that the price is right and the stay is but for one summer. I rented a window air conditioner to make the place breathable; Oklahoma summers tend to be sultry. I had to combat june bugs and other wildlife in the carpets, while cockroaches cavorted in my kitchen. My kitchen stove featured an old-fashioned oven whose temperature was controlled with an oven thermometer and hand operation of the flame level. But at least I could cook some of my own meals, in contrast to my living arrangements in Delaware. Our workplace was situated right in Ponca City—a short drive from my apartment since the city was small.

My work consisted of measuring the rate of seepage of oil and water through sand. The purpose was to model the behavior of water and petroleum in oil fields. I gathered some data over the summer, which was probably useful to Conoco's research in that area.

The Conoco employees I knew were mostly nondescript white-collar professionals. They didn't fascinate me, but at least they didn't chide me about my clothes and conversation skills, as those in Delaware had. They were definitely not the organization-man models I had observed the previous summer.

In the Bible Belt, everybody went regularly to church and took their religious vows seriously. In Oklahoma, I came as close to the so-called southern way of life as I desire ever to be. I soon found that single women my age were exceedingly rare in Ponca City. Nearly all twenty-three-year-old Sooners either had been married for five years or had left the area, seldom to return, five years previously. That meant women were nearly as unavailable to me as they had been at Boys State in Dillon, Montana, in 1961.

The racial bigotry was the worst I had ever personally witnessed. As in Delaware, I had no TV, but I did have access to newspapers and office gossip. By the summer of 1967, the Vietnam War was accounting for a significant number of American casualties, and the rioting by urban blacks was getting hot as well. The Detroit burnings were especially infamous that summer. Everybody at work was angry and frustrated and eager to win the Vietnam War, even, if necessary, by attacking the Soviet Union. Mowing down the black rioters in Detroit and elsewhere with machine guns was also a popular concept. "Hitler had the right idea, just the wrong race" was one remark I heard. My dissent from those positions added to my social isolation, as did my open skepticism about biblical literalism. Since I understood that blacks had been mistreated for so long that some kind of explosion was unavoidable, I was known as a "black supremacist." Nobody liked my arguments that the Vietnam War was not winnable and that we should seek a least harmful exit—though, strangely, no one ever called me a Communist. Somebody called me an atheist because I failed to be frightened by the thought of hell's burning lakes of sulfur. These people's appreciation of freedom was clearly limited; personal liberty was not a plentiful commodity in that Bible Belt setting.

For most of the people I met, the Bible served as an adequate substitute for thinking and living. Entertainment and educational centers, such as Marineland in Los Angeles or the Smithsonian museums in Washington, DC, were utterly lacking in Ponca City. The only entertainment I could find was a church with a yelling, gesticulating pastor. That pastor was a good stand-up comic, and his absurdities, admonitions, and holy-terror stagecraft provided amusement that kept my morale from completely tanking. During one sermon, he admitted to having neglected to tend to the spiritual welfare of one of his terminally ill friends, who died before the pastor could make the proper motions. As a result, the pastor felt compelled to admit that his friend was "in hell this morning." Our pastor seemed not to suffer any pangs of conscience for being responsible for the eternal torture of his friend; Satan had allegedly conned him into defaulting on that duty. That facile solace accorded by the devil gave me occasion to chuckle, and I found that the pastor's gig made life among the believers more bearable.

Still, I could have found my summer in Oklahoma more agreeable but for the toxic combination of bigotry and religiosity that characterized many of the local people, which made it impossible for me to connect with them in any social way. I have known those who assert, "White genocide is massacring our people," and I have also known advocates of "Jesus loves you and will burn you forever if you have erroneous opinions," but the attempt of certain Oklahomans to run the two in tandem was positively revolting to me. These people completely miss the point of the story of Jesus and the Samaritan woman,[3] in which Jesus preaches his doctrine to a Samaritan woman who has given him a drink of water. His disciples point out to him that Jews do not associate with Samaritans, but Jesus rebukes his disciples; he is ready to interface with anybody who will listen to his teachings. Racial and tribal prejudices did not apply to Jesus's ministry, and I can never abide those who introduce these primal vices into their Christian practice.

The Sooners I met brought to mind the southern white so-called Christians who populate African American tales of the American South—who called upon God in the morning to witness their reverence for his teachings and lynched a black man that afternoon. Bible Belt denizens also served as forerunners for twenty-first-century so-called Christians who converted the depraved bigot Donald Trump into Jesus's herald, dismissing objections to the strange transmogrification with an airy "We elected a president, not a saint. We know that Donald Trump is a believer." What sort of a God would allow his flock to fashion him in this way? What kind of a God would bless such execrable hypocrisy? When man creates God in his own image, God inevitably becomes a slave to his worshippers.

Oklahoma has a colorful history regarding race relations. The Tulsa race riot of 1921[4] and the fleecing of the Osage tribe's oil wealth in the 1920s[5] will be touched upon in more detail in chapter 10. But spice is added to the state's history by the May 25, 1911, lynching of mother and son Laura and L. D. Nelson near Okemah, Okfuskee County. Awaiting trial for the son's shooting of a sheriff, they were kidnapped and lynched by a mob, which may have included Charley Guthrie, the father of folk singer Woody Guthrie and grandfather of actor Arlo Guthrie. Postcards were made and sold depicting the grisly scene. I can understand why that monstrous family history haunted Woody and Arlo. Then there is the tragic and fascinating tale of Oklahoma's achievement of statehood in 1907, during which the prestate tolerance of African Americans was brutally trampled into the ground, and racism was firmly woven into the structure of the state government and society.[6] These stories of Oklahoma's past accorded perfectly with the racial attitudes of many of my coworkers that summer.

The two employees with whom I did form bonds of a sort were my lab chief, Tom, and an Asian Indian immigrant called Harish. I liked Tom in spite of his Sooner State beliefs, because unlike many of my coworkers there, he never got emotional about our political and religious differences, nor did he ever make ad hominem attacks. He took me seriously, and he and I could talk about other things besides Oklahoma psychological quirks. He kept me up on company happenings, and I even visited him at home once.

Harish told me he wanted to learn to drive, so I gave him driving lessons. I wasn't a good teacher since I lacked patience, and I had had no training in that pursuit. Nevertheless, he drove me around for a while and got so that he could operate my car somewhat. Unfortunately, one day he hopped a concrete parking lot space barrier, creating a dent in my flywheel housing. The flywheel gear teeth sang as they brushed against the dent, and I had to have the dented flywheel cover replaced. Unfortunately, my temper and my shortage of patience got the better of me at that juncture. I expressed displeasure at Harish's mistake—reproach rather than naked anger. I would probably have forgiven him and resumed the lessons after a little while, but that possibility never came up in our later conversations. I still ran around with Harish for the rest of the summer, but I wish I had been more forbearing about my student driver. I hope Harish wasn't too scared away from driving by my ineptitude as an instructor.

At the end of the summer, I left with no shaking of hands. The job was a disappointment, the locale was a disappointment, and I believe I disappointed Conoco. My low morale approached depression as the summer wore on, which made me less effective in the lab and less adroit at finding things to do outside of work. Often, I would just listen to classical music in my apartment or take drives into the country for a break in the routine. The pinched face of an airless dictatorship of God and the supposedly superior white man is what the Bible Belt presented to me; I could never thrive in that closed little world.

Reflections on My Internships

I am grateful for the opportunities accorded me by the chemical companies to get actual working experience. My summer jobs offered me a broadening in a way that touched relatively few college students at that time. I was able to move away from the academic environment and see how private industry operated for chemists. The jobs were useful in narrowing my search for what I wanted and what I did not want as far as a career was concerned. Summer job programs were a good investment for the companies, both from their standpoint and from the students' standpoint. The companies could get some production from the students and get a feel for how they would stack up as permanent employees. The students got an idea how to operate competently as part of a workforce for private industry: to show up for work on time every day, even on days when they would rather have done other things; to put in a full and productive eight-hour shift; to interact well socially and professionally with management and coworkers; and to handle their own finances and lifestyle independent of professors and family. That was a deficiency for many twentysomethings in those days since university training was thin to nonexistent in those areas. In my experience, universities, at least in fields similar to mine, emphasized training of new university faculty researchers and the use of students as inexpensive lab instructors and lab workers, at the expense of readying students for all types of professional endeavor. This is a problem that persists to this day, but happily, it is now being challenged and corrected at some universities in response to twenty-first-century realities.[7]

In addition to the career opportunities, these jobs showed me how diverse our country really is. I noted a separate and distinct culture characterizing each area in which I worked. Experiencing these different cultures was a pleasurable awakening for me. Since at that time I had never visited a small, homogeneous country with which to compare the United States, this diversity did not strike me as an American marvel until later in my life. Looking back, though, I can see that it is one of the great features of our country that we can contain so many different styles within our borders without chronic or excessive instability arising from friction among them.

I did not make a career with any of the companies listed above. During graduate school, spokesmen from du Pont and Conoco repeatedly requested interviews to follow up on the summer jobs, with a view to possible permanent employment. I finally consented to interview, but I did not get job offers from either company. I was not interested in joining the force of organization-man management ladder climbers in Delaware, and I certainly did not want to spend a lifetime out in Oklahoma. The Shell option fell through for another reason, to be recounted in the next chapter.

CHAPTER 7

CAREER 2: DRIFTING AND DREAMING

This stage of my life was a real crossroads. I was not one of the fortunate students who slid effortlessly from school into a career. Three years were to elapse between the awarding of my MS in chemistry and my arrival at what is called economic maturity—that is, working at a job in which the employer expects the employee to remain for a number of years, pays the employee enough to buy a house and start a family, and offers benefits, such as health insurance and the prospect of advancement. In short, I needed a career, not just a job.

There were reasons for my state of drift. First, I had lost much of my interest in my field of training over the years, which was a great disincentive for me to strive for a job in that field. My work experience had convinced me that a career in academe was out of the question—I had to work in industry. But I was not interested in managerial politicking, so I would have had to be an industrial lab researcher. But given my lack of facility with my hands and my lack of patience with physical apparatuses, how could I work out as a lab technician? Second, I had no professors willing to boost me with their colleagues, since my fading chemistry fire prevented me from finishing my PhD and networking among the faculty at Ohio State. Third, chemistry, along with other sciences, was a crowded field in which to seek employment. By the late 1960s, employers could be as choosy as they liked, given the great number of scientists being minted by universities compared to the number of available scientific job openings. By the early 1970s, this congestion had been compounded by the winding down of the Vietnam War and the tapering off of the Apollo moon program, which dumped thousands of highly skilled and experienced scientists onto the market. Since so many chemistry careers did not interest me, what kind of a career did interest me? I had no idea.

My situation at that time illustrates a major drawback of university education. While four-year university programs carry a lot of cachet and certainly offer extensive training in critical and analytical thinking, their lengthy time span carries the risk of major evolution of the student and of the job market during the educational program. Both the job market and I had altered dramatically from 1962 to 1968—in ways unfavorable for my chemistry career prospects.

Nevertheless, it is obvious to me that in the twenty-first century, some sort of post–high school tertiary education—four-year university, two-year community college, or trade school—is essential for any kind of job beyond menial minimum-wage dead-end work. For many reasons, not every student is well suited for a four-year university education. Some are not fit for the long, intensive study grind, and some simply can't afford the monetary payouts required. On the other hand, not all well-paying jobs require four-year university degrees. Alternatives to four-year university programs, such as community colleges or trade schools, are worth considering as tertiary education paths. Students now and at all times should examine themselves carefully to see where they want to go and what they want to do when deciding if and when to attend university and which field to pursue. They need to understand that they will inevitably be changing careers at least a few times over their work lifetimes as technology advances, global conditions change, and they themselves evolve. Gone are the days when one could collect a high school diploma, get a kindly uncle to put in a good word with some international brotherhood, and park for forty-five years in a routine job that pays a middle-class wage (if those days, in fact, ever existed!). In the twenty-first century, almost any static job at which a newly minted high school graduate can become proficient after two months of on-the-job training and expert after six months will go for subsistence pay. Furthermore, employers will always be tempted to replace expensive old-timers with cheaper youngsters in such jobs. Real pay and real security will come only with dynamic jobs that require significant schooling beforehand and offer opportunities to grow and evolve.

Before leaving Ohio State, I interviewed with the US Naval Oceanographic Service and naval officer candidate school. I was attracted to these organizations because they promised travel—an activity that had recently caught my interest. While I awaited answers from them, I worked at the ranch, as during previous summers, stacking hay and maintaining fences. I am still to this day awaiting an answer from the US Naval Oceanographic Service; that job simply never materialized, as happens with many government jobs. During the interviews for officer candidate school, it was clear to me that I was being tested largely for personal enthusiasm for the great victory in Vietnam. I did not expect, nor did I get, a favorable outcome.

Later in the summer, I got in touch with Shell Oil Company, my employer for my first summer job. I interviewed in Los Angeles and in Denver. The people in Los Angeles and I were not interested in each other, but I felt I could be of some use in Denver. I interviewed with the department head and several of the lab chiefs. The proposed work interested me, and I thought the interviews went reasonably well. But I felt that one question asked by the interviewer tripped me up. It was a standard-issue interview question in those days: "In what sort of position do you see yourself after five years with us? Ten years? Twenty years?" I thought then, and I think now, that is a supremely silly question; we have no idea how we—or the company or the world—will look in five, ten, or twenty years. It signaled that the interviewer was looking for a management ladder climber, a career path I had already rejected for myself some time before. I answered that I wanted to do lab research. The interviewer, who struck me as an organization man of the du Pont sort, probably blackballed me at that point on the grounds that I was not management material. But at the end of the interview, we went through the niceties, and he said we had mutual interest. Six weeks later, I got a letter declining my services. A long delay before a rejection reply was standard in those days. The bald hypocrisy of the company reply expressing regret and promising to let me know of any future openings was irritatingly patronizing, and I have had a sour impression of that interviewer ever since—not because the interviewer didn't hire me but because he was dishonest with me. He should have indicated his lack of interest then and there in Denver rather than expressing a desire to hire me and then going through the motions of sending a rejection letter containing a clumsy attempt at a soft landing after several weeks. Mealymouthed dissembling has always been a prominent characteristic of organization men, and it is one of the major complaints I carry against them. But there is a more practical negativity here: such a delay in notification is spectacularly inconsiderate if a candidate is awaiting or receiving offers from several companies and needs to know as soon as possible about a rejection from one employer so he can process prospects with others.

I base this surmise about Shell's behavior on the fact that I was occasionally on the other end of this game during my computer career. The differences were that I never expressed interest in a candidate who did not interest me, and we did not let weeks elapse before sending the blackball notice. Reflecting on the Shell episode, I recognize that my morale would most likely have suffered in Denver had I been hired, because of the psychological games I would have been compelled to play in order to prosper among these organization men.

At last, I tried the one resource said to be available to floundering young men: enlistment in the military. I made preparations to join the navy as an enlisted man. Everything went swimmingly; we agreed that in light of my scientific training, I was to work aboard a nuclear submarine stationed in Florida. Then I went for the physical examination—and I failed! My right eye was too myopic, and I immediately received a 4-F classification (not physically fit for military service). It was a great disappointment to me; I had seen the navy as a good way to serve the country and obtain employment and saleable technical training at the same time.

As the summer wore on into the fall and the rejection notices kept piling up, I continued to work at the ranch. I avidly watched the presidential race between Richard Nixon and Hubert Humphrey. It was the first election in which I was eligible to vote, and in Sweetgrass County, we were all, naturally, rooting for the Republican Nixon. Nixon's victory seemed to presage a change in direction, particularly in Vietnam—a change I felt was necessary. The Soviet intervention in Czechoslovakia in August 1968 came as a gut punch to all of us; it was obvious the Cold War was not winding down, and the world was not getting safer and more orderly. George Wallace's far-right candidacy did not help matters; it exposed tendencies in American politics that were to become dangerously powerful some decades later.

By November, every work opening for which I had applied had fallen flat. *Now what?* I thought. It was decision time for me. What was I to do with my life? Hanging out at the ranch and living off my parents was out of the question, as was living around Sweetgrass County and taking odd employment here and there indefinitely. I had the feeling I was stepping into a void. All that education—for what?

At length, I decided to try for a career in oceanography. I went at it without enthusiasm but with a sense that at least I was moving in some direction. I applied around and was accepted at Oregon State University, my father's alma mater, with a work stipend to support me financially while I was there. I left the ranch and began my studies in Corvallis, Oregon, at the outset of January 1969.

My intention at the time was to go through to a PhD in oceanography. I was set up with a physical chemist called Dr. Pytkowicz as an adviser. I took some courses and even found a dissertation topic: how amorphous silica crystallizes under pressure.

At that point, I had my most memorable personal experience with academic arrogance. I wanted to create a mass of biogenic amorphous silica for my experiment (an experiment that eventually failed because the extreme conditions I needed were too difficult to produce, measure, and control), and I decided to culture diatoms (silica-shelled marine microorganisms) in order to collect the silica. Needing ideas on how to culture diatoms, what kinds of diatoms would be appropriate, and more, I wrote to an eminent diatom specialist, asking where to get reading materials and experimental methods. In reply, I received a small card with a short note: "You will need to take years of courses before you can talk to me about this topic." Bang! Ouch! She put me in my place. This is by no means the only encounter I have had with overinflated academics; it is only the most prominent. Too many academics believe their moral and intellectual superiority to the great unwashed masses is so self-evident that they need never demonstrate it. They consider the virtue of their endeavors to be so axiomatic that the cultivation of social and political skills is unnecessary and irrelevant. Most professors are not part of an organizational hierarchy as much as they are autonomous individuals running their own research under the generally loose watch of university administrations. This arrangement diminishes the need for, and atrophies the practice of, cultivating other people's goodwill in the way one must in a corporation or in the military.

Professors' dealing as knights to pages with graduate students like me is well and good; it is also common. After all, graduate students are low in the academic hierarchy and powerless to retaliate. But what happens if the recipient of a broadside like this is an inquiring legislator who knows little about the science but votes on budgets that include this scientist's research funding? What if it is a newspaper reporter asking honest questions on behalf of the general public? This academic above-the-fray superciliousness does neither the scientist nor science in general any good, since it cedes the public discussion arena to our already overly ample national supply of creationists, climate-change deniers, and antivaccination cranks. The latter, whatever their deficiencies in scientific lore, always know better than to make social blunders of the above sort with their audiences. But more culpably, professors who imagine they are above social etiquette can indirectly cost lives! The antiscience climate among the general American public, originating to some degree from alienation of academics from average people and exacerbated by the Trump administration's anti-intellectual policies and rhetoric, contributed substantially to the butcher's bill from the COVID-19 pandemic in the United States in 2020–2021.

I noted before and have noted since that exchange many more instances of this behavior by academics, especially from older individuals like the one who sent me that note. A real dialogue between the public and scientists is necessary to mitigate the problems caused by the scientist-versus-general-public antagonism frequently deplored in scientific journals.[1] The forward movement of science must be a cooperative effort among all segments of society. Hopefully more of the younger scientists of today understand their own and the public's interests well enough to avoid such ill-judged actions. Unfortunately, even after more than four decades' absence from the academic world, I still occasionally uncover a complaint about arrogance, provinciality, and territoriality in academe.[2] I suspect that some remnant of this unpleasant aspect of university life will be with us always.

I took an extraordinarily interesting course in earth sciences from Dr. Van Andel. The course fired up my interest in geology, though not enough to overcome my general tiredness and my wish for a total change in pace. I aced the course. Dr. Van Andel's final test was for me to write a research proposal.[3] He was so impressed with my proposal that he told me if there had been a grade higher than A, he would have awarded it to me. I gained an invaluable ally and a resource for my final push for a real career. In the near term, I took courses for a year, stumbled through most of them, and eventually gave up in weariness all attempts at a PhD after a year in Corvallis.

During the first half of 1969, I had my introduction to intimacy. I dated a fellow graduate student a few times, and we spent some nights in her apartment. She was several years older than I was. I was nervous and clumsy, but I sensed she was uptight as well and a bit squeamish.

We went together for a couple of months, sharing her apartment a lot of the time. We played Scrabble, cooked dinners together, and patronized what little Corvallis had to offer for entertainment. But as time went on, we drifted apart. She was good company for a typically lonely graduate student like me, but I was also an immature wandering boy of the sort one encounters in Philip Roth literature and other tales of youth pampered and not prepared for adult life. We remained somewhat on speaking terms after the end of our romance, but she was clearly hurt by the course it took. The emotional aspect of female sexuality was something of which I had heard vaguely at the time, but I had never internalized it as relevant to my situation. Nothing from my misogynistic, sexually repressed experience in the 1950s and 1960s induced me to appreciate that a woman is likely to develop emotional ties to a man with whom she shares a bed just one time. As to the future of our relationship, I don't think we were made for a lifetime together, as our ambitions and visions of the future differed widely. She was content to spend a life in Corvallis, puttering in a lab, while I envisioned large cities, lots of travel, and a flourishing career (what kind of a career, I still had no idea). Nevertheless, I am not proud of that episode; it showed spectacularly that I needed character development.

In the middle of 1969, I moved into a rented lower floor of a house with another graduate student, Terry. We got along well; like me, he had started out with PhD aspirations but ended up at loose ends. I lived for the rest of my Corvallis tenure in that house.

Near the end of July 1969, I took a job as a burger flipper at a local college bar called Price's. I remember the date because at the time I started my job, we all watched the first Apollo moon landing on the bar's TV. It was an immensely proud moment for our country and a relieving positive occasion that punctuated the depressingly endless grind in Vietnam and the riots and controversy at home.

The money from that job adequately supported me after the loss of my stipend from Oregon State University. Since my customers were mainly college students, my income rarely included tips. But it was a tame job for the most part; the clientele never rioted, as sometimes happens when college kids get too lubricated. Occasionally, I had to eject old drunks who fell asleep or got sick.

No hard liquor was served; the only alcoholic beverage was beer from kegs and cans. My work schedule at the tavern was from 1700 until either 2100 or 0100, the closing time for the tavern. The hours were informal; I could show up when I was available, as long as I put in at least twenty hours a week. During my first several months on the job, I spent my copious spare time browsing through the Oregon State University library, reading books and magazines on sundry topics, or wondering what I was going to do with myself. Burger flipping and beer pulling in a small college town obviously did not constitute a situation I envisioned for a lifetime, but the job did give me a chance to catch my breath and ponder my future. The looseness in my work schedule gave me the opportunity to spend time looking for a real career.

At length, after consulting with a career adviser, I decided I wanted to teach at a community college. An MS in the relevant field was the standard requirement for the position. I could put my hard-earned chemistry credential to work. It looked like a rewarding job, enlightening young people without the endless hassle of a faculty position at a four-year university. I could use the summers to travel and enrich myself while earning my living and making my mark during the other nine months. Southern California was the place to pursue the career, I thought, having been enchanted by the area during my first summer job there. What more ideal combination could I have wished for?

Accordingly, I got hold of an adviser to guide me in the ins and outs of applying for a job at a community college. He provided me with the forms and a list of the community colleges in California, and he wished me bon voyage. I laboriously typed out application letters and résumés to about a dozen community colleges in the Los Angeles and San Diego areas. For the career, I needed a California teaching credential, which was granted upon my production of my master's degree and my passing a test on the US Constitution.

I was granted interviews at several community colleges in Southern California, and I drove down there with high hopes. Before the interviews, I checked out the campuses of some of the colleges to see which campus I would prefer when the offers came in. That was where everything went south.

The interviewers grilled me unmercifully about my experience. Where had I taught before? What was my general philosophy based on my previous years of teaching? I replied that I had taught chemistry to undergraduates in labs at Ohio State University, which the interviewers dismissed: "That doesn't count!" They wanted *real* teaching experience. I was nonplussed; one has to start somewhere, doesn't one? If everybody needed previous teaching experience, no new hires would be possible. One and all rejected me—or, rather, based on my lack of experience, they put me so low on their list of teachers available for openings that I was guaranteed never to see an offer.

Subsequently, I learned through the grapevine—not from any of the interviewers—that community college teaching positions, at least in California, were plums to be handed out to high school teachers who stayed put in their professions long enough, played by the rules loyally enough, and networked with community college bureaucracies extensively enough. It even appeared that some of the community colleges were run by the very boards that ran the high schools! The teaching loads in community colleges were lighter, and the students were more motivated and more intelligent, than was the case in high schools. After all that driving, typing, and preparation, I found I was applying for a senior position in a closed fraternity whose high-level employees had all been promoted from within as a matter of policy.

When I described the incestuous relationship between high schools and community colleges to the adviser who had sent me on that chase, he replied, "I could have told you that." He must have read the inevitable question on my face, because he added, "I thought it would be better if you found out for yourself." What I found out for myself was that he played head games with me.

So it was high school teaching first if I wanted to teach at a community college. Well, I could live with that; if that was how the game was played, I could play it also. I sent my papers to a few high schools in Southern California, and what do you know? I got an offer almost immediately. The only interview I needed to undergo was a telephone conversation with a school official, and I was in!

The school was in interior Southern California, residing within Edwards Air Force Base in Kern County. All the students were children of military personnel—military brats, I later found out. But I will get to that issue presently. The name of the school was Desert High School, and I drove down to pay a visit to get acquainted with the layout and make myself known to the school personnel with whom I would be working.

Following the advice of the school official, I took a few education courses at Oregon State for the summer quarter of 1970. All but one of the courses were credit-mill attendance-only-required courses, which did little to enlighten me on teaching techniques and much more to get me in on the educational dogma of the day, which was called Freedom to Learn.[4] The teacher was to be a mentor and encourager rather than a pedagogical instructor. At the end of the courses, the instructors merely asked us what grade we thought we deserved and what we had done to deserve it. In most cases, they gave us the grade we thought we deserved—that is, an A. I only got a B in one of the courses for some reason—what an injustice.

The exception was a good physics course. It was taught at a level suitable for high school teachers but informative for me nevertheless. I took the course because I was slated to teach physics at Desert High

School, and the school officials advised me that the course would be appropriate, as my degree was in chemistry, not physics. The professor of the class gave us a rundown on the special and general relativity theories using a geometric approach, which made the concepts much clearer than the mathematical equation derivations previously presented to me in undergraduate school. I aced the course, not because I asked for the grade but because I earned it!

A harbinger of what was to come appeared in the reactions of some of my acquaintances in Corvallis when they learned I proposed to go into high school teaching. A friend of my roommate, Terry, was already a teacher, and her first rejoinder was an emphatic "If you don't like it, get out of it!" Dr. Van Andel's immediate reaction was "If you find this job is not right for you, contact us right away." A police officer who regularly patronized Price's Tavern, whose mother was a teacher, said he was crying for my sake. These people sounded almost as if they were saying, "*When* you don't like it …" Did they sense something about me that suggested to them I might not relate well to adolescents, particularly those with average or subpar intellectual candlepower? I didn't ponder the warnings much at the time.

I said my goodbyes to my beer bar colleagues and to Terry and arrived in the Edwards Air Force Base area at the end of August 1970. A trailer was available to rent in a trailer park in Rosamond, a village in the Antelope Valley high desert on the western edge of Edwards Air Force Base. It was an agreeable place and available at an affordable price. I went to the Desert High School campus and met the principal and the vice principal. I had been told before I arrived what I was to teach: physics, algebra, and general math. I had looked over some of the textbooks and had immediately been struck by the elementary level of the general math material. It was fifth- to seventh-grade stuff; was this, in fact, a high school? As I talked over the issues with the two officials, the principal warned me that some of the kids would be "awful low," as he put it—"in the first percentile" for math capability. That made me somewhat nervous; I had never dealt with that type of audience before, and it promised to be a real adventure. The head math teacher later confirmed, "Some of them aren't going to move and aren't going to want to move." But I envisioned the flunk-outs quietly dozing in class, never learning, and then failing while I dealt with the others as well as I could. That was how things had operated when I went to high school. I was in for a lesson of my own!

My classes consisted of a physics class of about a dozen seniors, a freshman algebra class of about thirty-five, and three classes of general math—one freshman and two sophomore classes with about thirty students each. Five classes constituted the norm for all teachers; we taught for five fifty-minute periods and got to rest for the other two periods during the seven-period day. Nobody was on hand to mentor me or any of the other new teachers; we were expected to swim as well as we could upon being thrown into the water. As the newest of the newbies, I didn't even have an office or a classroom of my own; I held classes in the classrooms of teachers who were resting during the periods when I used their rooms. I stashed my papers and equipment on a desk in the janitor's room—barely more than a closet—while I dashed from classroom to classroom all day. At the end of the first day, I was exhausted. How was I to make a living out of this?

As time went on, I learned to conserve my energy so as not to end each day in a meltdown. My classes quickly separated into a dichotomy. On one hand, the physics and algebra classes were filled with kids who were motivated and obviously headed for the good things in life. In those classes, I did a somewhat passable job of teaching. I had some beginner's glitches, such as losing my temper on occasion or getting momentarily disorganized, but I was able to impart the material to most of the students, who were by and large receptive and cooperative. We even liked and respected each other; when the students were asked later in the year to evaluate their teachers, I was one of two teachers on the faculty who had classes that were unanimous in giving them good marks—in my case, those two classes. A couple of my physics students even had me write recommendation letters for them to the universities they wished to attend. With some mentoring by senior staff, I could probably have done well in the physics and algebra. It is even conceivable that teaching could have become a career for me if those classes had been typical. I could have given the students a boost and felt rewarded by having positively influenced successful people.

On the other hand, the general math classes—about two-thirds of my share of the student body—were otherwise known as *remedial*, a word that means just what it says. Most of the students were there because they lacked the math skills they should have had at their grade level. I was theoretically to remedy or cure their deficits. Deficits indeed! During my first week, I took one of the sophomores aside to tutor and evaluate him at his request. Among other things, he could not tell me what two and a half multiplied by two was. That was a long way even from the level of math I was supposed to be teaching, and I knew then that this individual would probably not make it. He was the worst I met, but there were many others almost as deficient.

Some students who were bright and advanced enough to be in meatier courses were in those classes just because they wanted to take life easy and ace the class without significant effort. Some were merely loafing through high school in general and had no intention of pursuing higher goals after graduation. Whatever the case, elevating slow learners to passable levels of math proficiency, when most of them had no desire to be elevated, was not what I had bargained for. I certainly had had no training in the endeavor! But conscientious as I was, I wanted to do as good a job as I was able. If my lack of enthusiasm and capability for such classes crippled me in that effort, the lack of a mentor to guide me through the inevitable pitfalls made the crippling irretrievable. My experience convinced me that master teachers' mentoring of the juniors is important for the quality of a school. I don't know how widespread mentoring is these days, but I sorely felt its lack back then. I got advice on an informal basis from a fellow math teacher called Rich, who also served as a crying towel for me during crisis moments. I was thankful to have him as a confidant.

I learned right away that the flunk-outs were not the docile sleepers I had known when I went to high school. They were noisy and disruptive. I learned too late that with remedial students like these, it is necessary to establish a strong authoritarian presence from the first day. But it is debatable whether a mentor providing foreknowledge of this fact could have helped me. I have never enjoyed being a dictator any more than I appreciate dictators trying to subjugate me. I hated trying to force students to learn as much as they hated being forced. I suspect that in many cases, their pain was augmented by having been called stupid to their faces for much of their lives.

Two things became clear to me over the next few months. First, I was expected to warehouse the remedial math students and wash them through the class as well as I could. The administrators continually admonished me that the students were stupid. But they then badgered me to take charge, with no details as to how to accomplish that. I was supposed to appetize them for the material (shades of Freedom to Learn—how relevant was that dogma there?). Lacking both training and competence for handling marginal students, I often wondered what good I was doing for anybody. Second, it was obvious that many of the students needed individual attention and could probably have benefited from it. But how was I to administer individual attention to perhaps sixty of my ninety remedial math students who needed it? Whenever I explained the way to solve a problem and then assigned a problem for the class to work, I invariably was faced with a chorus of "How do you do this?" and a forest of raised hands. Try as I might, I never was able to explain to some of them; extensive repetition of the explanation on an individual basis was likely what was needed, but where was the time? Fortunately, my classes contained a supply of Good Samaritans (always girls) who comprehended my discourse and volunteered to explain and demonstrate the procedures to the dimmer students in a one-on-one setting, even as I did the same. Thus, we taught as a team effort, and the need for individual tutoring was slightly mitigated. We were able to impart a slight amount of knowledge in this way.

Some of the general math students had undeniable gifts by which they could have been set on the path to truly successful careers through rigorous tutoring and creative inspiration—which I was not equipped to provide. One of them had a visual-arts bent that he may have parlayed into a real career. But the majority were, as the principal frequently warned me, headed ineluctably for dead-end, low-pay blue-collar jobs; long-term welfare; or even the penitentiary. That reflection was a distinct disincentive to me. Babysitting sixty-odd slow learners, laboring mightily to salvage them, and meeting with success in maybe a dozen cases while letting the rest go their own way as if I had never existed seemed to me to constitute about 80 percent wasted effort.

Discipline was a chronic problem in those three classes. The students conversed and walked around, even when I commanded otherwise. Compounding the problem was my frequent loss of my short temper, which sometimes led me to express frustration through four-letter words. Doubtful as my prospects were in that atmosphere, given my reluctance to be a martinet, the problem was made more difficult by the shortcomings of the administrators as disciplinarians, who were supposed to back up teachers faced with intractable students. One of my female students was terribly downcast, thinking her goose was cooked, the first time I sent her to the office. After that, she regarded that procedure with contempt. One of my male students related to me how the administrators would try to sound stern and commanding but would come across instead as comical and slapstick. As often as not, when I sent a student to the office, he would return immediately with a note to the effect that "He says he didn't do this. You can't be accusing these kids without proof." So we needed a court of law for kids who had not learned the first thing about living under rule of law!

Leafing through a book on educational techniques in the teachers' lounge one day, I came across a chapter about slow learners. The chapter gave several good tips on how to encourage slow learners embedded in a class of average students. But what caught my eye was a sentence late in the chapter: "Grouped slow learners are something else again and are sometimes given to new teachers in a perverted application of 'seniority rights.'" It is ironic that as a new teacher, I got some of the most difficult students in the school, with neither prior training nor contemporary mentoring, while more skilled and experienced teachers, who by dint of seniority had earned a partial right to choose their classes, got students who were easier and more rewarding to teach.

The upshot of all this was not only chaos in my classes and in the classes of a couple of other teachers but also low morale generally among the faculty at Desert High and a local reputation that the school was too loose in discipline. The parents were mainly fully cooperative with me and wanted their kids to behave and learn, but they were also frustrated.

The kids too were frustrated—and disgusted over the state of affairs. The other teachers sympathized with me and with one another. Even some of the kids obviously pitied me. It was a sad situation.

To keep up my energy, I escaped to Los Angeles every Saturday—a seventy- or eighty-mile drive—to go to attractions: the La Brea Tar Pits, Knott's Berry Farm, and more. I also took lessons in Russian from an old Polish gentleman who had been an officer in the tsar's army before the Great War. Those were my diversions, and they helped me to stay right side up.

About three months into my five-month teaching career, I contacted Dr. Van Andel at Oregon State University and related my predicament. His response was "A tale of woe if I ever heard one but not unexpected. Perhaps there is a solution." He sent me a brochure about a new oceanographic study called GEOSECS, then being started at Scripps Institution of Oceanography in San Diego. I called up the chief investigator, Arnold Bainbridge, and we arranged an interview.

The interview did not go as well as it could have; I later learned the chief investigator found me too introverted. He kept putting me off when I called him about the situation, but he passed my papers to another investigator who was looking for help, Dr. Charles D. Keeling, for his perusal.

Just as the Christmas two-week holiday arrived, the principal called me into his office and asked me to resign at the end of the semester—that is, at the end of the following January six weeks hence. I had no objections to departing as demanded; I was clearly not cut out for the shepherding of slow learners or for teaching at all in the Desert High School environment at that time. But I was unsettled; nothing had yet materialized at Scripps Institute of Oceanography.

During the January that marked the terminus of my teaching career, I drove to San Diego to get a personal take on my situation there. I ran into Arnold Bainbridge, the GEOSECS principal investigator, just as he was meeting with Dr. Keeling. I heard Dr. Keeling say, "Adams is the first choice." Mr. Bainbridge jovially gestured to me, and I talked to Dr. Keeling for a bit. I got the offer, and I agreed to start in the middle of February 1971. Thus, I landed on my feet; I had a job awaiting me at the end of my sad teaching career.

As I look back on this episode, I can see that even had I been assigned nothing but motivated and intelligent students, teaching itself is a physically and mentally demanding job. I understand why a three-month vacation each year is a necessity and why my sisters, Nina and Emily, retired from their teaching careers well short of the age of seventy, when one can maximize Social Security benefits.

One important takeaway from my teaching job was my first real, sustained, multi-individual contact with African Americans and Hispanics. The military, unlike lots of other American institutions at the time, was integrated. I had several minority students in my classes, and a faculty member was African American. It never occurred to me to feel any tension with any of them; I just reflexively saw them as people. I probably benefitted from my early childhood experience of not having had stereotypes and superstitions assiduously pounded into my brain. I never sensed racial tensions among the students either; no doubt the military enforced its norms to the point where the norms came naturally. That was a great benefit to us all since there was plenty of tension elsewhere in the country at the time. I feel that contact with minorities benefitted me by erasing any lingering subconscious conflicts I might have had. From then forward, I have always interfaced with minority individuals exactly as I interface with all others—with no discrimination, no forcing, and no artificiality. As my life has progressed and as I have traveled the world and worked with minority employees all over the country, I have become progressively more warmly welcoming of diversity in our society. The rights of minorities to full participation in our society are now one of my chief political passions. It is abundantly clear to me that full minority rights are a major requirement for our country's continued functioning as a democracy and as a modern world power in the twenty-first century.

As I left Edwards Air Force Base, I held lengthy farewell conversations with some of my students. My physics students and many of my algebra students were sorry to see me go; even a few of my general math students sympathized with me. If freedom to fail is one of the hallmarks of true liberty, I certainly exercised this particular freedom repeatedly and with a vengeance during that three-year chapter of my life. Failure can be educational as long as one learns one's limitations and finds out what one does *not* want to do. I had had a full curriculum of courses on these topics; the secret is to keep exploring and trying to ascertain where one *does* fit. I was neither stigmatized nor blackballed because of my long period of uncertainty. I was to be judged on how I performed now, not in the past. I was about to embark on a career as a chemist in Southern California yet!

CHAPTER 8

CAREER 3: WHITE-COLLAR PROFESSIONAL IN SOUTHERN CALIFORNIA

At last, I was settled into a career. I was thankful I had gotten the job at all. The economic depression affecting technically trained people was still in full swing; every other piece of mail arriving at Scripps Institution of Oceanography was said to be an unsolicited résumé. There were about twenty-five competitors for my position. To this day, I remain deeply grateful to Dr. Van Andel at Oregon State University for pushing my name with the people he had known when he worked at Scripps. He was an indispensable jump-starter for my career.

The work consisted of monitoring the concentration of carbon dioxide (CO_2) in the atmosphere at various points around the globe. Our long-term stations were at the South Pole and on Mauna Loa, a volcanic mountain on the Big Island of Hawaii. Dr. Keeling had been measuring atmospheric CO_2 concentrations at these places since the late 1950s. Other stations later added were a ship in the northern Pacific Ocean, off the coast of British Columbia; a research site in New Zealand; and a ship in the Southern Ocean. We also measured CO_2 levels on the pier at Scripps on the rare days when the Southern California air was clean. During my tenure, we added stations at Fanning Island (in 1972) and Christmas Island (in 1974) in the central Pacific Ocean.

My work colleagues were a chemist called Peter, a physicist called Carl, and an electronics technician called Dave. Later, we added a computer programmer called Bob. We worked together to analyze the air, keep the machinery working, and model the results.

I did the work of analyzing the air samples for CO_2 content, and I managed the receiving of air samples from various stations. I wrote computer programs—mostly in the FORTRAN language, with a little ALGOL and BASIC thrown in—to examine the CO_2 concentration data at various stations and plot the data as a function of time over years. This was my introduction to computers, which were to become a passion in due course.

In collaboration with Dave, I constructed a few electronic devices to automate our data collection and thus received a small introduction to the workings of electronic circuitry. I took a rough-and-ready course in glassblowing so I could fix routine cracks and breaks in the glass racks used for our air analyses without having to call in a glassblower and wait for several days before we could again use the apparatuses.

The result of all the sampling and analysis was a huge data set comprising CO_2 abundances in the atmosphere stretching back for many years at multiple locations. The main takeaways from the data were as follows:

1. The concentration of CO_2 in the atmosphere is rising yearly at an accelerating rate. In the late 1950s, the concentration was around 310 parts per million, and now it is more than 400 parts per million. The Keeling curve, named for Dr. Keeling, illustrates this rise.[1] Reputable scientists agree that human activity drives this increase.

2. The CO_2 atmospheric concentrations at each site are subject to an annual cycle. In the spring, land vegetation flourishes and pulls CO_2 out of the atmosphere, leading to a fall in the CO_2 concentration during that part of the year. In the autumn, the concentration rises as the plant material dies off and releases CO_2 back into the atmosphere.

3. The amplitude of this annual cycle varies with latitude, being more intense at high northern latitudes, where the amount

of plant life varies more widely over a year than at tropical latitudes.

4. The annual cycle in the Southern Hemisphere (New Zealand, South Pole) is about 180 degrees out of phase with the Northern Hemisphere cycle, naturally, since the seasons are out of phase.

5. The annual cycle amplitude has been increasing with increasing atmospheric CO_2 concentration since more CO_2 leads to more plant life and therefore more vigorous spring flourishing and more intense fall die-off.

Later in my chemist's career, I was tasked to set up and supervise our stations in the central Pacific. Carl set up the station on Fanning Island in 1972, and I set up the Christmas Island station in 1974. I trained, or retrained, personnel at these stations to collect air samples in glass flasks and ship them home to us in California. These personnel were Gilbertese natives who had been imported by the British during the nineteenth century from the Gilbert Islands around Tarawa for the tending of coconut plantations on the islands. The Gilbertese—and the coconut trees—had remained after the departure of the British.

Fanning and Christmas Islands are a couple of atolls that comprise part of the Line Islands. They are a few hundred miles north of the equator, near the Hawaiian longitude. Today they are known as Tabuaeran and Kiritimati, respectively, and are part of the Republic of Kiribati, inhabited by Gilbertese. The annual CO_2 concentration cycle at both of these islands tracked the Northern Hemisphere concentrations, though the amplitude of the cycle was very small since vegetation mass does not vary much over the year near the equator.

During that central Pacific adventure, I got my first personal contact with scientific misconduct, about which we read so much these days. The first year's air samples from Christmas Island, supposedly taken twice a month for a year, showed perfectly flat CO_2 concentration over the year—no annual cycle and no Keeling curve rise. I noted that the dates and times recorded for the air samples were suspiciously uniform: always the first and fifteenth of each month and always at 1200 hours. I called everybody's attention to the curiosity, and we later found out the sampling person on Christmas Island had one day driven the entire year's air sampling flasks out to the sampling site and filled them all with sampled air. He then had concocted dates and times for each sample and sent the mess back to us. I contacted a scientist with whom I had worked in setting up the sites, Dr. Martin Vitousek. He related that the individual had done the same thing to him—sat in his room and generated fictional weather data. So we had to replace the technician on Christmas Island and trash all the data he had falsified. After that time, the data looked better. In 1978, I went to Christmas Island again to confirm that everything was going according to plan. We had a conscientious operator at the time, and I was satisfied.

Another adventure occurred around 1974. We had been coasting along, recording atmospheric CO_2 concentration data over the years. Then, to our chagrin, we discovered a major omission dating from the outset of Dr. Keeling's monitoring; all our data had been biased for years. Measuring CO_2 concentration in air against known CO_2 concentrations in CO_2-nitrogen gas mixtures had been Dr. Keeling's method all along. This turned out to be an apples-and-oranges comparison; CO_2-nitrogen mixtures are not air! The major gases constituting air are nitrogen, oxygen (O_2), and argon (Ar). CO_2 molecules do not interact the same with this mixture as they interact with pure nitrogen. This caused the infrared analyzers to yield erroneous results for air CO_2 concentration— an error of about 1 percent. So we did some experimenting to arrive at precise and accurate values for the corrections needed, and we thus arrived at a good correction value for the atmospheric CO_2 concentrations gathered over all those years.

The error in the infrared readings for CO_2 caused by air gases turned out to be a function of total ambient pressure. Through further experimentation, we concluded that an additional 0.1 percent correction had to be added in to compensate for the effect of running Mauna Loa analyses at eleven thousand feet of elevation—about two-thirds of an atmosphere ambient pressure. We published the results of our investigation of the air gas effects in a paper.[2]

The upshot of all this science was that we established a good record of CO_2 concentration trends in the atmosphere at various parts of the globe for some decades. The Keeling curve thus generated established that anthropogenic CO_2 was accumulating in the atmosphere. Since

CO_2 traps the sun's heat in the lower atmosphere, this accumulation is blamed for the increase in global temperatures observed over the last fifty years and for some of the recent extreme weather phenomena. I served as one of the authors for several papers published on this topic, and I can feel that I did my little bit to establish climate change as a scientific fact and to undermine the position of climate-change deniers.[3], [4]

Dr. Keeling passed in 2005 after gathering this impressive set of environmental data. Our group is scattered to the four winds now. CO_2 monitoring continues today aboard NASA's *Orbiting Carbon Observatory-2* (*OCO-2*) satellite. This satellite measures CO_2 concentration by measuring how much reflected sunlight is absorbed by the CO_2 in the atmosphere.[5] CO_2 at many locations can be monitored, thus making a comprehensive picture available and pinpointing local CO_2 sources and sinks. This effort is large and involves many personnel and much equipment, but it is a necessary observation of one of mankind's biggest footprints on this planet. I believe the *OCO-2* project was made much more probable and politically acceptable by Dr. Keeling's little multidecade shoestring operation, which initially exposed the anthropogenic CO_2 rise to public gaze and on which I spent many years.

California was a happy place for me at that time. I had a good, steady job after my drifting and anxiety of the previous years. I was living in singles' apartments—hardly the abode of grown-ups—but I at least felt I was getting somewhere.

During that period of my life, I read voraciously on national and world events: the end of the Vietnam War, Nixon's impeachment crisis, the various elections, and more. I voted in all elections in which I was eligible. Two events marked this as an era of liberation. One was the election of African American Tom Bradley as mayor of Los Angeles, as he beat out racist Sam Yorty. The other was the victory of Billie Jean King over Bobby Riggs in a man-woman tennis match. These were both satisfying results for me, indicating that we were maturing as a society and slowly becoming more inclusive. We had, and still have, a long way to go, but these were important steps.

At the other end of the liberation scale, I followed the arrest and expulsion of Alexander Solzhenitsyn from the Soviet Union. I had been an avid reader of Solzhenitsyn's works for some years, and I admired his defiance of the corrupt, ineffectual Soviet police state. This contemptible act by the Soviet government showed anew how unfit it was to occupy a seat at the table of civilized nations, if the imposition of dictatorship in Czechoslovakia several years before had not already demonstrated this unfitness.

I acquired a couple of hobbies that occupied me in addition to my reading. I took up sailplanes and actually worked my way to a private pilot's license. My workmate Carl introduced me to it, and I spent many happy hours soaring on thermals (rising warm-air columns) generated by heated ground in the Southern California semidesert. Eventually, I tired of the sport; real expertise in soaring requires much dedication, including long hours fixing and customizing equipment. My reluctance and incompetence in working with my hands diminished my enthusiasm for the sport. As far as piloting itself was concerned, I was too high-strung and apt to freeze to deal effectively with the tight situations that inevitably arise at times during flying. I was too slow to change my plans as necessary when conditions abruptly altered. For example, if I lost altitude due to a downdraft, I tended to be tardy in changing my flight patterns and plans as demanded by the loss of space between me and the ground. So I left off sailplanes after about three years.

My other hobby was square dancing, which started out as an experiment in continuing my country dancing of the past in Montana. I soon discovered there was a world of difference between laid-back, undemanding country square dancing and the disciplined quadrille-style exercises practiced by city folk. I had to go through several weeks of lessons in order to memorize the many special maneuvers so I could jump into them reflexively when directed by the dance caller. But I eventually became expert enough to give a good accounting of myself at any dance. This hobby soon became a prime source of physical exercise for me, which was a definite benefit; white-collar jobs typically are deficient in this regard. I was even elected to offices in square dance clubs. This experience required extensive speaking to crowds, and it banished all remaining traces of the stage fright that had plagued me earlier in my life.

My social interactions finally blossomed during that phase of my life. I formed real long-lasting friendships with my coworkers at Scripps. Every Friday evening after work, the personnel at Scripps would have a beer keg party on a pier attached to one of the Scripps buildings. The party was typically attended by several dozen Scripps employees, and we talked over the world situation and various other topics. On occasion, my coworkers and I even had dinners together.

At the ripe age of twenty-seven, I finally got into my first serious relationship with a woman. I met Marion Pierce at a forgettable singles' gathering, and we hit it right off. She was twenty years my senior, but such things never bothered me. In fact, I found it a plus; not having spent her impressionable years in the 1950s, Marion lacked the manlessness panic I had found so off-putting among women my own age during school. We could conduct our relationship without consulting the orthodoxies of our youth. She was fluent in Spanish, and she owned a bookcase full of books, through which I leafed from time to time.

Unfortunately, Marion was afraid to be around people she didn't know well. I got her to go on one sailplane flight with me, and I tried to get her to accompany me in square dancing. My entreaties were never successful, but she encouraged me to continue my own hobbies. Strangely, she urged me to date as well. It was as if she felt she didn't deserve me. She felt unsettled by the age difference between us and argued that I should search for a "good woman." So I continued to date, though I had no intention of leaving Marion.

Early in our relationship, I started feeling uncomfortable about not being entertaining enough for Marion, and I apologized for this shortcoming. Marion's response startled me, and it has stayed with me ever since. She said that all she wanted was my company. My self was enough for her—no stand-up comic routines or ritzy excursions necessary! This ran counter to all the cultural statements and personal observations of my past. I had assumed women were looking for a meal ticket and children in return for sex and flattery—strictly transactional. Either partner could break off the relationship the moment he or she decided the transaction was unsatisfying—perhaps leaving behind a brokenhearted mate. So ran the 1950s literature, the college stag-party discussions, and the song lyrics and story lines. So behaved too many women I had encountered. During my early adulthood, the idea that a woman could want me simply for me was so preposterous that the idea never entered my head. The fact that Marion was middle-aged and had been through some relationships was an advantage. Through hard experience, she had shed the 1950s culture that afflicted many of the women I had known in school, and she started me on the road to recovery from the effects of that culture. We genuinely loved each other, and we stayed together for about four years.

Thus began a four-year facet of my life of which I am not proud. I dated extensively, usually with women I met at square dances, while I was going with Marion. They were mostly ten to twenty years older than I, and most of them had endured unions that had shown them how unblissful supposed marital bliss could be. They expressed a healthy skepticism of the joys eagerly anticipated by their juniors at my universities. They were out looking for a good time, and maybe a new partner, in square dancing. These observations cemented my bias toward older women. I felt at the time that this fun life was deserved compensation for the ridiculous Victorian sexual norms that had characterized and cramped my life up to then. Perhaps my female partners felt a similar liberation.

Nevertheless, after all their talk of being liberated, two female square dancers with whom I was intimate over that four-year period developed strong attachments to me, just as had happened in Oregon. We never made promises to each other about permanent relationships. I never consulted myself as to whether these women would make good lifetime partners for me. But it seemed the women, even after talking a good line about being fancy free, saw the intimacy in retrospect as a promise of commitment in spite of themselves. I had to tell them about Marion, to whom I wanted to remain faithful. Naturally, the revelation hurt the women, scotched the new relationships, and made me feel wretched. I see parallels between me and the third type of pest I described in my college chapter (chapter 5). Full appreciation of women's emotional reactions to intimate encounters evidently required me to take several lessons in etiquette. Lessons they were—needed lessons— and good character was certainly not manifest in me there. It was reprehensible behavior, and the fact that previous female acquaintances had played this game with me provides neither excuse nor cover.

During that period, I dated a woman whom I sensed had a real affection and appreciation for me. She was an African American coworker of mine at Scripps called JoAnne. But I was still immature, still acting wild, and still going with Marion, so I consider this woman fortunate that we never went down any false paths. I remember her with respect and affection to this day. She had me buy and make things for her when I went on trips, and she was the first African American I dated. On one occasion, I took her on a sailplane ride. This was in the early 1970s, when such a dating arrangement could have gotten us into trouble from some quarters. But the race issue concerned me not at all. Much later, I heard from her boss that she had died of cancer at the age of forty, about ten years after we parted ways. Today it pains me terribly that such a sweet person suffered that unjust end; she deserved much better.

Finally, I met my match (in several senses) at a square dance. I met and dated Marky Poindexter, and she was much more aggressive and outraged about side issues than the other women. She let me know it with both barrels. I had never, after all, wanted to hurt anybody; I just wanted my partners and me to have fun. The previous women had merely hidden their feelings better than did Marky. After discussions and ruminations, I realized my relationships with Marion—and the square dance women—would never go anywhere, and Marion appreciated my honesty also. So we broke it off, though both of us were teary and sorry. But it was best for both Marion and me; we kept in contact over the phone for a few months, and then the contacts tapered off. Much later, I checked the obituaries and found that Marion had passed on May 3, 2008, at the age of eighty-three. My relationship with her had one positive effect: it erased the misogynistic wariness I had accumulated over my school years. For all her issues, she showed me it was conceivable that a woman could love me for me, with no ulterior motives, no psychological games, and no self-dealing. That made it easier for me to form sincere relationships with women afterward. Marion did me a great favor in that, and I hope her life was happy and fulfilling after we went our own ways.

With some psychological adjustment—and no dating—I settled into my new role as Marky's faithful man. It was clearly a salutary turn; looking back on my singles period, I consider myself fortunate I did not continue the singles' lifestyle. I noted many individuals then and since who never let go of that meretricious way. The square dance world was rife with that sort of male, and they were sad cases indeed. They stumbled uncomprehendingly through life, never acquiring either fulfillment or meaning. I, on the other hand, can look back on a satisfying relationship that greatly enriched my life. Marky and I had enough in common that we could fulfill each other and keep a healthy relationship going, even over the inevitable rough spots. Rough spots there were; I had to shed all nostalgia for the singles' scene and never go back to it. The terrible Adams temper rose on occasion. This psychological realignment took several years; I had to grow up voluntarily. Not just any woman could have done this for me. There had to be some community of interest, personality, and character for this reworking of me to succeed. Patience and understanding on her part were necessities. Based on my observations in my earlier life, I conclude that such qualifying women were hard to find in my case; Marky was a rare bird indeed. She was twenty-two years older than I—slightly older than Marion—but neither of us felt that to be awkward.

Marky earned her keep as an accountant. She owned large bookcases full of books, and she had been a translator of Old English (pre–William the Conqueror English) literature. She was rather fluent in French and was an avid reader of British literature. In religion, she had none and wanted none. In politics, she was rather Republican but ferociously pro–abortion rights. We never married, because Marky would have none of anything ecclesiastical. I was OK with the arrangement; I felt that a ceremony and a piece of legal paper were not really relevant anyway. If a relationship is stable and healthy, these accoutrements make no difference. If a relationship is unstable and bound to fail, marriage by itself will not salvage it. I greatly appreciated Marky's liberated attitude toward the issue—such a blessed contrast to the husband-hunters of my college days!

Marky had to adjust as well, but I believe it was for our benefit. For example, I directed her to quit smoking. Smoking had been a habit of hers for decades, but secondhand smoke is hard on my eyes and throat and probably on other parts of me also. Thankfully, she realized the good side of this change of lifestyle, and she was strong and determined enough to kick the habit without noticeable physical or psychological withdrawal. Maybe she felt I was worth the trouble. At any rate, I have no doubt the health of both of us profited as a result.

After Marky and I got together, we vacated our respective apartments and moved to a country village about fifty miles east of San Diego, in the mountains by a lake called Cuyamaca. We desired a semirural setting with four seasons, and the 4,600-foot elevation gave us as close to that kind of environment as we could find in Southern California. We got snow regularly in the winter, though a snowfall rarely remained on the ground for more than a few days. The scenery was beautiful, and the people were mostly friendly. We settled in as villagers, and we frequently went for boat rides on the lake. We hiked in the surrounding mountains when the mood seized us. I joined the village volunteer fire department and got some training in ladders, engine operation, and cardiopulmonary resuscitation. Marky and I couldn't be very active in village life, since we had about a one-and-a-half-hour commute each way to our jobs in San Diego. That made for twelve-hour days, but weekends were all to ourselves. Square dancing tapered off and then disappeared as a result of the time squeeze.

Marky introduced me to a couple of new hobbies to replace sailplanes and square dancing. We took up backpacking, and over our years together in California, we hiked extensively in the Sierra Mountains of California. We would carry freeze-dried foods, tents, sleeping bags, and other gear into the mountains and hike for several days at a time.

She introduced me to Great Books discussion groups. Great Books Institutes constitute groups of people who all read an assigned set of books and then get together to discuss the readings. The book subjects are usually literature and fiction, with some philosophy thrown in. The idea is to read carefully and comprehend fully and then to clarify the material through the discussions. We were expected to educate one another as we pooled our ideas about the reading content. We would spend weekly evenings in San Diego to attend the book discussions and short ourselves on sleep that night, since we would never arrive home much before 2230 after such a gathering.

After several years at Scripps, and after much experimentation had been performed, I started feeling restless. For an academic research chemist, any real promotion from routine lab work required a PhD, and that was not in my cards. I had completed all the exciting research and all the computer programming I could see coming down the road. I was only in my early thirties, and another thirty or forty years of glass valve manipulation and recording of numbers was scarcely appealing for me. I started casting about among the people I had met as part of my Scripps work, looking for a new job as a chemist, but nothing ever materialized. Nobody wanted to hire a lab chemist holding a mere MS, and it took me a couple of years to figure that out.

At that point, Marky intervened to find me a new path. She was a genius at locating obscure notices in periodicals, and one day she exclaimed, "Hey! Earn that MS in computer science!"

"Yeah, yeah," I replied.

"Send in a check for a thousand dollars, and get your MS in the mail!"

There was the advertisement all right, but what did it mean? She pushed me persistently to check it out at least, and finally, I agreed to look into the matter. The degree offered was from a university called West Coast University, which was based in Los Angeles but offered evening courses at select classroom locations around Southern California. It was an accredited university that offered a wide variety of curricula. The head man at the San Diego branch of West Coast University said to me, "Just apply, and you're in." So I applied, and I was in! Actually, that course of action made sense; computer programming was the activity at Scripps that most inspired me after the completion of the chemical experiments. *I might as well make a full-time occupation of it*, I thought.

Since the long commute from Cuyamaca would have made the studies impossible, Marky and I moved back into San Diego to attend school; Marky went for her tax accounting certificate at the same time. As it turned out, the studies taxed me to my utmost even without the driving; I spent about forty hours per week—a second workweek—keeping up on the course requirements. No thesis was required; we just took one and a half years of courses relevant to computer software engineering: computer algorithms, architecture, and executive functions; a couple of ferocious compiler courses; and a set of courses on generating requirement documents for system engineering. It was all rewarding and exhausting. The course lasted from the spring of 1977 to the fall of 1978, and this time, I was a successful graduate student. I graduated summa cum laude, and I felt that along with my Scripps programming experience, I had acquired a lot of expertise to offer to a computer enterprise.

As I was approaching the end of my master's program, I searched around and landed a job with Sperry Univac. I left Scripps in June 1978 to become a full-time computer geek. I retained ties with my Scripps coworkers as long as I remained in San Diego, even attending the Friday beer parties on occasion. Carl had left a couple of years before, but Peter and Dave provided me with company.

My new job required I hold a secret clearance from the Department of Defense to access classified data. This was quite an adventure to obtain; I had to fill out several feet of forms describing my entire life and relationships. Some of my family later commented that they had actually been contacted by the FBI in their homes. I went through many hours of training on how to handle classified information and how to keep it away from unauthorized people. My clearance came through after a few months, and I could get to work in earnest. My first assignment was to a project called NATO Sea Sparrow, a missile designed to defend ships against aircraft and antiship missiles. However, the project was canceled before we got started, and I was moved onto a different project called Target Data Processing (TDP), a shore-based submarine surveillance system maintained by the Naval Ocean Systems Center (NOSC) in San Diego. I remained on that project for the next four years, until I left San Diego.

For a few reasons, it was natural for me to end up in the computer industry. The nature of the work fit me; it was mind work rather than hand work. I have already noted my disinclination for meticulous work with my hands, and I thoroughly enjoyed solving software problems, which never required mastery and maintenance of often cranky laboratory apparatuses. High-quality software requires a meticulous attention to detail and orderly, even persnickety thinking—ideal for someone like me so afflicted with rectitudinal fever!

The computer industry was youthful relative to the chemical and other more established enterprises; elaborate social rules and castes had not yet evolved. In my youth, I had observed that getting a job in a chemical firm was much like joining a selective college social fraternity: at least as much emphasis was placed on fitting in and being a team player as on actual contribution to the firm's economic success. Computer firms, on the other hand, tolerated and even welcomed introverted geeks like me; we were seen as assets rather than as social black sheep. There was never any pressure for me to join the management ladder climb, there was never an imperative to wear the proper clothing, and there were never lectures about my lack of skill in small talk.[6] The computer companies were content to let me contribute in my own way, and I was content to contribute. Importantly, in computer firms, I never observed any of the systemic racism I had noted in chemical firms; if it was there, it was too subtle for me to detect. Blacks, Asians, and Hispanics all appeared to be treated strictly according to their performance at work.

My job was to maintain and modify software that drove the display devices used by navy personnel to track submarines, and occasionally to modify executive operating system software. The language was called CMS-2, which was closely tailored to run on a navy computer called the UYK-7. We were very old-fashioned in those days; nothing off-the-shelf was used. We built all the software from the operating system through the device drivers to all applications and test software. This experience tamped into my mind the concepts of computer architecture and operating systems that I had picked up at West Coast University. I also learned the nuts and bolts of building a deliverable software suite: compilation to build machine code, loading and linking to compress the compiled units into a viable system, and the transport of this system onto a storage medium (tape or disk) for use in installing the software into a military facility.

TDP/NOSC was a mature system—that is, we were not creating a new software suite but maintaining and modifying a fully developed system. New requirements would arise, which we would implement.

Occasionally, I was tasked with adapting the system to accommodate a new piece of hardware, but mostly, I programmed new functionality desired by the navy. It was rather routine and closely supervised; opportunity for spreading my wings was limited. Nevertheless, the job was a good beginning education for a software engineer. I always got outstanding ratings for my quantity and quality of work and my ability to work independently with minimal supervision. I appreciated the latter, as I have always chafed under micromanagement, even during childhood. In spite of this, I was often compelled to take time off to provide progress reports—not because the managers didn't trust me but because the military likes to see charts and graphs that detail over time how effectively their money is being spent.

As a form of protest against this pervasive military bean-counting, I kept for many years the following sign on the wall next to my desk at work to display my general philosophy regarding my software efforts:

Effort Estimate for Me to Complete a Difficult 500-Line Program:

1 Month

Managers Track My Progress:

2 Months

Managers Provide Assistance:

4 Months

One takeaway from my initial association with Sperry Univac was the fact that the military is very cautious about introducing cutting-edge hardware into its systems. They don't like the possibility of a system crashing during a military engagement because the bugs have not yet been worked out in the electronics. All hardware was tried and true—and a few years behind the latest and greatest. This made military software development unattractive to many eager young college graduates, who wanted to work on exciting brand-new technology. These employees tended to see our operation as a graduate school where they could spend two to four years getting practical experience before jumping to a civilian software company to follow their dreams. On the other hand, military software generation provided a stable working environment for a couple of reasons. First, the work orders arrived in a slow, steady stream, allowing us to be long-term salaried employees rather than the piecework programmers in civilian operations, who often faced unemployment upon completion of a task. Second, military software development, being a federal-government-funded activity, is not sensitive to the vicissitudes of private consumer confidence and tends therefore not to be affected by economic volatility.

Our software development involved bureaucratic paperwork as well, particularly at the time of system generation and delivery. But I appreciated the workplace stability, and I could easily handle the form-filling and the occasional frenetic efforts to meet deadlines and specifications. Only near the end of my career did that stability deteriorate. The causes and results of that unhappy circumstance will be discussed in the next chapter.

I formed friendships with a few coworkers, notably Craig and Dave, a couple of executive programmers, and I kept in touch with them for several years after I left San Diego. One incident deserves relating, as it touches upon the status of women, and it provided an important professional lesson for me. One of our secretary typists, Ronnie, was clearly much more intelligent than her work position indicated. When filling out my first annual performance review form, in which I was to justify my need for a pay raise that year, I noted that I had made required changes to the software and coded new functionality. Ronnie looked over my form and said, "Don't you want to say that you added vital new features to the system and made it much more user-friendly and useful in its mission?" She suggested I list the specific vital features I had added.

"Uh, gee, yeah, I guess. Yeah! That's better!" was the gist of my reply.

I concluded from the exchange that perhaps the high quality of my work was not as self-evident to management as I had supposed. In my annual reviews, I needed to advertise my wares as vigorously as I had in my original résumé, and I took this lesson into all future performance reviews.

I heard from other employees that Ronnie had a great reputation for sprucing up other people's language. She deserved to be more than a secretary, and I strongly believe that an observant manager should have been on hand to notice her and encourage her to get the necessary training and become a power in the corporation. She may have done so before or after I left. On the other hand, maybe she was not liberated enough to try. But I saw her situation as a terrible waste of a fine mind. How many millions of women have suffered thus?

Marky and I moved back to Cuyamaca upon finishing our schooling, and she did taxes for me and other people during that time. I reenlisted in the fire department, but again, the long commute limited our options for being real participants in the community. Life in Cuyamaca, plus our many weeks of backpacking in the California Sierra and probably nostalgia for our childhood homes (mine in Montana and Marky's in eastern Washington state), generated in me a taste for rural and village living—with cultural opportunities nearby, of course!

After four years of programming for TDP/NOSC, I felt the need to move on. The work offered limited opportunity for advancement and visibility, and I was getting resentful of having to tutor employees whose titles were senior to mine only because they had occupied their jobs longer. Besides, the fifty-mile commute was finally getting on my nerves. I needed a change of scenery. Fortunately, Marky was flexible in that regard; she was almost as open as I to trying out new lifestyles. So I got in touch with an employment agency, and they located a job for me in Moorestown, New Jersey, with Computer Sciences Corporation (CSC). The promise was of more responsibility, more prestige, and more satisfaction. I jumped at the chance, and we packed our things and moved east. Fortunately, in those days of corporate largesse, CSC paid the several thousand dollars necessary to haul us and our baggage three thousand miles across the country.

An unfortunate casualty of the move was the aborting of a musical career Marky and I had started. We owned a couple of recorders (wooden woodwind instruments), which had stood on our desks for a few years, and we'd decided to learn to play them. After a year or so of lessons, we had progressed to the point where we could read sheet music and play alto and soprano recorders. Perhaps under different circumstances, we could have made this a major hobby. But my career move cut across those plans, and the crush of work schedules and new hobbies in New Jersey prevented us from resuming the pursuit. Today my musical occupation consists of picking out songs on an electronic keyboard. Sometimes I feel some regret at the path not taken. In any case, we said our goodbyes to our friends in Cuyamaca and San Diego. The farewells were not particularly lachrymose, as we planned to visit regularly. A new adventure beckoned!

CHAPTER 9

CAREER 4: SOFTWARE ENGINEER IN NEW JERSEY

At that point, my career took off in earnest. In the fall of 1982, I was hired to help modernize the Aegis naval destroyer software. I got into the project just in time to participate in a major expansion of the navy's capability, ordered by President Reagan to counter Soviet aggression. The navy and Sperry Univac had just come up with a new, expanded version of the UYK-7 navy computer, the UYK-43. I was to be a member of a team tasked with developing the pilot operating system for the new machine, plus working out the kinks and bugs from the UYK-43 itself. My partners in the enterprise were four newly hired colleagues called Bob, Frank, Glenn, and Barry. Ralph and Dick were assigned the development of the system-building suite—the software that takes compiled system program units and lashes them into a runnable system and then loads the system onto a storage medium for transport onto a UYK-43 aboard a ship. We worked together mostly smoothly, though personalities often clashed; we were an opinionated and independent set! The team leader was an Italian-born engineer called Ralph Mattei. His management skills kept the team working effectively, and as I look back on that operation and on the subsequent careers of the individuals on the team, I marvel at Ralph's capacity to get a project successfully completed by such a willful and disparate group.

All application programs were developed by Computer Sciences Corporation (CSC) in Moorestown, except General Electric (GE) in

Syracuse, New York, was developing the submarine part of the Aegis system.

Marky followed me to New Jersey and was an invaluable companion. She had a hard time finding work, since we were in the middle of a sharp recession caused by the Reagan administration's clampdown on inflation and on the speculators who were banking on its indefinite continuation. Those people were hurt, I think justifiably, but Marky was also hurt—unjust collateral damage. But inflation—and interest rates—eventually came down out of heaven after a few years. After several months, Marky found work as an accountant in Philadelphia. Unfortunately, she fell in with a series of toxic bosses—domineering, prone to blaming her for their mistakes, and outstandingly poor at people management. She went through a couple of them over three years before settling into a steady job.

The East Coast was a bit of a culture shock for both of us. We were both native to the West, which had not been settled as long as the East. People in the East were less spontaneous and more formal in their relationships with others than in California, Montana, or Washington state. After we got to know them well enough, we got along well.

Marky got us started in Great Books discussions again. This activity was noticeably more widespread and popular in New Jersey than in California. One could, and many did, make this activity a full-time occupation. There were several large operations in Philadelphia; Wilmington, Delaware; New York; Boston; and other cities in the area. Annual gatherings of Great Books participants, ranging in length from a single day to a week plus two weekends, were held all over the area. This became our chief avocation.

We did a brief stint as square dancers, but square dancing didn't captivate us as it had in California, and we soon dropped it in favor of Great Books. Likewise, backpacking fell by the wayside, partly because the mountains there were not nearly as large or spectacular as the California Sierra but also because we were older and less energetic. The appeal of sleeping on the ground and eating freeze-dried foods had dulled considerably by that time.

Our jobs consumed more of our psychological energy than they had in California. I was now a serious, ambitious professional. The work was so satisfying that I spent much time and energy in taking on extra assignments to prove my worth and have fun at the same time. Ralph Mattei divided up the work in developing the operating system among his team. I took on my own share, and I ended up assisting other people and taking on their work when they left our group for better things.

The company directly interfacing with the navy was the Moorestown-based arm of Radio Corporation of America (RCA), and we were subcontracted to RCA. RCA furnished the lab space to hold the new UYK-43 computers, and they wrote the system and software requirements that served as a guide for our implementations. The RCA arm in Minneapolis, Minnesota, designed and built the UYK-43 machines, and we did much commuting between New Jersey and Minnesota to work out design and performance issues of the machine. Although the basic machine architecture was already established, we were able to furnish input to RCA regarding details of the hardware and performance of the firmware (baked-in computer instructions for system load and error recovery). I acquired much expertise in operating system programming—that is, software that internally governs the operation of a computer but does not interface directly with human application users. We had to alter our executive software continually to meet the requirements of the application programmers who actually had navy missions to accomplish. Our group got praise from all quarters, and I received an Excellence Award from the navy for my pains.

After four years of that effort, I got restless and started keeping my eyes open for new opportunities. Fortuitously, I got a call from a coworker of mine from my Sperry Univac days in San Diego. He was managing a group in CSC's San Diego office, which was reworking the submarine surveillance software (TDP/NOSC) I had helped to build before moving to New Jersey. It appeared CSC had outbid Sperry Univac for the work and was staffing up for the effort. Since Marky and I had both been hankering for San Diego for some time, we were both delighted. Marky had a reasonably steady job, but the firm that employed her was declining and losing customers. Therefore, she was not unhappy to leave. We said our goodbyes to our respective employers, and off we went at the end of 1987 for a little nostalgia. We even contacted our village friends in Cuyamaca and were able to secure a house to rent in that village for our stay. Marky soon found a good job in a good firm in San Diego, and everything seemed to be coming up roses.

That effort lasted a little more than a year, and it marked a psychological turning point for me in several ways. Marky and I had recently collaborated in reading Thomas Wolfe's classic *You Can't Go Home Again*, and the force of its message hit me hard. We were never ostracized by our friends, as was George Webber in the Wolfe novel; however, the changed conditions in San Diego and my own evolution turned that excursion into the past sour.

The commute between San Diego and Cuyamaca, never a pleasure, became a nightmare. Formerly, the commute had taken about one and a half hours each way, as we could find unclogged side roads to get us through San Diego. In the summertime, the sun was still above the horizon when we arrived home, and we could enjoy a beautiful mountain sunset. But by 1988, the side routes had all been discovered, and they were parking lots just like the freeways. The commute was around two and a half hours each way, and we invariably arrived home well after dark. That problem had undoubtedly been present and gradually worsening before we first left for New Jersey. One tends not to notice gradual trends when one is continuously living them. But a five-year absence, during which we had had civilized commutes, made me more sensitive to the aggravation.

Another problem, which we had been fortunate enough to dodge before, became obvious: service for appliances and housing repairs was maddeningly inconvenient out there in the village fifty miles outside the city. The few local service providers tended to be not too serious about their jobs; they left answering machines for messages from potential customers. I wondered whether they ever listened to those messages; my messages never seemed to net a response. Service could be had from San Diego repairmen after a long struggle, but the struggle made me wonder whether the rural-life game was worth the candle. These observations stand to reason; service providers who were any good tended to have all the business they could handle in San Diego. Why should they trek all the way out into our mountains to fix a faucet or patch a roof? I remembered my father's rural lifestyle: in addition to ranch work, he did his own building, masonry, plumbing, wiring, fence upkeep, and machine maintenance and even much of his own veterinary work on his cattle. One must be a manual polymath to live an authentic rural life, and I was anything but handy. I thus started losing my taste for rural and village life. Reflecting on all this, I remember a remark by my father that I would probably prosper better in a city than in a rural setting. How right he was!

Our Great Books experiences in New Jersey had introduced us to many scholarly people who could sharpen and broaden our minds. This was a marked contrast to the largely working-class company I had kept in my square dancing and sailplane flying hobbies. Minorities, particularly blacks, tended to be more integrated and accepted in New Jersey suburbs than they were in San Diego, and I'd interfaced with them more on the East Coast than I ever had on the West Coast. In coming back to Cuyamaca, I found myself drifting away from our neighbors there as a result of that broadening. I rejoined the village fire department, but the fellowship from previous years was lacking. Several months before leaving San Diego, I dropped out of the department. I noted in 1988, and recalled from previous times, instances of appalling bigotry among some of the Cuyamaca villagers, particularly toward blacks and gays. One of the villagers broke up a romance between his late-twenties son and a local woman because she had a half-black son from a previous liaison; he wasn't "ready for that," he said. Another villager was almost incoherent with rage at the first tentative policy steps toward accepting gays into the military. By 1988, this behavior had become completely repugnant to me, and it added to my estrangement from Cuyamaca. Though I never developed real antipathy toward our friends in the village, the distance was obvious, even as Marky and I visited some of them from time to time for several years after our final exit from California at the end of 1988.

All of these 1988 annoyances might have been borne, except for the biggest factor: my first experience with a failed computer software development project. From the outset, it was clear to me that the CSC San Diego TDP/NOSC project was critically ill. For a military software development effort to succeed, either the project managers developing the system or the military planners ordering the system (and preferably both) must have a good idea of what the system is to do and how the system is to do it—in other words, what the system specification should say. The management at CSC San Diego was accustomed to software house culture, wherein small jobs (i.e., projects that occupy two to six programmers for a few months) drive the business. In no way was CSC management prepared for a many-pronged effort involving dozens of programmers, designers, and specification specialists cooperating intensively over a multiyear time span. The navy representatives were wholly unfamiliar with the works of military software. They had no idea how our software was supposed to work or even how to specify requirements for a military system.

CSC was supposed to write the system specifications and display them to the customer to see if they fit his needs. Due to the inexperience on both sides, we were starting all over again every few weeks to write the system specifications. We would produce the beginnings of a specification, and the customer, not knowing his own needs, would puzzle over it. There would be discussions and then another restart from the beginning. Numerous meetings of the CSC software staff soaked up additional resources to no real purpose.

Compounding the problem was the presence of several programmers who were mere hackers, who liked to smash lots of code together with neither design nor direction. They harbored hostility to both software design and software production process. Some of them were Apple computer enthusiasts who insisted, in direct violation of management's orders, they were going to develop all their software on their private Apple machines brought in for the purpose. In an attempt to salvage the situation, I drew up a process manual to try to introduce a little organization into our software development effort. The management approved of what I did, but some of the programmers threw tantrums. "You don't have the authority to enforce any of that stuff!" was their splenetic reaction. Chaos reigned, the blind were leading the blind, and nothing ever got off the ground during the year I was there. (But I got good training in the Ada programming language, which was the up-and-coming language for military projects at that time.)

After ten months of frustration, I got wind of a new submarine project starting up in New Jersey. I used a holiday weekend to fly back to interview for a job. Getting onto the project was not difficult since the people already in the project knew me from my previous four years on the Aegis project. I was immediately hired to start work at the beginning of 1989. As if in synchrony with my activity, the CSC San Diego project started to disintegrate in earnest right after my interview. The navy ordered a nearly complete shutdown of that waste of taxpayers' money, and I volunteered to be among the people to be let go—a large majority of the crew. It was back to New Jersey for Marky and me. I hated to pull her away from a good San Diego job, but we were a committed couple, and there was nothing in San Diego to support me. The recession of the early 1980s had ended, and Marky soon landed a good, rewarding job with good managers in Philadelphia after we arrived there. All trace of nostalgia for California, whether San Diego or Cuyamaca, was purged from my mind by that episode. I was glad to get back to New Jersey, since we had formed real social bonds with many of the people there—coworkers and Great Books friends.

Marky and I rented our last rental house at the beginning of 1989. Then, in 1990, since we were now committed to New Jersey, we bought a house. At the ripe age of forty-six, I was a homeowner for the first time. I have lived in this house ever since.

My new project was called BSY-2, which was an upgrade of the software that governed operations aboard Seawolf-class submarines. IBM (International Business Machines) had taken a crack at the development earlier and had come up with basically nothing, so the navy gave the work to RCA, with General Electric in Syracuse, New York, and CSC in Moorestown, New Jersey, as subcontractors—the same suite that had been working the Aegis upgrade. Again, we were tasked with generating software specification documents. This time, we were successful in document generation. I then moved on to a task leadership role in building a tool for navy personnel to use in designing the layout of tactical displays—the console screens that sailors use to perform their assigned shipboard tasks. Our plan was to integrate the tool into the BSY-2 software suite.

The BSY-2 project eventually failed but for reasons different from those that had killed CSC San Diego's dreams. In this case, the management and customers knew what they wanted, but the builders of the various components of the BSY-2 software never communicated with one another. Each group was so jealous of its privacy that interfaces between the functions could not be designed; they were slapped together using guesswork. I'm not sure how or why that situation developed, but it was well established by the time I was on the project. RCA was supposed to coordinate and control the effort, but obviously, they lacked the management heft required to knock heads together and compel the various groups to communicate and coordinate.

The people doing the software that gathered data for tactical display were a small, obscure outfit in California. Visiting their site once in order to get specifications for my display layout design software, I met a group of happy hackers throwing computer code around with little organization or purpose. Two years of their effort had yielded nothing of real value. I made our display layout design tool known to them, but they rejected it out of hand and cut me out of their loop completely, as I was supposedly intruding on their territory. A couple of their people had thrown a display layout design module together, more as a lashed-up debugger than a real sailor-friendly shipboard tool. They were resolved upon delivering the homemade module along with their other software. It was just as well; the display people themselves were constantly revamping their software design, and I couldn't possibly keep up with their fluid database anyway. So I stood there holding out my precious display layout design tool with nobody to buy it. It was yet another communication failure in that star-crossed project.

On that project, I made one of the memorable mistakes of my career. While I was developing the display design tool, I allowed myself to be hustled into making an unrealistic promise. One of the application managers told me they would be ready to use my display layout design tool in two weeks, and if I didn't have it ready by then, they would commit to using the tool being developed in California. I sighed and agreed to have my display design tool ready in two weeks. Several months of effort remained for both me and that manager, and I should have called his bluff, taken time to assess the exact amount of development remaining for my tool, and given an honest answer. My performance earned me a well-deserved tongue-lashing from my supervisor after the deadline for the completion of my tool was blown.

My supervisor had apparently made a commitment to his supervisor based on my assessment. It was a lesson I took to heart!

About two years into the work, General Electric (GE) bought RCA. In a fit of exasperation, GE moved the entire BSY-2 development to Syracuse, New York, cutting out the Moorestown, New Jersey, personnel. They got rid of the California display group and built the display handler again from scratch—which was really where the California people had left it anyway! The Syracuse effort eventually succeeded, as Seawolf submarines were deployed during the late 1990s.

During that period, I was introduced to the writing of proposals— papers addressed to the government proposing how we could best develop a system they wanted. We had some writing classes and a few mock-up proposal-writing sessions. I decided that activity was not for me. It was high-pressure and extremely political, and a gift of gab was essential. I may have gotten rid of my bashfulness, but I could never small-talk anybody or shade facts to make an impression and a sale. The art of the BS slinger was never mine!

Having two failed projects under my belt, I certainly had had lots of instruction on how not to run a project. Those were the only two projects I worked that produced nothing after years of effort. It was frustrating at the time, but looking back, I can see that it was educational for me. While on those projects, I learned some skills that served me well later on. I also got firsthand experience in observing poorly conceived and designed software development in action—experience I feel is more instructive than plodding along forever on a successful long-term effort. Certainly it is more adventurous!

My next project had been languishing before I got onto it, but it was rejuvenated by Saddam Hussein, dictator of Iraq. The project, called IPS, was an air force brainchild whose purpose was to allow automated inventorying of air force aircraft. The system was supposed to keep track of which aircraft were in which locations at any time, as well as the status of each machine. The software was to reside on several computers, or nodes, distributed throughout the world, and each node was expected to inventory its local aircraft and keep the other nodes apprised of the results.

The work had been landed a year or two earlier by an adventurous

CSC Moorestown head who had reached out into the non-Aegis world for work. The management of the project consisted of old Aegis hands who were used to working with friends in the navy. They were in over their heads in dealing with strangers in the air force, whose traditions and protocols differed from those of the navy. Thus, the effort shambled along for a couple of years without producing anything deployable.

Then, on August 2, 1990, Saddam Hussein invaded, occupied, and annexed the neighboring country of Kuwait. The world immediately went into an uproar, and the United States declared the annexation illegal and began preparing countermeasures. The Soviet Union, having learned the limits of its power in Afghanistan and Eastern Europe during the previous several years, did not prance and threaten on behalf of Saddam Hussein, as it would have done in its heyday. The United States had the field to itself. During January and February 1991, the United States put together a military coalition and liberated Kuwait in a military intervention labeled Operation Desert Storm.

The air force decided it had to have our IPS system deployed in Saudi Arabia for Operation Desert Storm. I was yanked out of BSY-2 as one of two rescuers sent on an emergency basis to get the system into shape for immediate deployment. That rescue effort was the closest thing to a death march[1] I ever encountered during my career.

After a few months of panic and sleeplessness, we got something into the field in time for Operation Desert Storm. Our software didn't work very well and, thus, didn't contribute much to the victory, but this is par for the course for software suites newly minted and put out into customer space for the first time. The going dictum is that one should never have any faith in version 1.0 of any computer program. Given that we had slapped the system together in a few months, we were lucky it was deployed at all. Once the deployment was made, however, the life of the development was guaranteed thereafter since the air force now had IPS in its arsenal and was therefore bound to pay us to maintain and modify it until it was actually useful.

I worked on the effort for about three years, mostly in the part of the software that handled communications among system nodes in various parts of the world. This gave me valuable experience in communications software and protocols. By then, we had fielded a reasonably good product, and I could feel a sense of accomplishment.

On the project, I was able to put to use the lesson I had learned on the BSY-2 project about the forcing of overly aggressive development schedules by users of my software. One day in June 1992, our project head asked me to estimate when I would finish an effort I was then working. I went over my specifications and came up with a Labor Day estimate. Then one of the senior management folks said, "But the department chief promised the air force that we would have this ready by July 16. So when did you say you would have it ready?"

I repeated my Labor Day estimate; I was not about to become a fall guy again! After much pushing and pulling, I ended up compromising and saying I would try to get it out earlier, but I would make no promises. I finished my effort around August 25, just before Labor Day, and the heavens did not fall in because the rest of the project was not ready in July.

The hustle to try to force a fast schedule is a common ploy, and it is almost always a bluff. The people who pushed me during the BSY-2 project were nowhere near two weeks away from using my display design tool. During my first four years on Aegis under Ralph Mattei's leadership, General Electric, the Syracuse-based contractor building the submarine component of Aegis, frequently tried to hustle Ralph this way. He never played their game, and we were always successful in coordinating our system development. This game did not register with me then; it came home to me later when I was a victim.

At that period of my life, I felt the yen to move on, and I looked about for a job in a new setting. I cast lines in New York, Massachusetts, and New Jersey and even landed a few interviews. But I found I had acquired an ailment common among experienced software engineers: gold handcuffs. That is, I commanded such a high salary that no one wanted me as a brand-new beginning software developer. I was no longer a fancy-free young programmer; I had to have prior experience to be as highly paid as I was, and that experience existed only with my present employer. "No interest; too much principal" was the allegedly witty remark made about me by one of the prospective new employers.

It was fortunate that none of the inquiries panned out; Marky had her massive stroke just as that expedition was tapering off. Had I been emotionally disabled by the ordeal described in chapter 1 just as I was beginning a new job in a strange culture, I would likely have flamed out and lost my career. As unforgiving as my present employer was, he was pure charity compared to a new boss who did not know me and for whom I had no past accomplishments. There would have been no slack cut whatever for a new technician who couldn't work at maximum strength.

Eventually, around the turn of the century, I moved back into the Aegis program where I had started in 1982. I remained on that project for the remainder of my career. During that time, I developed executive software and programs to facilitate the delivery of Aegis system software to the navy. Finally, the last decade of my career was devoted to developing programs that supported the radar aboard Aegis destroyers.

My career route detoured during that transition to radar software development. The radar management team was in over its head, and I was never integrated into the radar effort or even given any work. When I asked for assignments, I was invariably brushed off. Since I was not about to sit at my desk playing online games for pay, I cast about among other teams for work. I found a seat in the group that produced software delivery tools—programs to be run as part of tidying up Aegis software and packaging it for delivery to ships. They welcomed me with open arms and put me to work modernizing the tools and adapting them for new storage devices—small disks instead of magnetic tape cassettes. The work gave me a reintroduction to the FORTRAN language.

After I had spent a couple of years working in delivery tools, new management came to the radar software group. Since I was still technically assigned to the radar group, the new radar department head called me in for a chat. He asked how I was and said he assumed I was doing mostly radar work. I answered, "No, actually, I'm doing all tools work. The management here has never given me anything to do." Obviously, the department head wanted to correct the situation, so I said, "If you want me to stop philandering, you will have to be a better spouse." He assigned me to a few tasks himself, and I caught on with the new task leader. From then on, I was fully loaded with radar work.

The tools people were sorry to see me go, but in fact, I was not one of them anyway. I reflected at the time that applications, such as radar, are better stools to sit on for the long haul than support groups, such as delivery tools. In hard budget times, the applications, being direct assets for military missions, tend to survive, while the support groups tend to be shed to save money. The transition served me well during the layoffs to come.

At that point, an important consideration forced itself on me and weaned me finally from the need to jump from project to project every few years. If one changes jobs and projects every two to four years, one remains a freshman forever—constantly on a learning curve and never being held in high regard as a heavy hitter anywhere. Early in my career, spending a long time on one project had appeared to me to be static and not conducive to obtaining a wide range of experience. This is true for small- and medium-sized projects; spending years on a debugger or display formatter would certainly be stultifying. All possible learning about software like this is completed after a short time. But the Aegis application software was so complex and extensive that many years were required to get a good handle on how it works and thereby to be a proficient maintainer and modifier of it. The engineers who prospered in Aegis applications, such as radar, were those who had long remained on their applications. Untold years had gone to implementing hundreds of ingenious mechanisms within the software. A wide range of experience was available from the one application. During my ten years on radar software, I acquired the ability to solve problems well enough to make a good account of myself, but I was never one of the top-flight radar masters. Even the top-flight people had to struggle at times with the application.

During the radar phase of my career, I became experienced in generating software for off-the-shelf hardware and Unix-driven executive functions. These architectures had become all the rage in the military around the turn of the century. Our soldiers had finally realized that building their own hardware and their own special executive software was prohibitively expensive. Since Unix was the executive that drove the new off-the-shelf computers, executive programmers were no longer in demand in my work groups. I was required to master the C++ programming language, which supplanted all other languages due to its popularity among programmers. Some Ada remained on the more conservatively developed systems. During the last year of my career, I worked on an Ada radar project in which I was really happy and productive. It was a Korean navy effort to get ballistic missile capability on their destroyers. The effort lasted nine months, and it was one of the few projects I was involved in that delivered its product on time, on specification, and on budget. It was an excellent coda for my career and a great accomplishment for a new retiree to remember.

During my thirty-eight years as a computer professional, I always called myself a software engineer, and I strove to be sufficiently careful and conscientious in producing quality programs to entitle me to that appellation. I always tried to make my software logic clean and easy for others to read and debug. Nevertheless, personal observations made me fully aware of the reasons why electrical, civil, mechanical, and other types of engineers are nettled by the phrase *software engineer.* There were some interesting counterexamples among my coworkers! These people were not engineers at all, and they contributed to the poor reputation suffered by all software developers among other engineers.

The most common miscreants were those who hacked and slashed code with no rhyme or reason. They were known as hackers, or cowboys, because they fired their guns in all directions, leaving chaos and confusion. They would sit down and start generating program code by the thousands of statements with no prior thought for design. If they found they had left out a needed piece of code or if they found an error during a lab test, they would slap in the correction with no consideration for the rest of the program and, again, no design. Often, they would introduce new bugs into their software in the process. Nobody else could figure out what they were trying to do by reading their software code. The program parts that were to perform each function required by the navy were jumbled up together rather than being separated into one discrete program component (or procedure) per function. The names used for the variables and procedures did not indicate the purpose of the variables and procedures. Procedures were long, complicated, poorly organized, and logically sloppy—*spaghetti code* was a common epithet and a good metaphor. Software like this is likely to contain gremlins—that is, malfunctions that sporadically and spontaneously show up for an instant and then disappear. These gremlins are extremely difficult to corner, figure out, and correct, because they are infrequent and difficult to make happen and because the portion of the program in which the error resides is nearly impossible to determine.

More to the point from my perspective, the cowboys were often called upon to modify my software for some reason—to correct a bug in my software, add a new function, or integrate it into some new system. Cowboys could be a rigorous test for my temper. Not patient or self-aware enough to learn how my software ran before modifying it, they would sloppily jam in some code that would break a large part of my program. But the resulting software would usually end up (sort of) doing the functioning *they* wanted—just not so much of the functioning *I* had carefully constructed! Since the software had my name attached to it, I would be the one to catch flak from the test groups for my bug-filled programs. Since the cowboys seldom admitted mistakes pointed out to them and never offered aid in correction, I was the one who had to refit and rework the programs so that everybody's goals were achieved. Meanwhile, the cowboys would be off on some other effort. These people were incredibly hardworking, producing thousands of lines of code where others produced hundreds, but as can be deduced, they were also incredibly inefficient since so much of their product had to be reworked. Working around all these stumps in the road frustrated me, but I realized that somehow, I had to keep the Adams temper under wraps. Since I had to cooperate with these people over the long haul, it didn't do to start a running confrontation.

This cowboy behavior probably goes a long way toward explaining the ease with which criminals can sabotage our government and commercial software. A malicious actor who obtains detailed knowledge of a badly constructed program can easily take advantage of its many vulnerabilities to add damaging instructions that disable the software or turn it to bad purpose. The cowboys of my experience typically regard the development of functions for security and error recovery, which could keep evildoers at bay, as dull chores; they would much rather work on sexy application software that generates snazzy displays and other entertainment. They get sloppy and lackadaisical in constructing guardrail software. This problem is compounded by the reluctance of users to update their programs with fixes to these vulnerabilities when those fixes arrive; the users are always "too busy." Their systems thus tend to grow obsolete over time. For these reasons, I believe that bad actors will henceforward be a chronic and severe problem for our digital infrastructure.

Another prominent set of malefactors were the so-called artists. These were programmers who got the idea that the software they were developing was somehow an expression of their inner souls. They would spend months adding functionality to their software that was not in the specification and that the military customer had stated explicitly that he did not want. Their artistic temperaments would flare up when a manager or customer asked when the product would be delivered to the lab for testing or when a manager or customer placed a cease-and-desist demand on the extraneous software development. An angry confrontation might result, with the developer answering, "When I have it ready!" to the timeline question and "Sailors' lives are at stake here, and I'm going to do it the right way!" to the cease-and-desist demand. Alternatively, the answer might be a passive-aggressive agreement from the developer to change his ways, followed by no change whatsoever. I recall four examples of this type of production. In all cases, the result was the same: a tussle with the customer, a significant delay in the delivery of the product for testing and installation, the artist's removal from the project, and the discarding of his life's magnum opus. The artists were never cowboys; they carefully designed and lovingly crafted their programs. Their waste of taxpayers' money stemmed from the waste of their product rather than from extensive reworking of it.

Scope creep has always been a problem in software development. The temptation is always there to add things that are not in the specification but look technically attractive to the programmer. I was guilty of this myself: for the air force aircraft inventory system, I added a function to save the operator's manual text input from the display into a disk file so the input would survive a system reboot should a crash occur during the operator's actions. It looked nice to me, even though it was not in the specifications. But the customer is always right; if sailors' lives are at risk, that is the responsibility of the customer, not the software developer. The developer can certainly advise, but he can never impose! I had frequently negotiated changes to the software requirements in the past, and I should have done so that time. I was never called down on that occasion, but for the rest of my career, I was careful to follow the specifications when I generated software and to check with the customer before adding functions not listed in the performance specification.

Finally, we had the single-note players. These were programmers who followed the rules, produced reasonably good software, and were usually not a headache for customers, management, or coworkers. Unfortunately, they could cause problems if an imperative arose to move our efforts onto new hardware platforms or new computer languages or development suites. These people tended to get stuck in ruts, content to plod the same track endlessly for years, never growing in their jobs and never thinking outside their comfort box. Our single-note players were mainly specialists in the CMS-2 programming language. They wished to spend their entire lives on the old navy UYK-43 machines—and preferably on a small subset of the software. A few of them got a nodding acquaintance with Ada, but one and all refused to touch the C++ language or any of the new off-the-shelf machines being adapted for military purposes. This craving for comfort gets one only so far; if the skills of a single-note player become obsolete or if his pay rises too far above his static performance, he is in trouble.

During my stint on the air force aircraft inventory project, I interviewed someone for possible employment with us. I asked him, "What do you do?"

"I write device drivers for Unix" was the reply.

I pressed him further. "Have you developed any other types of software? Have you taken any task leadership positions? Have you ever negotiated specifications or design with the customer?"

To all, he answered, "No, I just write device drivers for Unix." He was a classic single-note player. We had no need for a writer of Unix device drivers in our shop anyway, so I nixed him to our management.

Most Aegis program managers with whom I worked were competent. They kept on top of their groups and on top of the software being generated. They knew who all the cowboys, artists, and single-note players were. Most of the time, they dealt with me fairly, acknowledging my performance where appropriate and chiding me where necessary. This saved my bacon on occasion; I never took criticism from managers when my software failed after a cowboy had sunk his hooks into it.

One memorable situation could have been the occasion for a major scandal. I recount it because it is a classic military screwup of the type familiar to all who have dealt with our armed forces, and it illustrates how software development management *should* behave. Our Aegis system is used by several foreign navies (Norway, Spain, South Korea, Japan, and Australia). We maintain separate versions, or baselines, of our system for each navy. They differ from each other because while all the navies want the Aegis system, not all the navies want the same Aegis functions. An engineer from our company got some ideas for improving one of the baselines. He generated a series of change requests for the baseline and started implementing them. Midway through the process, he was pulled off onto another effort, and there was no one else available to finish the task. But some ending resolution was necessary for the change requests; according to the paperwork rules, they could not be left hanging or be allowed to disappear into thin air. Accordingly, per instructions from the Pentagon, before the engineer left his effort, he marked all his changes as tested and ready for delivery to a ship, even though some were not tested and some were not even inserted into the programs. I was directed to copy the changes into a different baseline on which I was working and test all changes I copied. Naturally, most of the tests did not work, and I accordingly marked the changes as failed. But word of mouth came down from on high that we didn't have time for my shenanigans; I was to mark everything as tested and ready for delivery. I marked them as successes under protest; I sent out an email to all concerned, detailing my objections. Sure enough, a test group tasked to retest our entire system in preparation for deployment of the system on a ship confronted me over the failure of "my" fixes. At that juncture, management could easily have thrown me under the bus, saying, "Who? Us? How dare you insinuate that we would direct Adams to commit such a grave crime!" But everybody, including a chief scientist from my own company, came to my rescue. Moreover, the test group people, aware of the process imposed on us all, were ready to understand and forgive me. But I am grateful to my management that I got off unscathed from what could have been a sticky situation.

Over the course of my variegated career, I noticed a gradual change in the cultures where I worked. At Scripps, at Sperry Univac in San Diego, and during the first projects in New Jersey, work was made more pleasurable by the collegial atmosphere. For all our differences in personality and philosophy, we maintained friendships and met in social gatherings. There were the beer Friday evenings at Scripps. The software development companies staged parties and potluck dinners for the employees on holiday occasions, and time off was granted for attending them. We even traded gifts at Christmastime. After a good software delivery to the customer or after we had really impressed the customer with an awe-inspiring demonstration of our software, we would all go out to a local pub and celebrate for a few hours.

By the early 2000s, as our transition to off-the-shelf hardware was getting underway, a distinct cooling off of the social aspect of our jobs occurred. Much of it was no doubt due to an attempt by the military to eliminate fraud, waste, and abuse from its software development. The process for renewing funding for projects was made more formal and difficult, and actions that looked like inefficiencies, such as company parties, were slowly eliminated. The military attempted to force a quickening of the pace of software production, which made us all edgy. While customers' desire to get the most bang for their buck is justified and there were certainly areas of inefficiency in our old collegial ways, the sense of belongingness among the workers diminished, and morale probably went downhill. I believe productivity improved somewhat, but wasn't there a way to squeeze out the unproductive intervals from the workdays and still maintain us as human beings in a social organism rather than as production units in an industrial process? After all, it is well known that bad morale hurts productivity. I feel a nostalgic pull for all the successful projects, computer and otherwise, on which I worked from 1971 to 1995, but while there were many individuals in later projects with whom I maintained close bonds, I never felt the slightest wish to revisit the atmosphere of those projects. I feel a bit sad at a sense of loss in contemplating this evolution.

This evolution was accelerated and accentuated by a series of layoffs that occurred during the last decade of my career. The layoffs had the effect of making people more apprehensive and less apt to feel that they belonged. Certainly my psychological separation from the company grew over that period. The layoff day would be announced, and we would spend the morning tensely awaiting the arrival of a manager at our desks to ask us to come to the office for a chat. Usually around noon, the all-clear signal would spread among the troops who had not been thus visited, and a sort of relaxation would ensue. But there was always a residue of uncertainty: "Why was I spared? For how long do I hold a job?" I never had the survivor's guilt I have heard mentioned by others, though. Perhaps by the time of the layoffs, my social bonds with my coworkers had atrophied because of the diminution of collegiality.

The first layoff occurred in 2008, as a result of an order from some highly placed entity that we were to reduce our workforce by 25 percent. After it was all over, it was obvious to me that the main victims of the massacre were employees whose exact functions were hard to determine. As far as I knew, some of them simply occupied offices. As a result, I relaxed somewhat, feeling that my employment was secure.

The other three layoffs occurred in rapid succession (separated by several months) from 2012 to 2014 because of budget pressure. I got more nervous with the coming of each mass extinction. The majority of layoffs were a mystery to me until the last months of my own employment. At length, I could no longer contain myself, and I asked specifically about one employee whom I remembered as a good, conscientious hard worker, "What was wrong with her?"

"She was her own worst enemy" was the reply. "She kept telling us she couldn't learn new hardware and C++."

The response took me aback. You don't tell your boss that you "can't learn" material you need for your job!

At the time of my anxious inquiry, I was reassured I had never been close to being considered for the chopper. In fact, management said I was especially valuable because I could do C++, CMS-2, Ada, FORTRAN, documentation, or customer relations, whichever enterprise had the most need of me. The company problem was simply too many CMS-2 specialists who refused to move themselves into other areas where they could have been of better use—that is, too many single-note players. Much has been said about the virtues of having twenty years of experience, but these people tended to have one year of experience twenty times—a decidedly different ornament for the résumé!

Growing in the job and acquiring a multitude of skills have always helped people to rise in salary and in position. I feel that rises in real earning power should be connected as much as possible to rises in the quality and quantity of the work performed. An employee who expects real growth in his salary should progress toward greater responsibility, productivity, and visibility in his work. He should take particular care to become a self-starter and a good problem solver; these are in high demand everywhere. As one solves problems of progressively more significance and magnitude or takes on more leadership and responsibility, he should be rewarded with progressively greater pay. On the other hand, single-note players should be started out on a good living salary and given pay raises only to keep up with inflation.

The main takeaway from my career trajectory over the decades is that a way exists for individuals to combat the much-maligned wage stagnation in American life, especially in a booming economy. For those who feel their careers need a jump-start or their salaries have stagnated, steps exist for remedying their conditions. These steps involve leaving one's comfort zone and looking around for bigger and better things to do—in one's job if possible, but if necessary with a different employer or even a new line of work. Extra training may be required. A move to a different part of the country may be involved. Above all, one must form networks of people who like and respect him. It is almost impossible to land a good career if nobody in the world knows you! I went through just these processes during my years in the wilderness between Ohio State University and Scripps Institution of Oceanography and when my career as a chemist stagnated. In the latter case, I needed Marky to kick me a little, but I prospered satisfactorily for my entire career.

I recognize that being a middle-class white male gave me a head start and a continuing advantage throughout my career. Some have to strive harder than I did in order to succeed, and they have to be more diligent in seeking help. Even so, I have observed many successes among people from less fortunate circumstances than mine, and I have also observed many who came from privileged backgrounds who played their cards badly and flunked out. I still insist that individual spark—character and personal liberty—can determine much of the trajectory of one's career. There is never an excuse to sit around and hope or, worse, sit around and resent!

As tiring and frustrating as military software production could often be, I never regretted my choice to embark on the endeavor. Good character and personal liberty were consistently and amply rewarded. Performing diligent, free, and independent work and taking the initiative to learn new material to enhance my performance brought me great benefits. My career never suffered as a result of failure to cut corners, failure to go along to get along, or failure to play political games—though I was occasionally punished for committing those sins! The psychological rewards for rolling out a good piece of software after a hard year's effort cannot be overstated. All of these factors more than compensated for the head games, pratfalls, and bureaucracy. I derived satisfaction not only from the career in itself but also from the knowledge that I did my little bit toward bringing the Cold War to a satisfactory conclusion, keeping the United States militarily preeminent in the world, and preserving and extending liberty around the world.

I retired in January 2016 under my own volition because I felt the time had come, and I was getting tired. I had had lots of fun, but I was approaching my seventy-second birthday, and I wanted to leave the profession while I could still generate good programs, while company management still wanted more of my work, and while I still had a solid reputation for producing quality software. There is no sadder spectacle in the world than a professional who clings to his position after it has long been clear to everyone else that his day is done, especially if he once enjoyed a sterling reputation now shredded because everybody notes how he has performed lately. That melancholy ending was not for me.

At my request, I retired without fanfare, without a farewell party, and without a card signed by the entire workforce. Having been through too many tedious and artificial card-signings and retirement ceremonies where most of the participants neither knew nor wished to know the guest of honor, I sat at my desk on the last day and accepted gifts and parting handshakes from perhaps a dozen people who sincerely cared about me and appreciated the role I had played. I was grateful to them because they esteemed me for my work and my character. They were beautiful people who help me to remember my career with fondness.

My life with Marky proceeded smoothly after she got a steady accounting job with a competent manager. Our Great Books activity prospered, as we attended a weekly session in Haddonfield and occasional Great Books seminars elsewhere in the Northeast. We explored the Northeast corner of our country on bus tours, visiting Williamsburg, Virginia; the Finger Lakes region in upstate New York; autumn festivals in Vermont; and other highlights.

In 1995, we broke the ice on foreign travel and visited Britain. Marky had always been an intense Anglophile keen on British literature and history. Over the next few years, we took trips to England, Scotland, Wales, and Ireland. I was pleased that she was able to get direct experience of the country she had loved from a distance for so long. In 1998, she arranged a trip to the Canadian Rockies and a trip up the Inside Passage from Vancouver, British Columbia, to Alaska. She was still reluctant to visit the European continent.

Marky rebuilt my life in a number of ways. She ordered me to start saving in a 401(k) plan at my company and to start contributing to their pension fund. I had never thought of retirement much before that. Any investing I had done had been in money market accounts, which, in the early 1980s, paid handsomely, with interest rates around 18 percent. Since inflation was close to that figure then, I was just about breaking even. But Marky reminded me that my employer would be contributing to my 401(k), giving me a several percent pay raise. So I grew up and started salting money away for retirement. I am grateful to her for forcing the conversation; my retirement is considerably more comfortable with my pension and my 401(k) savings providing income. It is fortunate that she confronted me in my forties over the issue, rather than in my twenties. What twenty-six-year-old ever listens to advice like that?

In those days, credit card companies would not issue cards to anyone who had not already bought a great number of items on credit. Since I had paid cash for everything until then, the excessively picky policy of the credit card companies dictated that I should continue to pay cash for everything. Accordingly, Marky allowed me to put my name on her credit cards, and I was on my way to earning a credit rating. I was pleased that Marky recognized in me sufficient character that she could trust me with her credit cards and her creditworthiness. Naturally, I paid all my debts on time and in full; it never occurred to me to do otherwise. Now I have several credit cards and a great credit rating.

She had no fetters to living locations, and for that, I eternally bless her. In encouraging my successful career, she sacrificed her own to an extent. Her jobs in New Jersey were not as rewarding and remunerative as the ones she had had in California, and it took great consideration on her part to pull up stakes to move with me to New Jersey, where my career reached its apogee. I believe it broadened her culturally to live for a time on the East Coast, but there is no denying that her career suffered.

But most of all, I am grateful to her for pulling me away from that footloose and puerile lifestyle I led in San Diego during my late twenties and showing me the much greater satisfaction of a long-term one-on-one relationship with a woman. This experience matured me greatly and added considerably to my sense of having lived a good life and to the success of my working career. It enabled my character to evolve in such a way that I could handle her crisis adequately when it arrived.

By mid-2009, I had recovered from the traumas of my losses. So I went online and commenced a search for a companion. The experience taught me that character is required for successful participation in a healthy relationship. This character is obtained from loving parents who set examples for good character to their children, followed by careful cultivation of character in adulthood and continued association with good character role models. Many of the women I met at the time told me about childhoods featuring parents who were distant and even, in some cases, rejecting, never inculcating in their daughters the precepts regarding healthy relationships. These women went on to dysfunctional marriages with distant, unavailable, and self-absorbed men, some of whom were abusive or improvident to boot. My attempts to reach out to them made no impression at all. "The way to handle a woman is to love her," according to a line in the song "How to Handle a Woman" from the musical *Camelot*, and Marky made a remark to similar effect several times during our life together. But this is true only up to a point;

Marky well knew what love is, but there are women in the world whose background and makeup exclude them from the experience of and even the idea of love.

As I was about to give up on the dating service, I met Frances, my present African American partner, whose companionship has been a great growth opportunity for me. I had never realized how ignorant I was of the sensitivities and social mores of African Americans. Frances is a tremendous support for me, and I look forward to more Great Books and world travel, and a long and happy life with her.

CHAPTER 10

AVOCATION 1: HISTORICAL PERSPECTIVES AND COMBATING INJUSTICES: STORIES MY HISTORY TEACHERS NEVER TOLD ME

Having spent most of my lifetime observing the human scene, I have become a reasonably competent parlor historian able to impart lore to average audiences—while still unprepared to argue fine points with trained specialists. History is a constantly evolving analysis of the past for the illumination of the present and the instruction of the future; as attitudes toward the past change, so does the effect of the past on perceptions of present and future. My studies of history have been for the purpose of discovering how we got here—what made us what we are today and where we are likely to head. I have also tried to do my bit for the detection and correction of injustices—that is, the deprivation of individuals of their lives, liberties, and opportunities to pursue fulfillment—for no reason other than the demand of some abusive and dominant person or group. Throughout this activity, my main method has been to contribute to organizations that have the time and expertise to combat the injustices. At times, though, I have taken more concrete action.

I note a quote by John Stuart Mill: "Bad men need nothing more to compass their ends, than that good men should look on and do nothing."[1] The general spirit of this aphorism is agreeable to me, but I take issue with the meaning of one of its terms. In my view, those who look on and do nothing are not good men but accessories to the evil. In an attempt to be a good man, I determined to do the best I could to be part of the solutions to these injustices.

The first injustice that really stirred my emotions was the Soviet intervention in Czechoslovakia in the summer of 1968 in response to the attempt by Czechoslovakia to liberalize its institutions. I couldn't do anything about this injustice, but I read up on it. I had already obtained a general outline of Russian history and culture by that time. During the next few years, I read several novels by Aleksandr Solzhenitsyn, as well as a book by Andrei Amalrik,[2] which did much to guide me about Russia. Amalrik describes what he calls the "idea of justice" among Russians, which he says is one of the defining features of Russian psychology. This idea of justice is just a Russian version of have-nots' revenge—hatred of successful people simply because they are successful.

Later in life, I traveled to Russia a couple of times, and the Russians I met ruefully agreed with me that this attitude toward success is indeed a cornerstone of their thought processes. They were all familiar with the story of Dmitri's cow[3] in one form or another; in fact, one of them related this tale to me in the first place! This caste-derived mindset probably explains much of Russian behavior, both individually and internationally, and it probably originates in the caste system that has dominated Russian society throughout history.

The ignominy of Vietnam and the agitation of African Americans and other minorities for the rights theoretically granted to them by our Constitution gave rise during the 1960s and 1970s to a nationwide reassessment of our views of our own history. One of my educational experiences at that time was my reading of Dee Brown's history of the maltreatment of Native Americans by whites from 1865 to 1890.[4] It was an extremely painful read, a blistering indictment of slaughter and rapine of the Natives by whites. This account could not have been more totally at odds with the education of my early years—that is, since the Indians never invented the wheel, how could they have any rights at all? As I had never subscribed to that bigoted view, I had no trouble accepting the premise of Brown's book.

At that time, I was still building a career as a chemist at Scripps Institution of Oceanography and sailplaning and square dancing. I was not prepared to go full bore into activism, as I did in later life. I contributed to Native American causes, and I was careful to avoid the company of individuals who echoed the sentiments of my Victorian grandfather, Grandpa Ed, regarding the sacredness of inventing the wheel. But I was grateful for the opportunity to read that book, and to this day, I wonder whether it could have been published at all in the smug days prior to our embarrassment in Vietnam.

The next crisis that engaged my attention was the Russian invasion of Afghanistan. By the time this occurred, I was disenchanted with the Carter administration, whose fecklessness in the face of this provocation and in the face of over-the-top inflation and interest rates made the situation in Washington ripe for a change. I enthusiastically supported Ronald Reagan and the Republicans for the next several years on the premise that they would get rough with the Russians and bring our country out of its 1970s funk. After Reagan's 1980 victory, I contributed to Republican Party coffers and to nongovernmental organizations and lobbying groups who supported arming the Afghans to fight the Russian aggressors. I felt strongly that it was a golden opportunity to cut the Russians down to size after our defeat in Vietnam had caused their heads to grow too big for the world we live in.

Since the September 11 attacks by al-Qaeda in New York in 2001, I have heard voices raised to the effect that helping the Afghans to defeat the Russians was a strategic blunder that gave rise to terrorism. I have always rejected this attitude emphatically; terrorism has been prevalent in that part of the world irrespective of foreign interventions. The defeat of the Russians at the hands of the Afghans, I believe, contributed to the breakdown of morale while generating pressure for change in the Soviet Union; brought the Soviet Army into disrepute (thus probably emboldening the people in Eastern Europe and the Soviet republics to rise up against Russian misgovernment); and eased the eventual dissolution of the Soviet Union. While it is true that Afghanistan subsequently became an exporter of terror, and Saudi and other extremists got their training in that war, I still maintain that we did not fight on the wrong side in Afghanistan in the 1980s. No respectable analyst would argue that we fought on the wrong side in Europe in the 1940s, even though Stalin's terror empire became much more formidable after that conflict. I shudder to think how difficult our later confrontations with assorted Islamic terrorist nonstate actors might have been had the Soviet Union been available to arm, train, and finance them and to block our efforts to combat them.

Two more stories impinged on me during the 1990s: the Rodney King affair in Los Angeles in 1992 and the campaign to liberate the Amirault family in 1995 and years following. I was outraged by the Simi Valley jury's acquittal of the officers who were videotaped brutally beating Rodney King, a black man, and by the subsequent mishandling of the riots by the Los Angeles Police Department. I had spent most of my adult life living and working among the sort of people who comprised that jury—white middle-class suburb dwellers with no experience of people different from themselves—and their world view was fully reflected in their verdict. I felt the jury discounted the empirical evidence in the video less because of racism, though there was undoubtedly some of that present, and more because of the belief that a police uniform sanctifies an individual and immunizes him or her from all error and sin. These people take umbrage at all negative comments, and all humor, directed at the police. This authoritarian viewpoint is unsettling and offensive to me, especially in light of the many instances of police brutality against African Americans revealed on social media during the COVID-19 pandemic. I felt this viewpoint was badly overrepresented on that jury.

The verdict came to me while I was in South Carolina, installing software for the air force project IPS (see chapter 9). As my flammable temper rose up on the plane ride back to New Jersey, I recalled that Marky was notably to my right politically and had a marked bias toward law enforcement. Fortunately, Marky's cool head prevailed over my Adams one; she was as aghast at the verdict as I was.

I did not actively participate in the Rodney King affair, but I did take action regarding the Amirault case, which was first brought to my attention by a series of articles in the *Wall Street Journal*.[5] Child molestation cases were a fad at the time, and ambitious prosecutors had secured convictions on bogus charges against several child day-care centers. The Amirault case aroused my injustice antennae particularly acutely because of the sheer phantasmagoria of scenarios concocted by Massachusetts prosecutors, who coached and coerced parents and children into confirming the tales, and because of the tenacity and resourcefulness of the prosecutors and plaintiffs and their defiance of facts and simple justice after the hollowness of their cause was clear to everyone. Expendable people, junk science, corrupt police, and judges rendered incompetent by ideological zeal were all on horrific display in the case. I contributed to a legal fund for the Amiraults and followed the case carefully over the next few years. I called this case to the attention of the False Memory Syndrome Foundation,[6] a group that combats bogus child abuse cases based on supposed traumatic memories recovered under leading or even coercive questioning by therapists. Eventually the Amiraults were freed. I was gratified to see that the Massachusetts attorney general who pushed the awful case, Scott Harshbarger, lost his subsequent bid for the governorship to a nobody by a small margin. A native of Massachusetts later remarked to me that while he thought Harshbarger would have been a better governor than his opponent, he could never vote for Harshbarger after his Amirault caper. There were probably many Bay Staters who felt that way; since Harshbarger's loss was so narrow, it can be argued that the case terminated his political career.

The case benefited me in one specific way: I refuse to be scandalized by sex crime accusations until the investigations are complete and the facts are in. These damaging accusations tend to be believed in large part not because they are provable or even plausible but because they are titillating. Many are the reasons for making such accusations, including, frequently, actual sex crimes. Many people have been ruined by scandals like this, and thousands of black lives would have been saved between 1870 and 1960 if southern whites had been properly circumspect about lurid tales from their supposedly chaste women.

The Amirault and Rodney King cases persuaded me that my

attitude toward the death penalty had to change. Previously, I had held a middle-of-the-road conservative view on the death penalty: supportive but not zealous. Even now, I understand there are creeps out there who in principle deserve the death penalty, and I certainly set no store by lectures from the dictator-studded United Nations Commission on Human Rights. But after observing the antics of these juries, I had to ask myself whether justice could ever be served if crews like this were allowed to make life-and-death decisions in capital cases. Since the death penalty is infinitely irreversible, imagine applying it and then discovering that the relevant jury had muffed its duty as spectacularly as had the Amirault and Rodney King panels! Such proceedings would be nothing more than the lynchings that stain our national history. Given the universality of human error, it is much better to impose a no-parole life sentence, which can be voided when appropriate, than to kill someone by mistake! Even one such blunder anywhere is one blunder too many. I am now careful to support candidates for office who oppose the death penalty, and I contribute funds to political lobbying groups that share this viewpoint.

In 2009, I returned to the crusades against injustice by volunteering to work at the US Holocaust Memorial Museum in Washington, DC. This museum depicts the ultimate injustice: the murder of millions of Jews and others by the Nazis in their attempt to "purify" their race during the Second World War.

I had attended the US Holocaust Memorial Museum twice before I volunteered. On these occasions, I learned, somewhat to my surprise, that the intensity of my indignation at injustice was dulled if I sensed a culpability of some sort—or an unrelated moral failing—on the part of the victims. My fury burned hottest at the persecution and extermination of Jews who had fought for their kaiser and fatherland during the Great War. That was how the fatherland thanked those who risked life and limb for its preservation? On the other hand, I was much less moved by the persecutions of Jews who worked for revolutionary Socialist and Communist causes; as promoters of Stalin, how did they differ from their persecutors? No doubt I had always reacted to injustices in this differentiated way; I had long ago noted a remark by Aleksandr Solzhenitsyn in an essay[7] in which he describes his strong feelings of shame about Russian persecutions of Estonians and Lithuanians and his weaker shame about Russian persecutions of Latvians and Hungarians, as the latter two nations provided contingents of terrorists to aid the Russian Communist regime in murdering Russian dissidents during the 1920s. Perhaps we all are subject to allowing feelings of poetic justice to dilute our compassion in cases like this, but my first trips to the Holocaust Museum, which illustrated in one piece a large array of victims with widely varying qualities of character, brought this attribute of my thinking to my conscious attention.

The volunteer work of aiding visitors was rewarding to me in the same sense that a teaching career is rewarding: a few curious, intellectually lively individuals among the many were sufficient to make the entire hassle a positive experience. A minority of the visitors were interested enough in the message that we at the museum were trying to convey that they would seek additional information about the exhibits and the history. They would visit all the special exhibits along with the well-advertised permanent exhibit—a collection of artifacts depicting the history of the Holocaust from 1933 to 1945. I could engage with these visitors for hours, and I came away from such meetings convinced these visitors would leave our museum enriched by their experience. I believed they would go forth among the public and try to enlighten them as much as possible. I remain grateful to these lively people because they made me feel that my time and effort were well spent and that I really contributed to the general level of understanding of this awful history.

Unfortunately, the majority of visitors, like the majority of my students in my aborted teaching career (see chapter 7), attended only because of some external compulsion. Some of them may have been somewhat enlightened by their visit, but the fact that the lessons of the Holocaust seemed to be of secondary importance to them persuaded me that their visit did not enlarge them much.

This museum is a vital part of the effort to get the public to remember one of the most horrific events of history: the attempt to exterminate an entire people, the Jews. The motive behind this policy is difficult to pinpoint. The Nazis blamed them for all of humanity's misfortunes, but I doubt this animus motivated many of the actual participants, German or otherwise. Millions of non-Jews perished in this inferno as well, most notably Russian prisoners of war. A detailed history of this crime cannot be reproduced here, but I assert that it did not arise in a vacuum. Many historical streams flowed into this monstrous lake of fire, and many countries, including the United States, contributed to its ferocity. The survivors of this ordeal are fading fast; the minimum age for a survivor is now beyond seventy-five. A time will soon come when the Holocaust will be as surely ancient history as are the Napoleonic Wars, Abraham Lincoln, and the Greek city-states. It is vital for our moral health that this historic atrocity be remembered—as living history in the heart, not as cynical political slogans or arid enumerations in history books.

This museum also performs a vital service in calling the public's attention to crimes against humanity in other parts of the world. It assembles temporary exhibits to stand for a few years and describe horrors going on more recently than the Second World War: the Syrian civil war; the persecution of Burmese Rohingya; and the massacres in Darfur, Bosnia, Rwanda, and Cambodia. People should be made aware of these crimes by exhibits that they will remember and recount. Apathy and ignorance, among Americans and others, allow these atrocities to persist for much too long.

As part of my work for this museum, I did historical research for its special exhibit "Americans and the Holocaust"—what Americans could have known and how they reacted in the period from 1933 to 1945. My task was to find newspaper articles printed during those years that pertained to events of the Holocaust—for example, the German boycott of Jewish businesses, the establishment of the Dachau camp, and so on. Since I spent my formative years in Montana, my chosen area of research was Montana and the states bordering it: Idaho, Wyoming, and the Dakotas. The articles thus discovered came mainly from eight-page small farm-town newspapers. I started out not expecting to find any such articles, as these newspapers tend to concentrate on local marriages, births, deaths, and scandals. But among these gossip stories was an occasional Holocaust story—not in an international section, as in larger newspapers, but nestled in among front-page stories about picnics, school dances, county fairs, and the like.

Naturally, I noticed many other news articles not pertaining to the Holocaust as I pored over the issues of these newspapers. I found the material depressing. The Great Depression covered much of that period, and some people—notably farmers—were economically stressed for virtually the entire 1919–1939 era. But in addition to the economic poverty, I noted a distinct moral and intellectual poverty reflected in the newspapers and other media for the entire interwar period—the extinction of large characters on the public stage, with their places taken by mean, small people. Leadership vanished in the 1920s, along with positive pressure from public opinion—both of which, before the Great War, had made possible the progress in labor policy and the end of child labor, women's right to vote, liberalization of international trade, welcoming of immigrants, and other successes.

Americans in the 1920s were angry, confused, and frightened by the changes that had occurred in their world in recent years. Bewildering, disrupting upheavals had occurred all over the world in the years of the twentieth century prior to the Great War, including many innovations in the United States itself. For those who craved stability and certainties, that period was unpleasant enough. But the additional economic and psychological dislocations caused by the Great War and the great influenza pandemic that followed it were even more intimidating. To cap things off, the Paris so-called peace conference must have revolted many Americans by its shameless display of greed, vengeance, duplicity, and smallness of character. It was clear to every competent observer that this conference solved nothing and guaranteed nothing except more instability.[8]

Other peculiarly American disruptions perturbed Americans at that time. There was the Great Red Scare—the terror of the Russian Revolution and the atrocities being perpetrated by the Communists there—exacerbated by enthusiastic demonstrations by American leftists in favor of the new Russian regime. The fear of a Communist revolution in the United States enabled A. Mitchell Palmer, Woodrow Wilson's last attorney general, to round up leftists for deportation to Russia. The status of African Americans, always a problem, grew worse as blacks returning from the Great War demanded greater rights commensurate with their service to their country on the European battlefields. All the buffeting by the world led to a furious turning away from all things new or foreign by the American people, who sought refuge in nostalgia and repudiated all the progressive impulses of the previous two decades. They slammed the door on immigrants and clamped down hard on blacks. The 1924 Immigration Act (the Johnson-Reed Act) was an attempt to rejigger the country-of-origin map in the United States to resemble that of 1890. The idea was to exclude Jews and immigrants from Southern and Eastern Europe, whose arrival in the United States in large numbers since the 1890 census had led to hysteria over the "pollution" and "elimination" of the "white race"—Northern Europeans, that is.[9] The Holocaust Museum displays newspaper articles from that time calling for the preservation of the "old Northern European stock"—as if Americans were to be bred like show dogs and race horses, complete with collapsible hips and glass ankles! Lynchings of blacks went on as before; a sequence of photographs, including the infamous picture of the murders of Thomas Shipp and Abram Smith in Marion, Indiana, on August 7, 1930, greets the visitor at the entrance to the "Americans and the Holocaust" exhibit in the Holocaust Museum. The hapless Harding administration was bracketed on either end by the destruction of a prosperous black town, Greenwood, a suburb of Tulsa, Oklahoma,[10] by a white mob in 1921 and the destruction of another black neighborhood, Rosewood, Florida, by a white mob in 1923. Lynchings had occurred before and during the Great War, and they continued until after the Second World War, though with diminishing frequency as time went on.

The 1920s also saw the swindling by whites of Osage Indian tribe members out of the wealth the Osages had gained from sale of oil on their reservation in Oklahoma. These robberies were often accompanied by murder.[11] Unlike the perpetrators of the atrocities against blacks, these villains were more or less successfully prosecuted. In an ironic juxtaposition, one of the displays of good character to emerge from the 1920s saw the granting of full US citizenship to Native Americans in June 1924 via the Snyder Act, though full voting rights were not extended to them in all states until the 1950s.

Even the dedication of the Lincoln Memorial on May 22, 1922, was smeared by the spirit of the times. The disgraceful episode added a generous dollop of hypocrisy to the 1920s scene. Blacks, supposedly the beneficiaries of the Civil War, were manhandled out of prominent seats at the ceremony and forced into a distant "colored section." Their worst enemies, Confederate veterans, were accorded a special place of honor at the proceedings. The black speaker was not allowed to address any issues concerning blacks, nor was any of the largeness of character displayed by Lincoln in his efforts to save the Union mentioned. All the speeches by whites were panegyrics to a reconciliation between northern whites and southern whites—a reconciliation that certainly did not occur then and is decidedly incomplete even today. This memorial acquired real meaning years later when the African American contralto Marion Anderson sang there in 1939 and when Martin Luther King Jr. delivered his "I Have a Dream" speech there in 1963.[12]

There were bright spots even in the 1920s, such as the people who went after and caught the pillagers of the Osage tribe, and the sheriffs who, knowing full well the nature of his accuser, spirited the accused Dick Rowland away from the lynch mob in Greenwood, Oklahoma, in 1921. But the spirit of the era was better reflected in the Ku Klux Klan, whose resurgence had made it a national force, a national disgrace, and a self-styled "respectable" club posing as a Christian native-born society, an image that masked its ongoing murderous ways. To add to our degradation, this criminal organization, and the public esteem enjoyed by it and similar gangs, made it impossible to discuss, let alone admit and repent for, the atrocities committed against African and Native Americans until about 1970.[13] Thus, the American people were conditioned by the 1920s for ignoring or even condoning the still worse atrocities perpetrated overseas during the 1930s.

The 1930s saw the Depression hit and the arrival of President Franklin Delano Roosevelt on the scene. Unlike his predecessors, he had some leadership capabilities and was willing to try new solutions at least to cope with the Depression, but American public opinion had not changed much from the 1920s. Indeed, the end product of our labors for the US Holocaust Museum—the "Americans and the Holocaust" exhibit—depicts in full ghastly flower the degraded state of American public opinion, as well as the ideologues, conspiracy theorists, time-servers, and out-and-out crooks who dominated American life at that time. The 1930s were indeed "a low dishonest decade," as cited by W. H. Auden in his poem "September 1, 1939." But I submit that the Holocaust came on the heels of two low dishonest decades, which spanned the time from the Paris peace conference of 1919 to the outbreak of World War II in 1939.

During the 1930s, most people were poor, and it is difficult to be generous when struggling to live from day to day. Perhaps the daily grind prevented many people from even reading adequately about overseas events. Still, I have concluded from my own research that Americans in general were aware of the persecution of European Jews in outline form, if not in detail. People must have read articles about these maltreatments in small-town newspapers and possibly even discussed them.

Fallen far from the welcoming of immigrants in the 1890s and 1900s, the dominant American public attitude toward 1930s refugees and the Holocaust seems to me to have been "Thank God they are over there, and we are over here! What is happening is terrible, but my problems are more important than their problems, and in no way will I allow them to come over here and steal my food and my job. Let somebody else deal with it." This is a classic demonstration of low character—unemployment serving as an excuse for apathy toward industrial-scale mass murder!

Throughout the 1930s, there were plenty of American politicians and propagandists reinforcing this attitude, with only small, ineffective countervailing pressure. But the high point of that low decade, in my opinion, was the voyage of the *St. Louis* in 1939, which brought nearly a thousand Jewish refugees from Europe who hoped to settle in safer lands.[14] The Jews were denied entrance to Cuba, and the Americans would not take them either. Finally, the *St. Louis* sailed back to Europe, where many of its cargo later perished in the Holocaust. This drama is displayed prominently in both the permanent exhibit and the "Americans and the Holocaust" special exhibit in the Holocaust Museum.

The "Americans and the Holocaust" exhibit displays prominently in several places the racist hostility of Americans to Japanese, both those living in our country and those in Japan. The entrance to this exhibit flashes a photograph of a woman defiantly pointing to a sign reading, "Japs keep moving! This is a white area!" The criminal internment of Japanese Americans in concentration camps was popular and was well documented in the newspapers of the time. Few Japanese were murdered, and young Japanese males were often allowed out to fight in the European theater of the Second World War. The American persecutions were never as thoroughgoing as the German persecutions.

Isolationism was strong throughout the country, particularly in the states for which I did my historical research for the "Americans and the Holocaust" exhibit. An excellent account of the conspiracy theories and the logical pretzel-twisting Americans used to maintain the isolationism in the face of German provocations during the year leading up to the Pearl Harbor attacks in December 1941 can be found in Marc Wortman's book *1941: Fighting the Shadow War – a Divided America in a World at War.*[15] This observation led me to wonder what would have ensued if the Germans had bombed Pearl Harbor. I recognize that counterfactual history is murky wading, but I feel it is likely that in such a case, entering the war would have been much more difficult than it was in fact. After all, we did not declare war against the Germans when they sank the *Lusitania* in 1915 with loss of American lives, and Wortman's book paints a convincing portrait of American self-blame and pusillanimity when the Germans repeatedly attacked American ships in 1941. No German Americans were interned later in the war, and some of them actively worked for the Nazi enemy. Many Americans had German friends and relatives as well. Any declaration of war following a German Pearl Harbor attack would likely have been made over strenuous objections and challenges; possibly, such a declaration would have had to wait for further German aggressions.

When the Japanese attacked, however, a prominent reaction was "No little yellow bastard can do this to a white man!" Due to racial segregation, fewer Americans had Japanese friends than had German friends. Racism and isolationism, the twin devils of American psychology at the time, both demonstrate deficient character— indifference to the sufferings of people deemed not of one's own tribe. But after the Pearl Harbor attack, one abomination, racism, squelched another abomination, isolationism, and we entered the war without much protest.

I have dwelled on the period of American history from 1919 to 1941 at some length. This is partly due to the fact that my US Holocaust Museum historical research covered this period and induced me to discuss the two scourges that were so prominent then—racism and isolationism—and the symbiotic relationship between them and the Holocaust. But more importantly, the Holocaust and the events leading up to it offer an object lesson of what can happen when major worldwide social, technological, and economic upheavals occur amid moral and intellectual bankruptcy that cannot lead, cannot accept change, and cannot even get out of its own way. Bookended and morally defined by the 1921 Greenwood massacre that opened it and the 1939 *St. Louis* Jewish refugee spurning that closed it, this unlamented era primed Americans well for the horrors of the 1940s.

My studies of the Holocaust era led me to ponder the idea of a just war, or a morally asymmetric war. The Second World War has been widely touted as a just war, and I needed a definition of the term. In such a war, it really matters to the moral heft of the world which side wins; there really are good guys and bad guys. My conclusion is that the outcome of a just war must eliminate an injustice—it must enable previously shackled people to enjoy life, liberty, and the pursuit of fulfillment. The wrong side in the war is seeking to perpetuate an injustice—to maintain or extend bondage of humans.

Most wars clearly do not fit this definition. During the century between the 1815 Congress of Vienna, which shaped nineteenth-century Europe, and the 1914 outbreak of the Great War, which destroyed nineteenth-century Europe, a great many wars dotted the landscape. The majority of these Victorian-Edwardian wars were contests over real estate and prestige among more or less equally disreputable antagonists. The sum of the world's virtue was in no way affected by which side won, since these wars were not fought to liberate anybody from an unjust situation. It hardly mattered whether Emperor Nicholas I of Russia or Emperor Napoleon III of France directed the destinies of Turkish Christians and grabbed parcels of Turkish territory along the way. No celestial supervisors cared whether American or Spanish colonial officials oppressed Cubans and Filipinos. It was a decidedly neutral question whether the Alsatians lived better under a French dictator or under a German dictator.

I cite two examples of just wars—wars provoked by chronic injustices that had festered for centuries and resisted all attempts at solution or even amelioration. One injustice was European tribal chauvinism and violence, which imbued Europeans with the idea that they were entitled or even obligated to enslave and slaughter other peoples—in Europe, Asia, and Africa—to gain territory, plunder, and prestige or to vindicate this or that "true" religious faith or this or that "master" race. The other injustice was the American enslavement of Africans. These two injustices burgeoned ineluctably and eventually destroyed the orders they were disrupting. The creators and sustainers of these injustices used the degradation, enslavement, and murder of human beings as theoretical underpinnings of their governance. These injustices were vanquished, respectively, by the long twentieth-century war that began with the Balkan wars of the early 1910s and ended with the Balkan wars of the middle 1990s and by the American Civil War.

The first major act of the long war, the Great War of 1914–1918, was definitely not a just war. There were no thoughts of correcting injustices. A series of alliances and a mountain of armaments built up over the decades, feeding from and fed by a fevered nationalism and militarism infecting much of the populations and many politicians of Europe, led to an unstable equilibrium that was upset by the assassination of Archduke Francis Ferdinand, the heir to the Austrian throne.[16] This nationalism grew partly from arms races, partly from growing popular and official prejudice against other nations, and partly from news and propaganda about real events (or perceived insults to the nation) in colonial areas, notably Africa, where the race for territory and prestige heated up the atmosphere in Europe considerably.[17] The Great War ground on, and ground up people, for four years and ended in the farcical Paris peace conference. No existing injustices were corrected, but many more were generated by the conflict. Prominent among the new trouble spots was the Weimar German Big Lie—a lie that Germany had not lost the war at all but had routed the Allies in 1918 and was about to overrun France, when suddenly, the Jews and Communists seized power in Berlin and surrendered to the Allies. This Big Lie, promulgated by the German General Staff and later by Adolf Hitler, allowed the Germans to hide from their own defeat, and it did much to prepare them for the Second World War and the Holocaust.

The Second World War was clearly a just war. A victory by Nazi

Germany would have been devastating for the moral state of the world, as millions more murders and enslavements would have resulted, and the Holocaust would have continued to the final extinction of at least the European contingent of the Jewish people. This Holocaust would probably have engulfed other ethnic groups in addition to the Jews, since machines like the Holocaust rarely stop under their own power once they are started. (The Khmer Rouge atrocities in Cambodia from 1975 to 1979, the Rwanda genocide of 1994, and the Bosnia massacres of the middle 1990s were all terminated by foreign intervention, just as the Jewish Holocaust of the 1940s was.)

The Cold War between the West and the Soviet Union could be called the final great act of this twentieth-century long war. The Cold War was in itself a just war; a Soviet victory would have resulted in a Dark Age, and a singularly stupid Dark Age, given the stupidity of Russian rule generally. There were many mistakes and imbecilities from both sides during the Cold War: Vietnam on our side and the Soviet interventions in Eastern Europe and Afghanistan on the other side, with each side meddling in third-world quarrels for its own advantage. Nevertheless, our side was victorious and deserved to be victorious because of our superior moral weight; the freedom and the opportunities for personal meaning and fulfillment offered by Western countries; and the many injustices arising from the misgovernment, greed, and incapacity of the Soviet Union.

As a result of this long war from 1912 until 1994, European countries were forced to learn to get along with each other. Obsolete European world empires, which were an economic drain and a source of tension among Europeans, dissolved. The chronic, intractable European tribal nationalisms of previous centuries finally died a well-deserved death. Though freedom now seems to be unevenly robust and perhaps only temporary in some places, the end of the long war saw a general political, moral, and intellectual advance throughout the world.

The American Civil War was a just war. The destruction of the injustice of African American slavery was a secondary goal, though it attained more prominence and support as the war ground on and the victory of the Northern Union forces became steadily more assured. But Lincoln always insisted his primary goal was to save the Union. He assumed the liberation of the slaves would follow from saving the Union and the destruction of the proposed slaveholding nation known as the Confederate States of America. Slavery was indeed the moral driver of the war, according to prominent southerners before the war and contrary to later protestations by those same southerners after the war.

In fact, the correction of slavery's injustice by this war required more than a century to manifest itself. This unfortunate circumstance resulted from the right side—the United States—allowing the wrong side—the Southerners—to hijack the Civil War and Reconstruction narratives and preserve their deadening caste system, which is still visible today in many parts of the South. More culpably, the United States allowed the Southerners to reenslave the blacks for nearly a century after the collapse of Reconstruction. This tragedy arose from weakness and racism in the United States and the pertinacity and resourcefulness of Southerners in defending the morally destitute Southern way of life.

The upshot was that in my youth, we were treated to the Dunning school of Civil War and Reconstruction historiography.[18] The American Civil War was presented to me as a muddled, mushy romance tale about a tragic misunderstanding among loving brothers over tariffs and states' rights, a Southern agrarian Eden in which both blacks and whites lived in paradise until the Northern plunderers wrecked it, and the irenic reconciliation that would have occurred if only Lincoln had not been assassinated and if only those awful radical Republicans had not persecuted and alienated white Southerners during Reconstruction. Supposedly, the Civil War was not about slavery at all but about economic policy and governmental structure. Reconstruction was not an attempt to enable black Americans to live like human beings but a monstrous act of vengeance against "noble" white southerners. The black Republicans who held public office during Reconstruction were alleged to have demonstrated the innate incapacity of African Americans to manage their affairs. This Confederate Big Lie constructed by Dunning was convenient for both sides. It provided a fine cover for Northern benign neglect of blacks; Northerners could relax and blame all the subsequent evil in the South on John Wilkes Booth—Lincoln's assassin—and ignore this selfsame racist evil heavily infecting the North. This fairy tale also provided Southerners with a false moral equivalency to the

North during the Civil War, an equivalency they used to create the lachrymose Lost Cause myth to justify and legitimate their own war effort. If one accepts the Confederate Big Lie, then this war sinks to the low moral level of the other shabby scuffles of its era. Abraham Lincoln becomes yet another Emperor Nicholas I or Otto von Bismarck, aggressing against his neighbor for grubby territorial goals; this is exactly how white American Southerners wished everybody to view Abraham Lincoln.

Foner's biography of Lincoln[19] and other modern Civil War histories do a good job of debunking this rubbish; Lincoln's greatness and human shortcomings and the trouble he was having with Southern bitter-enders before his death are well illustrated by Foner. Foner makes much of his point, not emphasized in other biographies, that Lincoln's success arose largely because he had an open, lively, curious mind willing to learn new concepts and evolve opinions based on valid new information—an important component of good character. History thus contrasts Lincoln favorably with his more closed-minded contemporaries George McClellan, commander of the Union armies early in the war, and Andrew Johnson, who succeeded Lincoln as president after Lincoln's assassination.

The hell that was life for most African Americans within the Confederacy and after its demise is well documented in many reputable histories and fictions, as well as in the National Museum of African American History and Culture in Washington, DC. I also recommend an article in *Civil War Times* magazine[20] that clearly and devastatingly describes the Southern hatreds, self-pity, and vengefulness following the war—fully as venomous as the attitudes of the fabled radical Republicans in the North. Ron Chernow's biography of Union general Ulysses S. Grant[21] depicts the hatreds, corruption, and violence in the South during the Reconstruction era in a way that brings to mind the modern Middle East and Caucasus (see my musings in chapter 11 about the Palestinian-Israeli and Armenian-Azerbaijani conflicts). Unfortunately for Southerners, they, unlike the Northerners, lacked the military wherewithal to force their vengeance on their foes. The Southerners were compelled to hate Northerners quietly—and to murder blacks publicly—as compensation. Generations had to pass in order to clear the waters in that poisoned Southland well and to begin the reconciliation. Even now, there is more than enough toxic water to be found in that well.

In retrospect, I feel resentful about my early introduction to the Civil War era via this badly misleading Dunning orthodoxy. The Dunning school is as disruptive to American history as creationism is to paleontology, as climate-change denial is to climate science, and as the antivaccination sect is to immunology. One of history's most important purposes is to tell us who we are and how we got to our present situation. Distortions like the Dunning narrative give us a wholly false impression of our moral development and of our national character.

Eventually, after a generous decade volunteering to work at the US Holocaust Memorial Museum, age-related stamina loss made the job too difficult and disruptive, and I retired. But I also retired for another reason rich with irony under the circumstances. One evening, I was called in by the visitor services chief and informed that henceforth, all museum staff and volunteers were forbidden to talk among themselves about Donald Trump or any other political topic. I had always kept my political observations away from the visitors since, as a representative of the museum, I was bound to avoid irritating our customers. But why maintain silence about Trump among the museum staff? The museum itself had hosted a couple of special exhibits—"Some Were Neighbors," about bystanders who watched horrors but did nothing to save anybody, and "Americans and the Holocaust," about Americans who passively allowed the Holocaust to proceed—with the clear message that silence in the presence of evil is complicity. The permanent exhibit, which relates the history of the Holocaust, carries this message as well. Given the message of the museum's exhibits, I found it awkward to remain at the museum and not call out the evil that Trump represented. The COVID-19 pandemic forced the closing of the museum for more than a year; this hiatus gave me a pause needed to clarify my thinking.

My African American female partners made me made more acutely aware of the specific injustices, indignities, and oppressions visited upon African Americans during slavery before the Civil War, during segregation and Jim Crow laws before the 1960s, and during the present time. Materials presented to me have educated me in this particular injustice and have induced me to take what actions I can to help to rectify it. But their past has clearly imbued them with distinct psychological marks.

The hard history suffered by African Americans has left them distinctly skeptical about trusting white politicians with their allegiance. They have been left in the lurch throughout their history by myriads of dilettantes, milksops, and exploitative charlatans. All this is on top of their abandonment by the Republican Party, which claimed to be their protector, in the Great Compromise of 1877, in which the southern Democrats allowed Republican Rutherford B. Hayes to steal the 1876 presidential election in return for "southern home rule."[22] That is, the Republicans terminated Reconstruction protections and left African Americans entirely to the tender mercies of southern white racists. As a result of such experiences, African Americans are likely well trained in detecting phony saviors. Moreover, social and economic pathologies resulting from centuries of discrimination require special knowledge and care in order for redress to be effective—knowledge not common among our leaders. All this is probably why African Americans are slow to embrace newly introduced liberal politicians who are so earnest in proclaiming their commitment to African American equality—much to the frustration of those politicians.

In my own observations of blacks, I see a gritty, unsentimental realism and practicality, coupled with a general belief that their liberation will come exclusively from their own efforts, though they realize they need the federal government to prevent the recrudescence of the hostile environment for their efforts that prevailed until late last century.[23] They have just recently arrived at a threshold where many of them can see themselves as full participants in the American bounty and can be assured that society will reward them for their inputs. Understanding the brittleness of this new status, they guard it carefully; they are not about to surrender it for gurus or ideological pipe dreams. This practicality has become obvious recently: Joe Biden, who started out the 2020 presidential race as their favorite, saw his poll numbers with them tank pitilessly after he lost a couple of primary elections. He recovered after blacks themselves restored his status as front-runner. Blacks were markedly silent during the early 2019 outcry (mostly from whites, whose motives were not necessarily pure) over Virginia governor Ralph Northam's youthful indiscretion with blackface comedy; undoubtedly, blacks were aware that the ouster of him and his lieutenants would have left a Trumpian Republican in the governor's mansion. Taking a page from the Jews after the Holocaust, blacks are quick to publicize and denounce any injustice perpetrated upon any of their number. Recently, blacks have become more amenable to pooling their efforts with other marginalized groups, such as Asians and Jews, in order to augment everybody's political strength. Blacks never get wildly ecstatic about any candidate, even if he is one of their own, such as Barak Obama. The idea is to solidify and enhance their status, purely and simply.

A related injustice needing attention is white ignorance about African American sensitivities. This white narrowness often makes itself manifest in what are now called "microaggression" and "whitesplaining." A microaggression is a small act committed by one individual that might or might not be intended as an insult or a threat but that another individual might, for historical or cultural reasons, interpret as such. A microaggression occurred at a lunch that Lois and I attended. We were about to sit down at a table, when one of the white women seated at the table indicated the seats were reserved for her friends. Lois reacted with fury; since foul-smelling blacks have been a white myth for centuries, she probably read the woman's gesture as "Go away! You stink!" Whitesplaining consists of lecturing African Americans on their need to see their situation from a white perspective, as if they are not entitled to a perspective of their own, based on their own history. In this case, a whitesplainer would say, "I didn't mean it that way, and Lois should have known better! She needs to stop being so sensitive!"

In another episode, Frances and I entered the Grand Hotel in Big Timber, Montana, with a view to acquiring lunch. Frances soon took my hand and led me away. She later informed me that the locals already in the dining room had ceased their conversation and turned to stare at us. In African American history, whites suddenly going silent and turning to stare at a black newcomer was often a prelude to violence. Perhaps open and welcoming greetings from Grand Hotel employees would have defused her atavistic alarm, but dismissive whitesplaining would never have reassured her.

The misunderstandings among ethnic groups in the United States are many and great; helping African Americans to achieve equality is an endeavor to be approached with humility, patience, and willingness to learn, not with condescension or a desire for accolades.

I salute my partners for educating me away from my previous cocoon. My efforts here consist mainly in listening to my significant women and learning how to behave and in contributing to organizations that push for African American and other minority rights. The organizations include the Southern Poverty Law Center, the National Museum of African American History and Culture, and the National Museum of the American Indian. These museums form a good partnership with the Holocaust Museum in that they all illustrate starkly what can happen when man is allowed to become bestial.

Thus have I tried to make a difference in the world on behalf of liberties and good character. While the results of my attempts to right wrongs have undoubtedly been minimal in their effects compared to the efforts of others devoted full-time to rectifying injustices, I have not been a total bystander.

CHAPTER 11

AVOCATION 2: TRAVEL TAKEAWAYS: STORIES MY GEOGRAPHY TEACHERS NEVER TOLD ME

During the latter part of my life, I started traveling the world. I had always wanted to globe-trot and learn about the various cultures and histories of foreign countries, but my career-building and Marky's reluctance obliged me to put the hobby to one side for a few decades. I have since made up for lost time, and I have visited forty-six countries[1]—with hopefully many more to come.

Before my fifties, I had done a minimal amount of foreign travel: driving trips in Canada and Mexico and business trips to Kiribati in the central Pacific. Since 1995, my foreign travel has been under the auspices of educational travel services: Road Scholar, National Geographic, and Smithsonian. Travel agents set up my itinerary and arrange for eating and sleeping establishments they know are good. Travel guides and bus drivers know their way around the local area and can get us into the best places to visit. I appreciate the hard work these people do, and I want to observe and learn without the risks and distractions suffered by freelance travelers, who must be their own travel agents, tour guides, and drivers.

My purpose has been to learn about the countries I visit. These trips always feature reading lists, from which I read selected works in order to get advance information about the target countries. This travel has constituted the bulk of my primary source, or firsthand, learning about the world since starting this hobby, as opposed to secondary source, or reading of literature by others. These excursions have broadened my world outlook, along with according me much pleasure over the years.

I will touch upon highlights of my trips that I consider both interesting and enlightening. The material may appear eclectic and perhaps disjointed, but I hope nevertheless to spread some of my insights and observations around. This account is not a full panorama of the workings of the countries visited. An exhaustive recounting of my travels would be exhausting; besides, there is no point in repetition of data that can be accessed by Googling the country. Instead, this chapter will be a recapitulation of personal observations and impressions I consider worth discussion. Where appropriate, material from travel-related lectures and readings will be included.

I will say at the outset that I have never suffered a bummer overseas trip. Some have been more pleasurable and fulfilling than others, but I have acquired some education and enjoyment from each one. The guides in every country I have visited have been careful to shield me from any misadventures arising from the internal situation in the country, such as violent demonstrations, civil conflict, police harassment, or bureaucratic problems. The tour officials were professional; they related the good and bad aspects about their countries as they guided us around. This type of honesty not only provides a greater quality of education but also earns the country a better name among the traveling public than unalloyed good news, which only makes intelligent travelers suspicious.

The hotels and restaurants were all clean but variable in accommodation and convenience. Never did I have trouble with bedbugs or cockroaches, even in third-world countries. Where necessary, I received the appropriate preventatives for the diseases endemic to our destinations, such as typhoid, cholera, hepatitis, and malaria. In Asia, I had to buy bottled water and use it for all hygienic needs, including tooth brushing. African tap water was usable for hygiene but not recommended for drinking; we drank bottled water there. In Europe, Chile, Australia, and New Zealand, the tap water was potable everywhere, except for the Caucasus and dicey parts of Russia. I maintained my digestive health most of the time, but on a few occasions, I ingested something that compelled me to take an antidote and maybe a rest from my travels.

There is a reason for all this coddling of traveling foreign nationals. Many of these countries depend to a large extent on tourists spending money for their economic health. No country that desires to buoy its economy via tourists wants to earn a bad reputation by sending someone home deathly ill from local diseases, beaten half to death by police or rioters, traumatized by a stay in a nasty dungeon, or half eaten by bedbugs.

Marky's hesitations about language barriers turned out to be baseless; in the twenty-first century, English has now become the world's premier language, and it is a second language to a great many people all over the globe. This was brought home to me by an experience I had in Austria. Searching for a newspaper (*Blätter* in German), I went into a *Tabak* (tobacco) shop and hesitatingly inquired, "Uh, *Blätter? Englisch?*"

In accent-free American English, the proprietor replied, "No, I'm sorry. We don't have any English newspapers."

The reply startled me a bit then, but now I'm much more aware of the pervasiveness of English around the world.

In general, the European countries I visited tended to have their signs in three languages: their own language, English, and German. Exceptions included France (French only) and Russia (Russian only). I could stumble out a few words in French when necessary to make myself understood, and I retained enough Russian from my early adulthood lessons (see chapter 7) to be designated the travel group's reader of road signs, restaurant menus, and checks. I could also find my way around Tikhvin Cemetery in St. Petersburg to visit the graves of such Russian icons as Tchaikovsky, Dostoyevsky, Anton Rubinstein, Borodin, and others. But still, both France and Russia contained enough English speakers to prevent us from getting into real trouble. I'm told the natives of all countries appreciate attempts to converse in their language, inept or otherwise. It shows respect. There are many ugly Americans who get impatient over language barriers and never try to meet their hosts even a tenth of the way.

A couple of exceptions stand out, however. Very early in my overseas traveling career—to Norway—I ran into a party of Germans from former East Germany. The Cold War was of recent memory, and these people had been made to learn Russian as a second language, not English. So I was compelled to practice my German with them. We were on a boat going north along the Norwegian coast. I was headed to Narvik, and the German party were headed around the North Cape to Kirkines, near the Russian border. I gave them my standard greeting: *"Ich kann nur genug Deutsch um zu sprechen wie ein Dummkopf"* (I know only enough German to speak like a fool).

This broke the ice, as they all took it in good fun.

I subsequently got playful in a less tactful way. I jokingly asked one member of the party, *"Haben Sie für die Stasi gearbeiten?"* (Did you work for the East German secret police?). Since I was aware that during the Cold War, up to one-third of all East Germans at least occasionally served as informers for the East German secret police, the Stasi, I should have known better than to attempt this particular jocularity. This infiltration of the general public by the Stasi led to much recrimination and breakup of relationships when the Stasi files were opened to the public in 1992, as many people discovered that someone near and dear to them had spent years tattling about them to the police. I was fooling around and practicing my German to see whether it was comprehensible to my travel mates. But the man to whom I asked the question not only had not worked for the Stasi; he had spent several years in an East German prison for violating some article or other of the Soviet military constitution.

I don't think he took my levity amiss, as he and his wife explained the situation to me in an affable manner, and they knew I was (1) joking, (2) distracted by the effort to get my German straight, and (3) a tyro who had not mingled much in alien cultures. We had good conversations afterward, but still, I am mortified whenever I recall asking that particular person about that particular dark past. It was a major microaggression, and it would have been such with anyone who had lived in former East Germany, regardless of how he and the Stasi had interacted. This gaffe did not spring from ignorance of German history and psychology; it was simply inexcusable thoughtlessness.

The other language problem occurred when I traveled to Chile and Easter Island. I hadn't slept on the airplane flying overnight from Philadelphia to Santiago, Chile. When we got onto a tour bus, I instantly fell into a dead slumber, and when I woke up, only the bus driver and I were on board. The others had gone out on a walking excursion, apparently after futile attempts to resuscitate me. Queries about my party to the bus driver produced no enlightenment, as he knew only Spanish. I don't know enough Spanish to get by on any level. After much searching, somebody who spoke English was procured for me, and she told me where everybody was. I went by myself on this walk excursion later in the trip while everybody else had free time. I suppose there is not much pressure to learn a second language in South America, since Spanish and Portuguese are spoken over huge swathes of the continent. Europeans, on the other hand, must learn English or German in order to communicate among many small linguistic enclaves.

In the Caucasus, Asia, and Africa, I never tried to go local, as the languages were totally unknown to me. But since there were plenty of English speakers everywhere, we all got along famously. I have never tried to learn the few phrases usually listed in the travel literature I receive, such as greetings and salutations, counting to ten, common questions and answers, and so on. Since I visit the vast majority of the countries only one time, this knowledge would profit me only for a few weeks, and there are many more substantive things I want to learn about the countries.

I have visited countries with almost all manner of internal freedom, from highly libertarian countries, such as Iceland and the Scandinavian countries, to tight dictatorships, such as Vietnam and Laos. I have never visited countries where the government kept the tour group paranoid and controllable by bugging the tour buses and hotel rooms, using members of the secret police as tour guides, planting spies in the tour groups, and encouraging local people to harass and entrap visitors. I hope never to be in such a situation, which would be neither educational nor pleasurable. There is no point in donating my tourist money to enrich regimes like these. From my readings, I understand that the old Soviet Union was this way, as is North Korea now. But if a country is serious about wanting tourists to swell its coffers, it must not maltreat visitors in this way. On all my trips thus far, I have always been allowed to inquire about any topic in the safety of the tour bus or hotel room; in a few countries, however, we had to watch our words among the public. The yen for tourist money motivates even the most repressive countries to shield us from police brutality, thus suppressing bad notices from returning travelers.

On my travels, I have seen economic prosperity levels all over the spectrum. From the richest Northern and Western European countries to the poorest East Asian countries, I have seen wealth and beggary. Indeed, since it is monumentally difficult for a poor country to hide its poor people, no attempt is made in this direction. Moreover, since I invariably read up on the countries before I visit them, I have enough forewarning to expect more or less what I encounter upon arrival.

Many of my trips overseas were to my ancestral homelands: the British Isles and Norway. The characteristics I appear to have picked up from my forebears in these locales are the British love of liberty and autonomy and the Norwegian desire to do the right thing (or rectitudinal fever, see chapter 2—Freudians call this fastidiousness "anal"). Perhaps my wish to rectify injustices (see chapter 10) came from genetic material from both of these places. In any case, I saw these characteristics among the populace during my visits to these countries. The inhabitants of the British Isles tended to be independent and individualistic, and the Norwegians were certainly anal. The peoples from these places are somewhat related by blood since the Vikings populated many parts of the British Isles during the Middle Ages.

British self-reliance and independence showed up in one important way. Hot water taps were labeled with notices: "This water is hot!" If I insisted on scalding myself anyway, that was my affair, and nobody was about to recompense me with a five-digit sum for my stupidity. More substantively, Marky and I were able to wander at will among the ruins of Tintern Abbey in Wales. We could drink in the timeless, majestic peace of this centuries-old monastery, undisturbed by guards frantically chasing us out lest a stone tumble onto us from the still-standing walls and give us an excuse to sue. We were able to wander into Shakespeare's babyhood home and see how his family must have lived four hundred years ago. Edinburgh Castle was ours to explore, with its fantastic view of Edinburgh. This British tolerance contrasts—favorably, in my opinion—with the United States, where safety is overblown because batteries of tort lawyers stand ready to rake in lavish livings from alleged suffering. This limits everybody's freedom of action.

This British abhorrence of shackles has shown up repeatedly in their history, as in the Magna Carta in 1215, which guaranteed that no absolute monarch would evolve, and the dethroning of King Charles I in the seventeenth century, coupled with the establishment of Parliament as a coequal branch of government. Their refusal to buckle when attacked by Nazi Germany in the 1940s is the most recent and most sparkling example. Their treatment of their colonial subjects and the Irish was certainly less than admirable. But still, I have formed the impression from my reading that their colonial subjects fared better than those of continental European powers, notably France, Belgium, Germany, and Russia. During the early twentieth century, British operatives led efforts to ameliorate the condition of the Congolese under Belgian misrule.[2] When the time came to free the colonies after the Second World War, the British gave up their empire with more grace and less resistance than did the other colonial powers.

British-Irish relations appear to be good-natured; so far, there is no fence between the six Protestant UK provinces and the rest of Ireland. During my trip there with Marky in 1998, we didn't travel to Northern Ireland, since the Time of Troubles, the civil war between Catholics and Protestants, had not yet completely died down. But Frances and I were able to tour Belfast in 2014. There was still enough acrimony that one had to be careful, but we had no misadventures there. The Republic of Ireland is as beautifully green as advertised. Unfortunately, when we visited in 2014, the Irish economy was distorted by their having adopted the euro as a currency. The price of the euro was such that Irish exports were overpriced, killing their trade. The Irish couldn't persuade France and Germany to weaken the euro to allow Ireland to export. As a result, our guide's only job was as part-time tour leader for Road Scholar, but she lived well enough thanks to subsidies from the European Union. I would find that lifestyle depressing, but I suppose one can get accustomed to many situations.

The Potato Famine of the 1840s loomed large during both my trips to Ireland. This catastrophe caused a major demographic shift in the United States, as Irish who couldn't eat immigrated to our shores and populated large parts of our country with Catholics. This bit of history sticks with me because of the animating principle of the British government regarding Ireland at the time—a deadly caricature of the conservative principle that holds that people should be independent and help themselves as much as possible. I certainly believe that people should be allowed to chart their own lives, but if they are starving with no recourse, aid is essential. The British, paranoid about food aid creating a generation of chronically dependent welfare Irish, denied all aid to Ireland and, thus, greatly intensified the famine. Unfortunately, the Irish added to their own problems by overpopulating the island and dividing up the land estates among all offspring for generation after generation, until each property became too small to sustain anybody. But still, the British policy of the 1840s was inhuman—and it was echoed in the United States during the COVID-19 pandemic. The Republicans were so solicitous of people's character that they forgot about people. They justified tardy and niggardly aid to COVID-19 victims by expressing the fear that a rescue plan would cause them to idle away the remainder of their lives on welfare. Better ten starve than one become dependent on handouts!

The Norwegian neatness showed up in several ways. The Norwegians never change the days of their holidays to abut onto a weekend, as do the Americans. Not only do Tuesday holidays remain detached from weekends, but if the holiday falls on a Sunday, that holiday is not noted. I was told that it is wrong to move holidays. On another occasion, someone sat on a low, thick-legged table, prompting an official to point at him and shout emphatically, "Excuse me, but that is a table!" This stickiness has descended to me; in my house, I had to train myself to avoid redoing tasks already completed by my partner, and I typically put newly cleaned dishes at the bottom of the stack, so all dishes will be used eventually. It distresses me to see a book opened and lying facedown or eyeglasses lying forward facedown.

On my first trip to Norway, I visited my maternal grandmother Mimi's childhood grounds, the Lofoten Islands. We took a bus to the end of the island chain; causeways between the islands enabled this land travel. Even in June, the weather was cold and foggy or cold and windy. For this reason, the Norwegians are earnest consumers of fat and sugar.

189

Protein comes mainly from pigs and fish. I encountered my favorite dish from my grandmother's days: *rømmegrøt,* a pudding consisting of the leftovers when sour cream is heated until the butter floats out. Rømmegrøt is flavored with sugar, cinnamon, and raisins, along with melted butter. It is well suited to the climate since it is exceedingly rich in calories, fat, and carbohydrates, especially with the aforementioned trimmings. Lefse, a sweet wafer, was also good. My fellow travelers told me that one is not a true Norwegian unless one likes lutefisk. I quickly discovered not only that was I not a true Norwegian by this standard but also that my grandmother probably did not like it either, since she never inflicted this dish on us. Lutefisk is a laboriously prepared dish for which one soaks cod for several days in water, then for several days in lye (a primary ingredient in Drāno!), and then in water again to remove the poisonous lye. The fish is then dried by storing it with salt and afterward baked. The result is a colorless fish jelly that tastes rather rancid and feels rather slippery. I will leave this pleasure to real Norwegians! Recent immigrants from South Asia have spruced up the bland Scandinavian fare in recent years. Many people here now enjoy dishes served with coriander, curry, bay leaves, cilantro, and other imports.

The main export from the Lofoten Islands is stockfish, which is cod hung on wooden frames (stocks) outdoors in the early spring. The wind dries out the fish over a period of several weeks, yielding essentially cod jerky. Some of this is eaten locally, but most is shipped to Italy—no refrigeration needed—where it is rehydrated and served in fish dishes. I found stockfish all right—edible but nothing to excite me.

The stockfish must be dried at just the right time of year. If it hangs out too early, it will freeze in the cold weather. If it hangs out too late, it will spoil in the warmer weather. Since my Lofoten trip, I have often wondered how climate change is affecting this industry; spring comes earlier and is probably shorter than the springs of old.

One Scandinavian trip was a North Atlantic cruise said to follow the trail of the Vikings as they made their way across the Atlantic around the turn of the second millennium. The Vikings, in creating a trade network that reached from Newfoundland to Constantinople, presided over one of the great medieval empires. We cruised through the Shetland and Orkney Islands of Scotland, noting Viking graffiti on the burial places there. After visiting the Faeroe Islands—a property of Denmark—we circumnavigated Iceland, stopping for hikes along the way.

The Mid-Atlantic Ridge is a chain of outgassing and volcanic mountains on the Atlantic floor—an upwelling of Earth's mantle through the crust, which is pushing the Old World and the New World apart at a rate of about two inches per year. The Faeroe Islands are a failed, extinct branch of this ridge, while Iceland is an active part of it. Ditches run through Iceland and belch gas from Earth's interior; Iceland is growing broader from east to west at the rate our fingernails grow, according to our guides. As a result, the Icelanders get about 85 percent of the energy to run their economy and society from geothermal sources provided by this volcanic activity.

All of the lands visited on that trip featured bleak tundra grasslands. The tragedy of this part of the world is climate change. Sadly, since the Arctic is warming up rapidly, the permafrost underlying this stark but appealing terrain is disappearing in many places, leading to sinkholes and methane outgassing.

A geologist accompanying us on the trip took us on a hike to the Arctic Circle, on Grimsey Island, north of Iceland. The Arctic Circle, which is the southernmost point at which the midnight sun occurs, is marked by a monument on Grimsey. This monument was erected in 1925; since then, the Arctic Circle has moved north at a rate of about fifteen meters per year. This motion occurs because of a periodic variation in the tilt of the Earth relative to its orbital plane. So we had to walk about three-quarters of a mile north from this monument in order to stand on the real Arctic Circle. I calculated that by the middle of the twenty-first century, the Arctic Circle will no longer cross Grimsey Island.

In stark contrast to the homes of my ancestors is Russia. I visited that country twice during the mid-2000s, before Vladimir Putin got serious about reimposing the leaden despotism usually characteristic of Russia. At the time of my visits, I found it a pleasant surprise; Russians and visitors to Russia whom I had previously met had guaranteed to me that I would be eager to leave soon after my arrival. I had also read many books and articles about Russia over my lifetime, and I had a reasonably good outline of the nation's recent history and culture. The thicket of paperwork involved in getting a Russian visa tended to confirm these forebodings—suspicious Russians needed to know and control my every move! But I found my trips to be superbly rewarding and educational; there was nothing of the old Soviet maltreatment of tourists on display that time. The Hermitage Museum in St. Petersburg could occupy weeks of a serious traveler's time. The Peterhof and the water gardens in front of it were marvels. Many of the architectural wonders in Russia and Eastern Europe were recent rebuilds; much had been destroyed by the Nazis during the Second World War. In the Communist era, re-creating past splendors was not encouraged; only since about 1990 has cultural consciousness returned to that part of the world.

The Russian travel authorities were willing to show us warts and all, as in other countries, and a remarkable freedom and frankness were discernable that my previous sources had never indicated. One lecturer admitted that immigrant Chinese were taking over much of Russian agriculture, leaving young Russians to move to cities. He added that their electronics industry needed some improvement. When I commented that in the Soviet era, such observations would have brought the police to his door, he agreed heartily. Our bus driver had an American flag magnet on his dashboard. One of our tour guides stated openly that she didn't like Putin at all. We were allowed to walk around at will without the police chaperones who had darkened many of the accounts I had read about Russian travel. Noting all of these things, I developed a small hope that things could look up for Russia after all.

I have been sobered, but not taken aback, by the recent restrictions coming into being under Putin. I have my doubts now about frank discussions inside Russia of Russia's and Putin's shortcomings and about Russian bus drivers with American flag magnets. Russia has been through several such false dawns in the past: the Khrushchev thaw in the 1950s before Brezhnev tightened the screws; the Silver Age for the arts in the 1920s before Stalin cracked down; the relative liberalism of Tsar Alexander II in the 1860s before his assassination and the reactionary rule of his successors; and so on. Putin represents yet another valley in this dreary cycle. Still, it is better for freedom in Russia now than in the Brezhnev era. Unlike in the recent past, Russians are allowed to travel abroad; during recent decades, I have seen groups of them touring Europe and the Middle East. Antigovernment protests occur in Russia on occasion. Perhaps over centuries, barring a major catastrophe, Russia will finally emerge from its freedom cycles to become a modern nation.

Another of my observations is that Russians are certainly not anal. The grass in their cemeteries and parks is allowed to grow more or less wild, and mud paths are not paved or asphalted. Though Russian hotels were as splendid as any I visited—probably part of the Russian effort to look good to foreign visitors—their public toilets near tourist spots were among the filthiest, barely breathable and definitely not for the barefoot. But each toilet house had its collector at the entrance, assessing each user around twenty-five cents for God knows what purpose. Supposedly strict rules at the Hermitage Museum in St. Petersburg required wearing plastic bags over the shoes to prevent footwear-borne grit from damaging the floor. Nevertheless, one day I forgot to don the bags until near the end of my tour, when I felt chagrinned upon beholding my bare shoes. But nobody else noticed or cared. Russian drivers are among the least anal I have observed; in clogged streets, those who were in a hurry occasionally hopped the curb and drove on the sidewalks to speed up their progress, attracting no attention whatever from the ubiquitous police.

In Moscow, there is a Park of Fallen Idols to celebrate their liberation from Communism. A huge statue of Feliks Dzerzhinsky, the first Communist secret police chief, dominates the scene. Busts of Brezhnev, Kosygin, and other Communist bigwigs are scattered about. A memorial to the slave labor camp victims sits in the middle of the park. But I was startled to come across a bust of Van Cliburn, the pianist who won the Moscow Tchaikovsky competition in 1958. Had he fallen from grace in Russia also? Nearby was a memorial garden to the fallen soldiers in the Great Patriotic War, the epic Russian struggle against Hitler; these veterans would hardly be in disgrace! Reflecting on my studies of Russia, I surmised that the Russians had simply decided, with no thought of the context, that these sites in the Park of Fallen Idols would be good places to pay tribute to Van Cliburn and the Great Patriotic War martyrs. Had this happened in anal Norway, these placements would have constituted definite statements about the status of these people!

The fabled Russian tipplers were largely invisible to us; I suspect these are more prominent in villages than in large, tourist-filled cities, such as Moscow and St. Petersburg, where the authorities may encourage them to keep a low profile. After all, the Russians want tourists to speak well of them upon return to their homes, just as in all other countries I visited. I did note that every large and small grocery store and every fast food stand sported an extensive liquor section. At my hotels, there was a bar that opened at around 0500 to accommodate those who needed eye-openers in the morning.

The Russians are said to be warm and sentimental—another major departure from my ancestors. Two incidents demonstrated this feature. At a lecture on Romanov history, it was pointed out that Empress Catherine II had a reputation as a bed-hopper. Therefore, there is controversy over whether Tsar Paul, her son, was really the son of her husband, Tsar Peter III. I asked a practical question: All of the remains are stored in the Peter and Paul Cathedral right there in St. Petersburg, so why not do a DNA analysis to settle the matter? The lecturer replied that this could never happen. The Russian public would not be able to manage an outcome proving that their last six tsars were descended from some horse master; better to avoid the risk altogether. On another occasion, at the obligatory attendance of a performance of Tchaikovsky's *Swan Lake* ballet at the Mariinsky Theater in St. Petersburg, we learned that the original story line ended in Odette and Siegfried being washed away and drowned in a flood after they swore their eternal love. Someone pointed out to the producers that they would never get a Russian audience for a story that ended like that; they had to change the ending to have the flood miraculously recede when Siegfried and Odette swore and sealed their love, so the two could live happily ever after. This Russian affinity for treacle is certainly not a prominent characteristic of my ancestral countries!

My travels in Western and Central Europe and the supplementary reading material showed to me an easygoing tolerance; people were remarkably relaxed about being in a mix of different cultures. This seemed to be true even for the Balkan countries, an eternal flashpoint.

I suspect there is still some resentment in the hinterlands, especially in the Balkans recently torn apart by the 1990s warfare. All in all, though, I found the tolerance pleasing to behold; it runs counter to European history over the centuries. Open borders between European Union member countries facilitate travel by the citizens and the shedding of their prejudices through contact with people from all over the continent. The long absence of warfare, enforced partly by NATO and partly by the presence of nuclear weapons on both sides of the Cold War, doubtless accustomed people to the virtues and benefits of tolerance and peace. Moreover, a free press and social media doubtless educate Europeans about conditions in other parts of the world where war and bigotry are enshrined, further inoculating them against these plagues.

I believe this acceptance of racial and cultural diversity stems partially from the fact that there are so many reminders right on their doorsteps of the consequences of ideological fanaticism. Mementoes of the long war of 1912 to 1994 are everywhere. Russia contains innumerable cemeteries and memorials to their fallen in the war against Hitler. France is scarred by the remains of the mines and trenches of the Great War and by emplacements in Normandy that recall the bloody contest there in the Second World War. The obvious newness of churches and other landmarks bespeaks the recent destruction and reconstruction. Holocaust reminders are everywhere; the Jewish Museum in Berlin speaks eloquently of this tragedy. I visited Auschwitz I, with its city of torture chambers and execution sites, and Auschwitz II (Birkenau), with its human bone gravel, barracks, toilets, and partially destroyed gas chambers. At Mauthausen in Austria, we went up the staircase of death from a quarry to the surface. Prisoners were compelled to carry 160-pound rocks up that staircase for the construction of Hitler's retirement palace. Needless to say, many were killed by the ordeal. We were crammed into the gas chambers there to better get a feel of what had happened. At a children's death camp called Salaspils, outside Riga, Latvia, the entry gate is inscribed with "Beneath this gate, the earth groans." Children there, as long as they were alive, were used as involuntary blood donors for the German Army. The walls of Anne Frank's family hideaway in Amsterdam are plastered with poignant stamps reminding us of the family who were betrayed by a lowlife and kidnapped by the Nazis. All were exterminated, except for Otto Frank, the father, who had served his fatherland in the Great War on the French front and was rewarded by the murder of his family.

More recent signs of the bloody past include the trace of where the Berlin Wall ran; this trace zigs and zags through the city. Pieces of the Berlin Wall were on sale everywhere. Checkpoint Charlie, once a heavily guarded gateway between the two Germanys, is now a museum depicting the paranoia of the Cold War. One of the most popular museums in Berlin is the DDR (German Democratic Republic, or East Germany) Museum, where Communist life in all its dreariness is depicted. The Baltic countries were full of occupation museums portraying Soviet misgovernment in those states. Torture chambers and Soviet-style statues of "heroes" characterized these museums, whose presence was said to be annoying to the Russians. When I visited Prague, Czech Republic, and Vienna, Austria, in 2000, the shabbiness of the Cold War was still apparent, particularly in Prague. Dysfunctional Prague streetlamps and mud paths in Prague parks reminded me of the lack of pride that characterized Communist rule. In 2016, Frances and I visited these two cities; the unkempt areas had been cleaned up, but tourist masses made navigation almost impossible. In 2000, I had made several treks to the roof of St. Stephen's Cathedral for a magnificent overview of Vienna, but in 2016, we could barely get into the tourist-packed cathedral in the first place; walking its hallways and roof were out of the question.

Persecution of minorities is officially forbidden in European Union countries. This policy goes far toward maintaining peace; countries that misbehave internally are likely to misbehave externally as well. European history is rife with examples of this truism, particularly throughout the nineteenth and twentieth centuries. The Baltic states of Estonia and Latvia, which have large ethnic Russian minorities (planted there by Stalin in the 1940s to bind these countries more tightly to the Soviet Union), are made much safer by treating their local Russians with respect. This policy averts the dangers presented by the presence of a persecuted, discontented minority who look to a foreign power for succor—another all-too-frequent feature of European political history. My inquiries on this topic were answered reassuringly, though; the

Russians in those two states, particularly the younger Russians, know well enough via social media and a free press what life is like in the motherland. They are mostly content with a good life undisturbed by Muscovite corruption and oppression. Hopefully everybody can avoid a ghastly racial awakening of the sort that spilled so much blood in that part of the world not too long ago.[3] The Baltic peoples naturally remain wary of their treacherous eastern neighbor but not dismayed. NATO, the defensive alliance between Europe and North America, is stable enough to have survived the recently silenced gabble of Donald Trump, though not without some apprehension regarding the possibility of another Trump-like grotesquery in the American future.

Occasionally, Frances and I saw signs of something uglier beneath the serene, tolerant European surface. Walking in Dublin, Ireland, one sunny afternoon, we were startled by an epithet shouted by an elderly woman. I didn't pick up all the words, but she was angry about Romanians. It was not clear to me whether she was complaining to us about immigrant Romanians or whether she thought we were foreign invaders, but her bigotry was abundantly clear. We all went our separate ways after her ten-second harangue, but it was a revelation to me nonetheless. In Russia, our group, on a walking tour, passed by an unhappy-looking gang of skinheads. At a dinner with my travel group in Riga, Latvia, I uttered the word *Chechnya* in the course of a conversation, the context of which I don't remember at all, and from the next room came a booming voice: "Why don't you shut your mouth?" Investigation revealed two tipsy ethnic Russians who spoke American English with not the slightest sign of an accent. Based on one overheard word, they probably imagined I was taunting them about their less-than-glorious campaign then in progress in the North Caucasus. Together, my travel group and I calmed down the pickled Russians by assuring them we were not heckling them. One of them then remarked, "You have to be careful! You're talking in a language that everybody understands." Cosmopolitan enough they were to pass as American speakers, but dour Russian chauvinism still prevailed.

Later on, there were the votes in Britain to leave the European Union, the election of Trump as American president, and the rise of authoritarian nationalist political parties in European countries—partly in response to the plight of refugees from violence and starvation and partly due to social and political changes that dismay and disorient marginalized people. The old Pleistocene tribal wild beast is with us still, alas!

I will now turn to parts of the world where peaceful tolerance and easygoing prosperity are not to be found anywhere—on the surface or underneath. I learned much about human conflict and bigotry during my visits to the Middle East and the Caucasus. These localities have been plagued by decades-long conflicts among tribes of different religions and origins over small patches of territory deemed sacred by all parties.

The Middle East has long been the seat of many chronic conflicts, but my personal observation concerned the conflict best known to the general public: the Israeli-Palestinian standoff. A history of this conflict is too much for these pages; I will limit myself to personal impressions augmented by many news articles and books I have read over the years on the subject.[4] My studies of the Holocaust are germane to this account since that historic atrocity largely governed how and when the state of Israel was formed in 1948. After the passage of generations, the scars of the Holocaust are still acutely visible on the Israeli people in all sorts of ways.

One of my most vivid memories is of a meeting our tour group had with a Holocaust survivor called Hannah (Goslar) Pick. She was a childhood friend of Anne Frank, and she described their relationship, using anecdotes to bring to life the iconic diarist. Unlike Anne, Hannah survived the Holocaust, but like Anne, she descended from a father who suffered the supreme Nazi obscenity. Having defended his fatherland in the Great War on the Russian front, Hans Goslar was arrested and allowed to die of disease in the Bergen-Belsen concentration camp.[5]

At the time of my 2010 visit, the Israel Philharmonic Orchestra was boycotting Richard Wagner's music. Wagner was a sulfurous anti-Semite, and he was Hitler's favorite composer. This boycott was lifted in 2012, before my second visit in 2014. Yet even now, Wagner is a painful topic, and performances of his music always generate controversy in Israel.

The Yad Vashem Holocaust Museum in Jerusalem was very moving. Its organization is different from that of the Washington, DC, museum.

One walks through a twisting back-and-forth path to see episodic exhibits, rather than a chronological walkthrough of Holocaust history. The children's exhibit is evocative; one walks through a dark building while hearing the names of murdered children.

Our group toured the obligatory biblical sites. These were mildly interesting to me, more from a historical standpoint than a religious one. Not being overly spiritual, I was not overawed by walking where Jesus had allegedly been.

We were shown a free and prosperous society, but underneath the surface lurks the Palestinian issue—the Arabs who were displaced from Palestinian areas to make way for Jewish settlements. This occurred on a massive scale in the 1940s in Israel proper and later—since the Six-Day War in 1967—in the West Bank areas conquered from Jordan. The Palestinians have a legitimate complaint about their treatment by the Israelis: they were thrown summarily out of their homes to fend for themselves where they could find room. The neighboring Arab countries, while doing little enough to help the Palestinians, threatened for decades to drive the Jews into the Mediterranean. Thus, the Arab leaders exploited local hatred of the other—the Jews—to maintain the legitimacy of their own corrupt dictatorships. Naturally, this sea of hostility surrounding Israel has for generations kept the Israelis on edge about another Holocaust. Riding our tour bus around Israel and the West Bank, we passed innumerable checkpoints and many concrete walls. I never witnessed any firefights, but I read about plenty of them.

Today there is much discrimination against Palestinians by Israelis. On one occasion, I asked a Palestinian about the program for establishment of autonomous Palestinian villages in the West Bank, in which endeavor he had been active. These villages are officially intended to give Palestinians some control over their own lives. He informed us that while Palestinians in theory were allowed to go through a paper trail to establish self-governing villages, in actual fact, no village had ever been allowed to complete the paperwork to get a charter. Other discrimination problems are cited by Freedom House[6] in its critical assessment of the state of Israel's democracy. By this shortsighted discrimination, the Israelis are passing up a great opportunity to nurture a group of Palestinians with the experience of life under a free, law-based system.

I believe the growing influence of the ultraorthodox Jews in the government and in society at large not only feeds the discrimination against Palestinians but also poses a threat to Israeli openness. Before our 2014 visit, Prime Minister Netanyahu had reached a compromise with the Palestinians about the Temple Mount. Part of this compromise was that Jews could pray at the West Wall but not inside the temple. This temple worship restriction has since been lifted, but at the time of our visit, the ban was a sore spot with the extreme orthodox Jewish faction. A group of them were confronting the Israeli police as we were waiting in line to visit the temple. The idea of the orthodox was to overturn this ban by physically forcing their way into the temple. We were kept waiting in the sun for about an hour and a half as the confrontation dragged on. When we were finally let in, Frances was caught in the middle of a physical wrestling match between the police and the orthodox but escaped harm. These orthodox insurgents clearly demonstrated a willingness to impose their values by force on others; and the failure of the Israeli police to deal immediately and firmly with them caused me concern that such ideologically extreme lawbreakers, treated so kindly, could damage Israeli rule of law and democracy.

But while the Israelis have been far from sin-free, I observed signs that the Palestinians had a hand in their own plight. The Palestinian governments have used their people wretchedly, both in the West Bank and in the Gaza Strip. Yasser Arafat passed up the opportunity of a century to lead his nation into modernity and thus gain a name as a great liberator of his people. Instead, he chose to be yet another in the dreary series of corrupt Arab looter-dictators who use uprisings against Israel as a tool to legitimate their own gangsterism, and his successors have followed his lead. Their goal is not to provide for the Palestinian people but to maintain their power and increase their wealth by looting public resources. They buy the loyalty of powerful groups and families in a classic instance of kinship-based governance. The ordinary people are shamelessly exploited and kept in their place by police brutality, and they know it.[7] This mess does everything to discourage investment and business activity and economic prosperity in the Palestinian areas. The massive corruption hurts the Palestinians in the eyes of Westerners who might otherwise be more inclined to assist the Palestinians in obtaining better treatment from the Israelis.

All of this misbehavior has augmented individual hatred by Israelis and Palestinians, instances of which Frances and I witnessed on our visits. As our plane came in for a landing at Ben Gurion Airport in Tel Aviv, I was treated to a wholly unsolicited but heartfelt five-minute tirade on the evils of Palestinians by my seatmate, a young Israeli woman. Later on, denied entrance to a Palestinian village in the West Bank because of unrest there, we instead had a Palestinian woman from the village board our bus and talk to us. She could not conceal her fury as she listed the crimes of Jewish settlers in the West Bank. Our two guides consisted of an Israeli and a Palestinian, who were supposed to give us hope by getting along with each other. Usually, they did, but occasional sparks flew. We attended a discussion staged by the Bereaved Families Forum, which furnished a Palestinian and an Israeli who had each lost a child to the violence. This forum, along with individual activists, is trying to build bridges. But the majority on both sides seem to be satisfied with apartheid and frozen hatreds: the Israeli right wing has kept power in the government for many years by whipping up nationalism, and Hamas in the Gaza Strip never seems to lose its followers. The leadership of each side takes a maximalist attitude toward the other in order to maintain its standing with its base of support. Often, the separation is enforced by the police, as when Palestinian policemen arrested four Palestinians for having a kaffeeklatsch with a group of West Bank Israelis in 2014, just before our 2014 trip to Israel.

There is much more to Israel than the Holocaust and the Palestinian conflict, of course. Israel is a technological powerhouse in the region, and she gets a large part of her water by desalinating Mediterranean Sea water. Israel is also a major supplier of citrus fruits to Europe. Last but not least, Israel is a major Western ally in the area—a supplier of intelligence and military power alike. It would be a giant world tragedy for Israel to descend into authoritarian rule, based on national security concerns or based on strict interpretation of Judaic law. This would damage Israel as a beacon for already rare liberal values in the Middle

East, a refuge for persecuted minorities from elsewhere in the region, and a center for technological innovation and social tolerance. Too much despotism scars that part of the world already!

The tragedy of the Israeli-Palestinian conflict is twofold. The tragedy of the Israelis is the shadow of the Holocaust, in which six million Jews—about a third of the world's Jewish population—perished. This stark history prevents Israelis from trusting Palestinians to work in good faith toward a solution to their conflict. They must preserve the Jewish character—and the Jewish majority—of Israel in order to provide a sanctuary that guarantees the prevention of another Holocaust. The tragedy of the Palestinians, in addition to their continued second-class citizenship and the loss of their homes, is that they have become far too conditioned to corrupt and chaotic government, and they possess far too little personal liberty, as a result of the centuries-long tutelage by their Ottoman Turkish overlords. Unfortunately, the behavior of the Israeli settlers in the West Bank—pushing Palestinians out of the way to make room for new settlements, as well as other demeaning actions—offers scanty enough education to the Palestinians in the ways of open and inclusive government. These two tragedies feed into each other, greatly impeding the way forward. The two problems must be solved together in order for a peace process to work. It will be a long, hard slog, even in the case of serious and imaginative peace processes. But the alternative is more of the same lackadaisical, bad-faith so-called negotiations punctuated by blatant discrimination on one hand, sporadic violence on the other, and occasional full-scale war. Unfortunately, I see this alternative as by far the more likely future. As was the case in the American South after the Civil War (see chapter 10), only the passage of many generations and the gradual dimming of popular passions will lead to a real peace.

Relations with Egypt and Jordan are more benign than in the past; that war threat has greatly receded. Israel and Jordan are now cooperating in an effort to restore the Jordan River and the Dead Sea, both tragically withered by excessive water diversion. During my 2011 visit, I had to get my Israeli passport stamp on a detachable piece of paper to hide from Arab neighbors, but in 2014, we could get a regular passport stamp and uneventfully cross into Jordan to see the magnificent Petra temple and monastery. The Jordanians were no longer concerned lest the accursed soil of Israel contaminate their fair land from our shoe soles! That tomfoolery was reserved for our trip into the Caucasus in 2013.

The South Caucasus consists of three countries: Georgia, in the north, lies east to west across the northern borders of western Azerbaijan in the east and Armenia in the west, forming a rough Greek letter π. Eastern Azerbaijan borders Russia in the north. To the southwest of Armenia is the Azerbaijani district of Naxcivan, bordering Iran and Turkey, which we did not visit.

During the 1990s, while the Soviet Union was unraveling, Armenia and Azerbaijan came to blows over a small mountainous Armenian enclave within Azerbaijan called Nagorno-Karabakh (a part-Russian, part-Azeri name meaning "Mountainous Black Garden"). Stalin had set up the enclave to avoid excessive conflict in a region populated by Armenians but surrounded by Azerbaijanis. In 1988, the Armenians in that area voted to secede from Azerbaijan and unify with Armenia. Azerbaijan responded militarily; both sides conducted mutual ethnic-cleansing operations; and after several years of war, Armenia ended up holding Nagorno-Karabakh and a good chunk of Azerbaijani territory surrounding it. The Armenians dubbed the area the Republic of Artsakh and assumed tutelage over it, but no UN member state, including Armenia, has ever diplomatically recognized it. Russia intervened to stop the hostilities and subsequently stationed so-called peacekeeper troops in Armenia. Armenia and Azerbaijan remained locked in a state of cold war over the Armenian occupation of the areas. Military hostilities flared up again in 2020, several years after our trip, when Azerbaijan regained some of the territory previously lost to Armenia— in the process demonstrating the limits to the control Russia has over the region. Russia was able to restore peace after a time, based on new cease-fire lines, and still maintains troops in Armenia. But there is much bitterness among the Armenian public over the war's outcome. This bitterness is probably not assuaged by the presence of an Azerbaijani War Park in Baku, wherein are displayed arrays of helmets captured from Armenian combat dead in 2020 and captured Armenian military equipment manned by dummies representing Armenian soldiers.[8] This little-noted frozen war has many parallels to the Palestinian-Israeli conflict.

This geography and history dictated our itinerary through the three countries. We could not cross the heavily militarized border between Azerbaijan and Armenia, of course; we had to go north through Georgia to travel between Azerbaijan and Armenia. So Georgia had to be the second of the three countries we visited. Azerbaijan had to be the first; if we started in Armenia and crossed over through Georgia into Azerbaijan, there was risk the Azerbaijani authorities would accuse us of having previously planted our shoes in Armenian-occupied Nagorno-Karabakh. Subsequent crossing onto Azerbaijan would thus contaminate Azerbaijani soil with cursed earth from that Armenian-blighted place. Accused of this trespass, we would not have been allowed into Azerbaijan, regardless of how well prepared our papers were. Thus, the journey had to start with Azerbaijan, followed by a northern loop through Georgia and then south into Armenia.

Frances, my soul mate, was a sensation all through the South Caucasus. It wasn't hostility; it was just the intense curiosity of people who had never before encountered an African American. They crowded around her as if she were an icon, and some were eager to have her pose with them for photographs. Hopefully the novel experience of contact with her afforded the people we visited a bit of broadening; such broadening is of great benefit to every individual and to the human species in general but particularly in the Caucasus and the Middle East.

We were warned never to discuss Armenia with our Azerbaijani guide. But he brought up the subject himself, and sure enough, he was plenty bitter about the situation in the west of his country. He was immensely proud of the fact that of the three South Caucasus countries, only Azerbaijan was free of Russian military forces. We spent most of our Azerbaijan time in Baku, on the Caspian Sea, where we were allowed to enter a mosque (in stocking feet). Oil wells populated the sea off the shore of Baku, and they are said to be a major source of Azerbaijan's national wealth.

North we went into Georgia, where scars of a different nature were apparent. In 2008, Georgia and Russia had come to blows over alleged Georgian persecution of the natives of South Ossetia and Abkhazia.

Russia occupied large parts of Georgia. At that point, the European Union and the United States intervened to lean on Russia to withdraw from Georgia proper to the borders of South Ossetia and Abkhazia, which have since remained under Russian occupation. That too is now a frozen conflict. George W. Bush, the US president who played a role in ending the hostilities with Russia and oversaw the distribution of aid to Georgia after the conflict, is revered in Georgia; a major boulevard in Tbilisi is named after him, and billboards portraying him were plentiful during our visit.

Also revered is Georgia's native son Josef Stalin, who became dictator of the Soviet Union during the first part of the twentieth century. We visited his childhood hovel in Gori, his personal railway car, and the Stalin Museum.

Things got ugly during one of our afternoons in Tbilisi. A gay pride march of some size was scheduled for that time. Since there is a surfeit of antigay feeling in the Caucasus, an equally large counterprotest materialized, and things got out of hand in front of our hotel. Since we were out on a walking tour with our guide early that afternoon, we missed out on the first part of the melee, but later in the afternoon, as we reached our hotel, we witnessed some confrontations—not much violence but plenty of yelling. About four hundred were injured over the afternoon—mostly police officers since they had been ordered to go easy on all demonstrators. As we were approaching our hotel, an elderly woman expressed hostility to us as Americans, but nothing rough occurred.

Upon crossing into Armenia, I was struck by the poverty of the countryside. Yerevan, the capital city, seemed to be prosperous enough, but in the mountains surrounding it, hovels predominated. An earthquake had devastated the region north of Yerevan in 1988, and after twenty-five years, not much rebuilding had taken place. The story from our tour guide was that Mikhail Gorbachev had visited the area in an attempt to find out how best to aid the people and the rebuilding efforts—in 1988, the Soviet Union was still a going concern, and Azerbaijan and Armenia had not yet slugged it out over Nagorno-Karabakh. From their misery and deprivation amid the rubble, the

Armenians cried out, "Make those awful Azerbaijanis give us back our sacred territory of Nagorno-Karabakh!" Gorbachev gave up and left.

Besides the chronic quarrel over Nagorno-Karabakh, some of the Armenians' hostility to Azerbaijan stems from religious differences (the Armenians are Orthodox Christians, and the Azerbaijanis are Muslims like the Turks) and from the fact that the Azeri language is closely related to the Turkish tongue. All of this makes the Azerbaijanis appear as new Turks to the Armenians.

The genocide perpetrated by the Turks against the Armenians in 1915 casts a shadow over the entire country, much as the Holocaust is always at the back of Israeli minds. A giant memorial to about a million Armenians—the great majority of the Armenians then living in the Ottoman Empire—resides in Yerevan, and we were allowed a (much-too-short) time period to visit it. Relations between Armenia and Turkey are strained as a result of this legacy. This Armenian Holocaust has been much muted in world literature compared to the Jewish Holocaust. I suspect the publicity of the Jewish Holocaust stems from the more open admission of guilt by the Germans. The Germans, stripped of hot-eyed nationalism by the occupying Allied powers and blessed by the passing of the German perpetrators and the arrival of younger Germans endued with more personal liberty by a free society, owned their crimes much more easily than did the Turks. The Turks, ruled through time with varying degrees of authoritarian nationalism, never have fully admitted either their involvement in crimes against the Armenians or the extent of the massacre. In the United States, the story of the Armenian genocide was further muffled for decades by ignoble power politics: the Turks were a Cold War ally against the Soviet Union. A desire to maintain the goodwill of this ally discouraged memorializing of the Armenians in the United States. But now, with the changing of the geopolitical order in Europe, an Armenian Holocaust Museum is permissible and is proposed for Washington, DC, in the near future. We can leave our appeasement policy behind.

The deserts of the Middle East and the mountains of the Caucasus were beautiful places to travel. But the plague of ethnic awareness causes much more human devastation than its exhilaration is worth! I had hoped that we Americans and the Europeans at least had learned from our sad experiences of the nineteenth and twentieth centuries. Unfortunately, there are plenty of people everywhere who decline to be enlightened. When will everybody grow up?

My travels in the Pacific region have left me impressed with the enterprises of the Polynesians, who colonized a large patch of the central Pacific Ocean between about five thousand and one thousand years ago—the dates are not firmly established. DNA studies trace their origin to Taiwan, through the Malaysian Archipelago and across the Pacific from west to east. The farthest outposts of their empire were Hawaii in the north, Easter Island in the east, and New Zealand in the southwest. They even landed on the west coast of South America. Along with the Vikings in the North Atlantic Ocean, the Polynesians built one of the great medieval maritime empires.

There is controversy over whether the Polynesian empire died as a result of overexploitation and killing of the ecosystems they occupied, especially Easter Island and New Zealand, or whether the coming of Europeans caused the collapse of their empire. Possibly, a combination of these and other factors ended the Polynesian glory days. We found out that the Polynesians were responsible for the extinction of the moa in New Zealand and the Easter Island palm forests (as well as the impressive construction of the famous *moai*, the huge, woebegone busts of statues we visited on Easter Island, known as Rapa Nui to the Polynesians). My guides told me that late in their empire-building activity, the Polynesians (known as Maori in New Zealand) first landed in New Zealand and found an immense population of moas—flightless birds of several species ranging from a couple of feet to ten feet in height and up to a quarter ton in weight. Upon this discovery, they decided, in typical short-term human thinking, not to bring along their usual complement of chickens, dogs, and pigs. After all, there was an infinite supply of food right there in New Zealand; why trouble to bring along additional livestock? Unfortunately, the moas were a slow-breeding species tame from lack of human experience and easy to hunt. Their overhunting to extinction left the Maori with rodents as a less-than-adequate protein source supplemented later, perhaps, with each other. Whatever their reputation for past industriousness and ferocity, all the

Polynesians I met in Hawaii, Easter Island, and New Zealand were easygoing and good-natured.

The Polynesians never made it to Australia; the winds and currents did not allow them to travel in that direction with their technology. The Australian aborigines are of South Asian descent. DNA studies have them migrating from Ceylon, off the coast of India, to Australia via land bridges that connected all these places when sea level was much lower. Any water channels along the way would have been easily crossed. These aborigines differ markedly from the Polynesians in appearance and culture. Frances and I got to experience both folkways on our Australia and New Zealand excursion.

I was grateful we got the opportunity to tour the Great Barrier Reef off the northeast coast of Australia. This magnificent array of fish and coral is one of nature's great wonders and a wonder that may well cease to exist beyond the twenty-first century. This ecosystem is being punished by climate change, which is causing ocean warming and ocean acidification. Future generations may see only piles of calcium carbonate unless more action is taken than humans normally take on problems like this.

My East Asian travels acquainted me with another tormented part of the world—a place where I might have become a veteran given a different life path! Throughout much of the nineteenth and twentieth centuries, Vietnam, Laos, and Cambodia were misgoverned by the French, who extracted farm products—notably tea and coffee—from plantations worked by locals. Thailand (otherwise known as Siam) was allowed (more or less) independence, while Britain colonized Myanmar (otherwise known as Burma), partly to keep an eye on the French and partly to grow foodstuffs for the home country. The Cambodians and the Burmese originate from the Indian subcontinent (indeed, Myanmar could almost be called part of South Asia since it borders India and Bangladesh); the other groups originated in various parts of China. The Burmese and Cambodians are darker-skinned than the inhabitants of Vietnam, Thailand, Laos, and China, and their facial features are different. Ethnic friction is a daily fact of life there. The reluctance of the European powers to relinquish their empires in that part of the world and the American fear of world Communism led to huge misunderstandings and military conflict—including the Vietnamese wars against French and Americans—lasting for decades. This conflict had died down by the times I visited, but the scars were readily visible.

Land mines left over from the wars peppered the area, though they are being gradually cleaned up. We as a tour group were never taken on hikes into the woods, and we were told that care must be taken on such hikes to avoid explosives. Another sign, and a demonstration of the impressive resourcefulness and industriousness of the Vietnamese, is the Cu Chi Tunnel complex northwest of Ho Chi Minh City (formerly Saigon). Not only do the tunnels run through the hard sand, but they connect semiunderground mess halls, hospitals, and barracks that are less visible and less vulnerable to air strikes than are surface works. In Ho Chi Minh City, we visited a museum that was once called the Exhibition House for US and Puppet Crimes. Since the United States is now helping to defend the Vietnamese claim to their own east coast (the western shore of the South China Sea) from Chinese naval encroachment, the name of the museum has been simplified to the War Remnants Museum, and its contents depict mainly French war acts, though there are still some US-related exhibitions. I hope they retained an honest and reasonably complete depiction of their perspective on the American war. It would be a shame for them to soft-pedal that part of their history in order to placate an ally, as did the US government for so long regarding the Armenians in order to placate Turkey.

Another tragedy was brought to my attention during my Vietnam trip. Our guide greatly admired Ho Chi Minh, the Vietnamese Communist leader, whose biography was presented at several points on our trip. I knew enough of Ho Chi Minh's story to know why our guide would admire him, even though I have heavy reservations about Ho Chi Minh's contributions to his country and to history, given the tyrannical nature of his government. Nevertheless, while I despised the utopian Communist ideology he claimed as part of his fighting purpose, I believe his relationship with the United States was a tragedy—born of American ignorance and French arrogance.

During the Second World War, the United States supported Ho Chi Minh's war efforts against the Vichy French colonizers and, of course, against the Japanese occupiers. At the end of that conflict,

Ho Chi Minh asked the United States to support an independent Vietnam, citing the Atlantic Charter as a blueprint.[9] President Truman never responded; the Americans had previously received word from on high—that is, from Charles de Gaulle, the leader of the Provisional French Government. De Gaulle, in an epic display of hyperbole and chutzpah, had met with the US ambassador to France to protest the US denial of help in reasserting French colonial rule in Indochina, citing the Russian menace in Europe.[10] His threat was obvious, even if posed with Gallic indirectness. We were persuaded, if persuasion was needed. The American leaders at the time, since they were de Gaulle's contemporaries, doubtless saw the world through his imperial European eyes and could not think outside the box and bury the Victorian era finally and forever. Abhorrence of Russia and Communism, which heightened American susceptibility to French blackmail, turned the Americans away from Ho Chi Minh. Racism no doubt played a part; since the French looked more like us than did the Vietnamese, they must have been viewed as more worthy of our consideration.[11]

More was the pity, since Ho Chi Minh admired Americans, particularly George Washington, whom Ho Chi Minh sought to emulate during his struggles with Western colonialists. But he set up a despotic government utterly at odds with Washington's experiment, and he was busily slaughtering non-Communist Vietnamese leaders at the time he made his request of the United States. Like most Vietnamese nationalists, he coveted Cambodia and Laos. All this made him much less sympathetic than he might have been. But according to both my guides for my trip to Vietnam and my Vietnamese lab partner at Montana State University (see chapter 5), his primary passion was always an independent and self-governing Vietnam, not an ideology imported from Russia and China. However, we brushed the Vietnamese aside and took the reactionary Charles de Gaulle line, supporting French cardiopulmonary resuscitation efforts on their dead empire until the French were routed from northern Vietnam in 1954 and then taking over the full effort from them after that. "Containing Communism," this policy was called, and for pigheaded detachment from facts, it was nearly matchless! The rest is history, which might have been much different and less bloody. I know that counterfactual history is risky (e.g., Ho Chi Minh might have broken up our friendship by continuing to kill his rivals or making moves to dominate his neighbors, even as we were aiding him). But prickly ally though he would have been, I believe that helping Ho Chi Minh would have helped us; we might have had a cordial relationship with Vietnam from the outset and, in the process, perhaps gained enough leverage over Ho Chi Minh to moderate his misbehavior. It is possible the Vietnamese dictatorship might have been diluted, and Vietnamese military adventurism diminished, if the Americans, rather than the Russians and the Chinese, had midwifed and tutored the Vietnamese nation. If all that had failed, at least we would have made the effort, and the results could not possibly have turned out worse than they actually did.[12]

Ho Chi Minh's last wish, according to our guide, was to be cremated and have his ashes scattered along Vietnam from the Chinese border to the Gulf of Thailand. Instead, the Communist ideologues who succeeded him mummified him and set him up on display in a glass case for leftist worshippers to ogle, like Lenin in Russia and Mao in China. I declined the opportunity to join a queue and look in on Ho Chi Minh; this tacky display was a gross violation of his wishes. The Vietnamese should cremate that mummy and scatter the ashes, as he specified.

The catfish-farming industry and the Ha Long Bay fishing villages and grocery stores floating on platforms, which kept us supplied during our cruise there, attest to an industrious and resourceful people. The many-times-rebuilt Long Bien Bridge over the Red River near Hanoi provides additional evidence of the strong Vietnamese work ethic. US bombers repeatedly leveled this bridge, and the Vietnamese kept rebuilding it with timber, stones, or whatever was available. When I crossed the bridge, I noticed it consisted of several segments, each constructed of a different building material. Sadly, there were poor lost souls in the riverbed, visible from the bridge—Vietnamese war veterans who had fought for the Americans and South Vietnam. They were tolerated to the extent they could pick out a miserable existence in the Red River bottom from whatever garbage was available, but that was the extent of their rights.

Hanoi is clogged by myriads of half-maintained motorbikes whose drivers mostly regard traffic signs and signals as suggestions rather than mandates. The motorbikes swarm just like pedestrians in a mall; they don't jostle each other, and they simply go around large vehicles like our bus, tapping their horns to let others know of their presence. The Vietnamese lack the American complex about rights and personal space that leads to much misunderstanding and tempestuousness in heavy American traffic streams.

In Cambodia, there was a really hideous scar: the remnants of the killing apparatus of the Khmer Rouge regime, which lasted from 1975 to 1979. This regime was finally ousted in 1979 by a Vietnamese invasion—provoked not by Khmer Rouge brutality but by repeated Khmer Rouge military jabbing of the Vietnamese along their border. The Vietnamese installed a puppet regime in Phnom Penh and fought their own Vietnam War—a remarkable reprise of the American effort in Vietnam itself. Both sides in both wars were aided by great powers, and Vietnam behaved with even less finesse in Cambodia, if possible, than the United States in Vietnam. Both supposed liberators were forced to withdraw, leaving behind embittered governments and populaces. Cambodia now tends to side with China in its quarrels with Vietnam, including ownership of the South China Sea (Vietnam's east coast). This is a cheap enough stand for Cambodia, which does not border the South China Sea.

On our 2010 trip, we got a tour of the Tuol Sleng Genocide Museum in Phnom Penh—a converted high school where people were tortured and murdered. Of twenty thousand people who went into the prison, seven survived. Shackles and iron beds adorn the rooms, and thousands of pictures of victims line the walls. We visited the Choeung Ek killing fields, where prisoners were transported to have their throats slit with palm fronds and then be buried in mass graves. This is the best known of about two hundred Khmer Rouge killing sites in Cambodia; about seventeen thousand people were murdered at Choeung Ek. Pits—the poorly filled-in sites of mass graves—and human bone fragments abound on the grounds, and the chief exhibit is a glassed-in Buddhist stupa containing about ten thousand skulls. The smell of death was still readily perceptible at Choeung Ek in 2010 after decades, and our Cambodian guide was psychologically unable to accompany us into the grounds.

Among those buried in these pits are Hout Bophana and her husband, Ly Sitha, whose story lends a personal touch to this massacre. After being raped by soldiers during Lon Nol's military dictatorship, which misruled Cambodia from 1970 to 1975, Bophana was then shunned by society for being a single mother. She was eventually married by a monk, Ly Sitha. So repelled were they by the rot of Lon Nol's regime that they imagined any change to be an improvement. Accordingly, they supported the Khmer Rouge regime. But upon the discovery of their love letters to each other, they were arrested, tortured at Tuol Sleng, and executed at Choeung Ek in 1977. Bophana was twenty-five years old. She is now regarded as a Cambodian national heroine.[13] Around two million Cambodians—about a quarter of the 1975 population—perished at the hands of Democratic Kampuchea over the period from 1975 to 1979.

For several years, the US Holocaust Memorial Museum in Washington, DC, maintained a room dedicated to victims of the Cambodian tragedy. This room contained biographies of many good people consumed by that awful machine. The museum performed a great service in calling public attention to the Cambodian massacre—in which the United States played a less-than-heroic role.[14]

Cambodia, like many Southeast Asian countries, is a dictatorship. Our guide assured us that Cambodia has a democratically elected parliament, and in a narrow sense, this is true. The ruling party, however, owns almost all the parliamentarians, allowing one or two opposition figures to sit in parliament and be noticed by foreigners and also to be massively outvoted on every issue.

The Angkor Wat Buddhist temples in Cambodia were spectacular, and much can be learned about the ancient Khmer by careful study of these temples and their surroundings. They testify to the enormous capabilities of the Cambodians in centuries past. Unfortunately, like Vienna and Prague, this priceless landmark is now overrun by tourists, whose millions of dollars help to juice the Cambodian economy and no doubt line the pockets of corrupt government officials. This tragic comedown for such a great work saddens me, but Angkor Wat is not the only great monument to be so diverted from its purpose.

Tonle Sap, the great lake in Cambodia, is an interesting geological feature. Its volume varies over the year by a couple of orders of magnitude, with its level rising about ten meters as the Mekong River floods during the monsoon season and causes the Tonle Sap River to back up into the lake—and falling when the monsoon ends, the Mekong River shrinks, and the Tonle Sap River reverses course and drains the lake. The local villagers make a living by fishing in this lake. When we were there, the dry season was in full force, and we took a motorboat through what was really only a mud channel to get from the village to the lake. Looming over us were villagers' huts on stilts about ten meters high. I noted an automobile or two parked in what would be several meters of water a few months hence.

This lake and the Mekong River are especially susceptible to the ravages of progress and climate change. Hydropower dams and drought resulting in smaller monsoons stunted the Mekong River's flow, threatening to disrupt the fragile Tonle Sap water-level cycle entirely and destroy thousands of local livelihoods. There is already alarm among the Cambodians.[15]

I concluded from my observations that the Vietnamese were more prosperous than the Cambodians. The Vietnamese had more vehicles, and every single Vietnamese hut, even in the floating villages on platforms on Ha Long Bay east of Hanoi, had the requisite color TV. Cambodian creature comforts were much scarcer, and our tour group was shepherded away from certain popular routes in Cambodia, lest we be set upon by aggressive beggars. French observers have contrasted the Vietnamese with their neighbors.[16] The Vietnamese taste for hard work probably explains much of the difference in poverty levels just cited. It definitely goes a long way toward explaining the Vietnamese victories in their wars against French and American forces.

Temples were all over the map in Myanmar, a primarily Buddhist country. Some of the temples were spectacular in their architecture, in color and design. In fact, these temples are as much a part of the East Asian landscape as cathedrals are part of the European landscape. Religious devotion constitutes one of the most profound experiences of mankind; religious monuments form some of the most spectacular architecture created by man. I have long since lost count of the number of cathedrals and temples through which our travel groups have guided me.

The Bagan city of temples was a highlight of our Myanmar excursion. We were supposed to enjoy the spectacular sunset there, but unfortunately, air quality is atrocious in Myanmar, as it is in China and northern Vietnam. Instead of setting magnificently, the sun sank gradually into a lake of coal smoke, turning redder and dimmer over a period of about half an hour before disappearing in the murk. Coal is burned abundantly in that part of the world, generating smog that is intensified in northern Vietnam by the burning of rice straw and by the aforementioned motorbikes that overcrowd the streets of Hanoi. Visibility is often no more than a few hundred meters. Any serious attack on climate change will require a revolution in the way business is conducted there. In order to be effective, any Green New Deal implemented in the United States must obviously be undertaken in conjunction with this East Asian revolution.

We saw only the pacific side of Buddhism on our trip, but unfortunately, the Burmese have been persecuting the Rohingya Muslim minority in the west-central province of Rakhine for several years. This persecution began in earnest about six months after our trip there, and it is now so severe that the US Holocaust Memorial Museum in Washington, DC, is calling the action a genocide and putting up a display depicting the atrocity. As tourists, we were not given access to that area—it probably would have been dangerous for us anyway. On our trip, our guides pointed out that while the military had at that time loosened its grip on the country, it maintained its hold on important power centers in the government. At the outset of 2021, the military staged a coup to reestablish the dictatorship. Aung San Suu Kyi, the state counsellor who had won many prizes for her opposition to the military dictatorship, was arrested and imprisoned, along with all her supporters. There is some popular unrest over this illegal act; the future is obviously cloudy.

The legacy of Aung San Suu Kyi is notably ambiguous. She had come under heavy fire from many organizations, including the Holocaust Museum, for her apparent indifference to the fate of the Rohingya. What to make of Aung San Suu Kyi is an ancient moral riddle: Should she have soft-pedaled the persecution of the Rohingya and fought to preserve what little was left of freedom and rule of law elsewhere in Myanmar, or should she have protested the massacres and expulsions of Rohingya and likely been bounced from office and perhaps imprisoned or killed, thus losing all her effectiveness? The stands she did take clearly did her no good; she was deprived of power and incarcerated regardless of her moral heft.

Upon our crossing the border from Myanmar into Thailand, the pernicious effects of racism and nationalism on the Burmese economy were obvious to me. Housing in Burmese villages consisted largely of rickety tree-limb-supported bamboo curtain walls to be annihilated by the first gale-force wind. Housing in Thailand, by contrast, was mostly what the United Nations delicately calls "permanent housing"— legitimate buildings constructed of concrete, bricks, and timber, as we know in the West. Statistics presented to us in lectures bore this out: in life expectancy, gross domestic product per person, infant mortality rates, export net worth, and more, Thailand outstripped Myanmar enormously. According to our guides' lectures, these disparities are a consequence of the xenophobic "Burma for the Burmese" philosophy promulgated by the Burmese military dictatorship. While Thailand is a dictatorship, it is open to the world for foreign trade, travel, and other international contact. International trade and intellectual broadening promote progress and prosperity; this is a lesson that some of our own Americans would do well to absorb!

My African adventures made me aware of problems regarding animal conservation, especially in the face of climate change. On safari in the southern part of Africa, we saw several types of African antelope, plus crocodiles, vervet monkeys, giraffes, hippopotamuses, rhinoceroses, zebras, baboons, painted dogs, lions, cheetahs and, most of all, elephants. It was a delightful education, but all flora and fauna were having a hard time of it since a prolonged drought (probably, though not definitely, connected with climate change) had left food and water scarce. Though Victoria Falls in Zimbabwe was just a shadow of its real self due to the drought, southern Africa is still majestically beautiful, especially around Cape Town in South Africa.

A major burden for Africa is its status until recently as a reservoir of slaves. Africa is inhospitable for modern economic activity, due to the harsh climate (which we experienced on our trip), the many endemic diseases, and the lack of arable land. For much of history, this prevented Africans from being much more than subsistence farmers and tribal warriors. In the seventeenth and eighteenth centuries, no African products were available for trade with other parts of the world, except human bodies, which were exported extensively to the Americas, the Middle East, and South Asia from the 1600s to the 1800s. The horrors of the Western Hemisphere slave trade are illustrated extensively in the National Museum of African American History and Culture in Washington, DC, as well as in many books. The physical weakness of Africa, resulting from this same history, finally led to the sordid struggle called the Scramble for Africa, which started out as nominally a crusade against slavery and ended as a brutal, pitiless carving up of the continent among rapacious colonial powers.[17]

In South Africa, we had another introduction to man's inhumanity to man. One of the highlights was the South African Apartheid Museum, which was modeled on our own US Holocaust Memorial Museum. We visited the Robbin Island prison where Nelson Mandela was held for eighteen years. In Cape Town, there was a museum depicting "colored" neighborhood life under apartheid. The sheer depravity contained in racism and white supremacy was on full display there. South Africa had willingly adopted the caste system based on skin shadings, the carefully cultivated hatreds, the economic and intellectual backwardness, the arbitrary police brutality, and the mulish imperviousness to facts that defined and dominated the American South.

Yet another instructive parallelism occurs here: one of the first steps toward South African apartheid was a deal between the British and the South African Boers struck as part of the ending of the Boer War in 1902. The status of black Africans was a sticking point in the negotiations; the British held out for some humanity toward the blacks as part of the settlement, while the Boers insisted on total subjugation. The British surrendered on this point for the sake of reconciliation, they shook hands with the Boers, and everyone agreed to throw black Africans under the bus.[18] This shabby agreement neatly recalled the shabby 1877 American Great Compromise between Republicans and

Democrats, which marked the beginning of American apartheid (see chapter 10).

All this certainly damaged the African people, though I believe it is much too facile to blame all of Africa's problems on European exploitation. Other issues supervene now that the last vestige of European colonialism—apartheid in South Africa—has been vanquished.

Our guides and many of the Africans we met deplored the governmental corruption that is such a drag on the economies of African countries. South African business owners especially were ruefully resigned but hoping for better days to come. We went through some schools and orphanages—going concerns no thanks to the governments, which want only their slice off the top. The African ethic, it seems, is that one serves one's family first, one's clan second, and one's tribe third. The general public comes in a poor fourth, if it comes in at all. This leads to a perception among African officials that the chiseling that we Westerners call *corruption* is not corruption at all; it is the essential and virtuous providing for one's family. A good father must bring home the necessaries of life, and other people's tax money is just as valid for the purpose as a warthog from the bush.[19] The idea of sharing national resources with all the country's inhabitants, including those of other tribes, is alien to most government personnel. The upshot is, among other evils, the tribal affiliations of government leaders result in a disproportionate share of resources going to one tribe or a few tribes.

The unreliability of African government officials has relegated the government bonds of South Africa, one of the most successful countries on the African continent, to nearly junk status. Zimbabwe and Zambia are in worse standing, especially Zimbabwe, which is still struggling with the legacy of the corrupt dictatorship of Robert Mugabe. These countries rely heavily for their functioning on income from tourism and on local and foreign private efforts, such as the African schools and orphanages and the NGOs combating AIDS and other diseases. The COVID-19 pandemic has greatly curtailed the tourism industry. But I get reports that the Africans themselves are still surviving and that the southern Africa drought has been broken by good rainfall, at least for now.

Adding to the problems caused by tribal identity politics are the boundaries of African countries, which were defined primarily by European colonial powers. These boundaries often include mutually hostile tribes within a country and often cut through historically tribal territories. This arrangement throws together people who do not want to belong to the same country and sunders people who do want to be together. Tensions within and among African countries are thus raised.

All of these factors leave Africa in a decidedly disadvantageous position; but I, and the African blacks and whites with whom I discussed these issues, sincerely hope for an eventual renaissance of this rich and variegated continent.

All during my travels, I have tried to adapt to local customs and devices as well as possible. But a couple of situations severely tried my broadmindedness. For one thing, I have never been able to get the hang of using chopsticks for eating. Chopsticks defeat all my efforts to be dexterous with them, despite multiple demonstrations on their use from fellow travelers. It is an epic struggle for me to get a morsel of food from a plate to my mouth using chopsticks; the morsel usually takes a detour back to the plate, to my lap, or to the tabletop. The chopsticks often end up in an absurd crossed position, and I have to reinsert them among my fingers—for whatever good that does! I typically opt for Western silverware where it is available. At one Vietnamese restaurant, though, only chopsticks were to be had. I gamely went through a meal with them, and I actually acquired some nourishment, but a large part of my meal was scattered on the tabletop around my dish, and I was unable to fish out the last remains.

My other problem abroad is Turkish toilets. The Caucasus trip provided me with my introduction to these contraptions, which consist of a basin about eighteen inches by twelve inches and about three inches deep, set into the floor. A four-inch hole resides at one end of the basin, and a water tank several feet above the basin connects to it with a pipe. Men performing number one have no problem; they can just stand and point to the basin. But the other three possible combinations are decidedly a culturally broadening experience. The idea is to place one's feet on either side of the basin and squat over it—a supremely uncomfortable undertaking. The one point in favor of Turkish toilets is that one need not sit on a toilet seat of indeterminate cleanliness.

Where only Turkish toilets are available, I can get through this ordeal, but I much prefer our Western toilets! No matter how cosmopolitan I become, chopsticks and Turkish toilets will always give me grief.

Traveling the world, with the proper goals in mind, can be an enormously rewarding experience. While my little essays about various parts of the world are not meant to convey any expertise on any area, they relate how I was able to educate myself. Traveling to learn puts my own life's adventures into proper perspective and allows me to understand that there is plenty of good, bad, and ugly all around. Even now, I am sometimes reminded of how cosseted I have been. Complaining to our Burmese guide one day about Donald Trump's authoritarian ways, I was brought up short with a simple question: "Have you ever been arrested for insulting the government?" Our guide had known real dictatorship, and I had to confess that I had not. I often wonder how this guide is faring under the new military dictatorship.

The best we can do is to contribute what we can to efforts to alleviate suffering where we see it and to publicize the pain. But however much or little we do, we must never be indifferent, airbrushing these injustices from our minds in order to concentrate on our own advantages and grievances. This inability to note what happens to us in the context of the world makes us petty and low in character, resentful, and easily manipulated by would-be tyrants.

At the same time, there is much beauty and grandeur to see. The majesty of the northern fjords and Iceland's stark loveliness, the Great Barrier Reef and rain forests in Australia, the Australian and Middle Eastern deserts, the Polynesian lagoons, Ha Long Bay in Vietnam, the beautiful scenery of South Africa, and the mountains of New Zealand and the Caucasus are all well worth visiting and treasuring in my memory. The magnificent tapestry of human history and culture is reflected in the grand cathedrals all over Europe, the temples in Asia, and the ingenuity of people all over the world in adapting to the environments in which they dwell. There is also the sheer pleasure of learning, which I find to be the chief personal reward for my travels.

Travels like mine, undertaken by more people, might make the world a little safer. There is the small consideration that many countries depend on tourist money to keep their economies afloat, but a larger issue is that people benefit from getting acquainted with other cultures. They get to know themselves better, and they become less narrow and less likely to support quarrels and wars. Greater intercultural understanding can make embarrassing microaggressions rarer. I have met hundreds of travelers over the last thirty years, and they are increasing in number as time passes. Perhaps in time, tensions around the world will decrease due in part to the traveling—let's hope anyway!

CHAPTER 12

ERA HORRIBILIS: DONALD TRUMP, COVID-19, ECONOMIC COLLAPSE, RACIAL RECKONING: STORIES MY CIVICS TEACHERS NEVER TOLD ME

Donald Trump's administration is now history, but its stench remains. The Trump era was a test and a trial for the entire world—and a nightmare for many. It was an era that starkly illustrated highs and lows of character and personal liberty—an era of the sublime and the abject, of the inspirational and the despicable. It was also a demonstration of the fact that democratic, liberty-based societies absolutely require personal liberty and good character of every participant, and it showed the danger presented to such societies by a leader who possesses not a trace of either. This administration and its present-day coterie of adherents represent to me a determined effort by the authoritarians among us to destroy our liberties by imposing a so-called pure vision of our country as a white people's society. The race-based caste system they envision is a clear indication of what we must escape and of the work still in front of us if we wish to be Americans true to our own national principles.

The dominant catastrophe of this era, and the catastrophe that exacerbated the others, was the administration of President Donald Trump. Even jaded as I was by 2016, I was shocked that someone like Donald Trump could gain the allegiance, and even adulation, of a large segment of the American population—large enough to get him elected president in 2016 and threaten the integrity of our country's institutions for four long years. By 2020, I was too shell-shocked to be shocked, but the sickness in our country was obvious: he could bully, swindle, infect our national dialogue with epic nastiness, compromise our national security around the world, destroy businesses with his xenophobic policies, and botch the response to the COVID-19 pandemic so thoroughly that thousands of businesses collapsed and hundreds of thousands of Americans died and, after all that, still persuade several tens of millions to vote for him in 2020 and support his lies and his violent attempt to stop the election certification in 2021. During my early and middle life, Trump would have been laughed out of either party had he sought a nomination, and had he somehow been nominated, he would have been cremated in the general election.

A history of these sordid years is not in the scope of this narrative, nor is a rehashing of other people's editorial opinions. We already have dozens of newly minted books and thousands of editorials from which to choose, detailing the crimes and missteps of this administration. I have read much of this literature myself, and nothing is to be gained by transcribing it.[1] Trump's spectacular cruelties and pathologies are well documented, and I need not recount these either.[2] The decades-long degeneration of the Republican Party and how it and Trump met in 2016 to form an unholy religious sect are subjects I need not reproduce.[3]

For all of its sheer awfulness, the Trump administration yielded an important set of lessons for those paying attention.

1. Liberty and Representative, Accountable Government

Immediately after the Second World War, the United States, as part of its strategy against the Soviet Union, became the spokesman for liberty and democratic government around the world. According to our Enlightenment dogma, all people around the world "yearn to breathe free," as the Statue of Liberty slogan puts it, and are willing to fight and die for liberty if only we would provide the wherewithal for the fight against the corrupt dictators who oppress so much of the world.

This dogma tripped up against snag after snag over the ensuing decades. The African nations, freed from European colonialism, promptly engaged in vicious tribal warfare, further inflamed by American and Soviet meddling. In most cases, these wars ended in tribal dictatorships. In the 1960s, the Vietnamese were notably ungrateful for our attempts to shove democracy on them (operating through a thoroughly corrupt, dictatorial South Vietnamese regime). After the collapse of the Soviet Union in 1993, this dogma gained some credibility by the relative success of Eastern Europe in adapting to democratic, libertarian norms, but even there, some shakiness was observable—notably in Poland and Hungary. Ukraine had chronic trouble from the start, and Russia and Belarus slipped back into dark despotism after a short period of anarchy. After the September 11, 2001, attack on the World Trade Center, the United States moved militarily into Afghanistan (and later Iraq) and bounced out the terrorist and robber baron governments and set about building democracy in those countries. None of this made any difference; the tribal rivalries and sniping went on as if we didn't exist. Undeterred, we gleefully watched the Arab Spring from 2010 to 2014, in which a series of corrupt Arab dictatorships were toppled. Anticipating a great green crop of democracies, we instead witnessed a crop of chronic civil wars—or, in the case of Egypt, a ridiculous, incompetent Muslim Brotherhood member, Mohammed Morsi, elevated to the presidency by the peasant vote. He was bounced out by the army after a couple of years to the cheers of the populace after he offered nothing to the Egyptian people except inept despotism. Only in Tunisia was there partial success. What a meager harvest for so much emotional and economic outlay by the United States!

But hopefully the Trump era will finally lay to rest this misleading universal-liberty dogma. The election of Donald Trump as president in 2016 exposed the seedy third-world underbelly of our own American electorate. Right here in our own country, there are people who lack the personal liberty necessary to function in a free society. A great many Americans were fully prepared to behave as wretchedly as did the Russian muzhiks in the 1990s, the Afghan villagers in the 2000s, and the Egyptian fellahin in the 2010s when freedom of thought, rule of law, and representative, accountable government were thrust upon them. Not only did many Americans vote their cultural and religious passions to elect an incompetent charlatan who went on to damage the lives of those voters,[4] but many engaged in political unrest and violence on behalf of that same charlatan. How could we, the United States of America, have put on such a lamentable banana-republic spectacle?

In the introduction, I listed the major attributes of WEIRD and kinship-based psychology,[5] and I believe that attributes of kinship-based psychology provide an explanation for the strange behavior of many of Trump's fervent base of supporters. (Note that I said "provide an explanation for," not "explain." More research would be necessary to tease out the full causes of this behavior.) For most of the time since the Second World War, they lived in communities that provided them with the highly structured environments, close interpersonal relationships, and authority figures they needed in order to cope with life. A race-based caste system, which guaranteed social status to all whites simply by virtue of their complexions, kept these people's self-esteem at healthy levels. But over the last few decades, the disintegration of these communities and the weakening of the caste system, forced by economic, demographic, and technological changes,[6] deprived these people of the stability and unearned social status they required and left them in a world that demanded much more independence and initiative than their paltry supplies of personal liberty would allow. In their agony, they cried out for a clan elder to moor and reassure them, and along came Donald Trump. These people are kinship-based—unfit for participating in a democracy—in several ways.

The most obvious obstacle to their participation in an open, liberty-living society is their intolerance toward people deemed not of their own clan (i.e., racism and other forms of bigotry). This hostility to so-called others is a hallmark of kinship-based psychology, and it contributes to their most important complaint against modern America: the increasing presence and strength of minority communities.

Second, the inability to understand or accept absolutes in truth or goodness characterizes many kinship-based Trump supporters. For them, no truth or goodness exists independent of their clan elder. I have watched interviewees state frankly that they regard Donald Trump as their North Star: whatever he says is true because he says it, and whatever he does is good because he does it. The most obvious example is their ready acceptance of Trump's Big Lie: that he won the 2020 presidential election and then was cheated of his victory by Joe Biden's trickery. This self-deception also served as a less painful alternative to the actual processing of their unpleasant reality: Trump's electoral defeat.

Third, the concept of rule of law is missing from many of these people's minds. Any law independent of, and binding on, their clan elder is unacceptable and even incomprehensible to them. According to his supporters, the clan elder is ipso facto incapable of error or sin, and the law consists solely of his desires. The most spectacular display of this mindset was their enraged reaction to the failures of Trump's efforts to reverse his 2020 election loss. That Trump could not order the election to turn out as he wished violated one of his supporters' most fundamental assumptions about their world. Unable to conceive an abstract law that compelled their clan elder to accept an unpalatable situation, they saw a voluntary, malicious *choice* by officials to deny Trump the second term to which he was divinely entitled. This supposed betrayal demanded immediate and violent revenge—leading to the riot at the US Capitol on January 6, 2021. This reaction to an election loss happens repeatedly in third-world countries among people who have not grasped the fundamentals of rule of law.

Finally, the Trump era illustrates a distinctly authoritarian mindset among Trump's base of supporters. Obedience, not independent thought and action, is their ideal—specifically, unconditional and constant obedience to their clan elder. Not unlike the Weimar Republic Germans in the 1920s and 1930s and the post-Soviet Russians in the 1990s, they create disorders while yearning for a strongman to impose a graveyard peace.

These reflections remind me of a conclusion drawn by Henrich[5] and reinforced by my own experiences: far from "yearning to breathe free," the majority of people in the world, including many in the United States, actually yearn for structure, stability, safety, and predictability. Caste systems provide these conditions, which is probably why caste systems are so ubiquitous and so durable. Castes defined life in the American South, Russia, and India for centuries. The prevalence of castes, and the exemption they bring from hard thinking, hard work, and resourcefulness, possibly plays a role in the recent worldwide decline in freedom cited by Freedom House.

For all this, it is clear to me that countries that respect democracy and rule of law and strive to inject personal liberty and good character into their domestic and foreign policies reap rewards among other countries. People really do respond well to these virtues. The United States has built up moral capital over the decades since the Second World War by striving—though not always succeeding—to govern itself in a moral way and to set an example for the rest of the world. If we make mistakes, we try to own and correct the mistakes. If we do well, we try to aid others in doing well. As a result, we have dozens of allies around the world—allies who are such because they *want* to be our allies. We have no need to maintain forces there to keep these allies friendly, so we can devote our resources to more constructive purposes. The people in these countries really care what happens to us—see their anguish when we were attacked on September 11, 2001, and when we foisted Donald Trump upon ourselves in 2016. Contrast this with Russia and China, the major bullies of the world. Who are their allies? Who would react with anguish if something happened to their leaders? Only countries they can occupy or otherwise force into alliances, countries that milk them for resources, and individuals who lack character and personal liberty.

This is why I am convinced that a second Trump term would have entailed the destruction of all of our alliances. A reelection of Trump after the damage he caused would have convinced people in other countries that Americans were content with Trump's repudiation of our allies and our national values. Accordingly, those allies would have repudiated us in turn, and world order would have disintegrated, whatever the fate of democracy and rule of law in this country.

2. Personal Reflections on Trump's Administration

One salutary effect of the Trump era was that I learned much about the functioning of government that I should have learned in my high school civics class taught by Mr. Collins and at Boys State (see chapter 4). At that time, I was too unfocused and immature to pick up as much as I might have. As Trump's dangerous antics compelled me to watch in nervous horror, I absorbed fascinating lore about legislative procedure and the structures and processes of government during that time.

During the Trump era, I felt compelled to be there for my country and to put myself at its service to an unprecedented degree. My first action taken in regard to opposing Trump and the damage he caused was dropping out of the Republican Party, of which I had been a member for all my adult life up to 2016. It was exquisitely painful to be forced to reregister, but the party of Abraham Lincoln, Theodore Roosevelt, Dwight Eisenhower, Barry Goldwater, William F. Buckley, Ronald Reagan, the Bushes, John McCain, and Mitt Romney had ceased to exist. It had been twisted into something wholly different by the cult worshippers who climaxed a decades-long Republican devolution by taking over the party under Donald Trump's aegis. By 2016, the party was ripe for this usurpation; all character, personal liberty, policy, governing philosophy, solutions to problems, and moral gravitas had been banished. The conservative virtues of initiative, self-reliance, industriousness, and honesty had been supplanted by surly bigotry, ideological extremism, conspiracy theories, and hypocrisy. The Republican Party had left me stranded outside.

I voted in all elections and made sure my ballot was properly processed, and I became active in the local Democratic Party in Marlton. I called my congressional representatives about pending issues, made contributions to organizations that committed themselves to countering Trump, put up lawn signs warning people away from Trump, and sent emails to friends and relatives, exhorting them to take note of Trump's evils. I spent several hours phone-banking voters to urge people to vote and even got a few letters to the editors of newspapers published.

But my most important activity was my effort to resist the rampant disinformation and situational ethics that characterized the Trump era and to try to help others resist. With all the lies floating in the ether, what is truth, what is goodness, and where do they lie? The answer is important for those who wish to survive an era like the Trump incumbency with their moral and epistemological compasses intact. In my opinion, the swamp of lies and amorality can be avoided by possession of a curious and resourceful mind and a healthy dose of personal liberty. Through discipline and training, such a mind can become competent in evaluating sources of information and moral instruction. A robust self-awareness allows the individual access to his own biases, psychological weaknesses, and knowledge deficiencies, enabling him to attempt to correct for these. Personal liberty, and the self-esteem that comes with it, endows the individual with confidence in the conclusions he draws from his studies and self-assurance in the presence of ambiguity and nuance.

Having never been particularly persuasive, I never argued points with others in one-on-one engagements. My approach to changing people's minds has always been to impart information for them to digest. But my early life experiences made it clear to me that most people do not want information; they want affirmation. In light of this, I opted out of this activity, leaving it to others who were more practiced at persuading.

The events of the Trump era compelled me to revisit my position on free speech. I had always been a full-throated First Amendment fundamentalist opposed to any hint of censorship. But lies and propaganda on social media brainwashed millions of isolated, vulnerable, and weak people.[7] This brainwashing led to the 2017 Charlottesville, Virginia, hate march; the 2020 El Paso massacre; and other spectacular hate crimes during Trump's tenure, culminating in the sacking of the US Capitol in 2021. The weaknesses in my position became obvious; untrammeled social media output could be hazardous. Some sort of media regulation is necessary for the maintenance of public safety and for the integrity of our politics. Precision and vigilance would be necessary in crafting legal limits to free speech.

Like all despots before him, Trump could not have inflicted any damage without the willing complicity of millions of enablers and followers. I was often startled at the intensity of my own antipathy toward Trump and his supporters. No other president, and no other cohort of voters, had aroused remotely similar feelings in me, and I had found much to fault in past presidents. I had good friends who supported George W. Bush and Jimmy Carter, for instance. I didn't care much for those presidents, but I never let my differences with their adherents get in the way of our relationships. Some past presidents had problems with character, but most were basically decent human beings, and all of them loved their country and wished to serve it to the best of their abilities. Not so Trump; in sheer self-absorption, in unfitness for office, in poverty of legacy, and in peril presented to our country, Trump was, in a qualitative sense, in a class by himself. Differing outlooks on his administration were not variations in opinion but variations in quality of character. To me, an honest discussion of whether Trump did a good job as president is no more possible than an honest discussion of whether slavery was beneficial to blacks or whether the Holocaust was a good thing. There is one and only one correct answer to those questions: no. These are questions to be answered without nuance or qualification; they are about right and wrong, up and down, good and evil. I speak for myself alone, but perhaps my sentiments were shared widely enough to account for much of the American political polarization so frequently deplored in our news media.

3. Other Crises

A quartet of calamities befell the United States during the last year of Trump's term—calamities that removed all doubt as to his unfitness for office: the COVID-19 pandemic, economic collapse, racial unrest, and the attempted coup in Washington, DC, on January 6, 2021.

The first calamity, the COVID-19 pandemic, should have been Trump's opportunity to redeem his low standing by showing brains and stamina and taking the helm of the effort to combat this disease. But he not only did nothing substantive in planning or action to help to tamp down this contagion; he made it much worse. If he had set an example by wearing a mask, keeping physically distanced from other people, and urging others to do the same, his followers would certainly have obeyed him, and hundreds of thousands of lives would have been saved. Instead, he denounced these safety measures as tyranny and urged his followers to "liberate" themselves from "despotic" state and local officials who tried to mandate such commonsense measures. He tried to silence scientists who warned that the pandemic was worsening, creating confusion among the public about how bad the disease actually was.

The COVID-19 pandemic gave rise to a second calamity—economic collapse—because people could not work together in a workplace and could no longer patronize restaurants, theaters, sporting events, and other public places without running the risk of infecting one another. Businesses closed, and jobs were lost. Trump never went to Congress to push for aid to stressed people and businesses, nor did he propose a plan for handling the economic fallout from the pandemic; he just sat and let Congress run itself and come up with desultory and reluctant measures.

But the COVID-19 pandemic and the economic slowdown did have one salutary effect: like a parent taking away a schoolchild's playthings and forcibly directing his attention to what was important, these crises, by removing diversions, such as everyday work, entertainment activities, and little parties and little quarrels, left the public with little to do but watch television. Television then focused their attention on a third calamity: a series of spectacularly hideous murders and maimings of African Americans, Asian Americans, and others. The cold-blooded killings of George Floyd, Breonna Taylor, and Ahmaud Arbery riveted the public's attention and sensitized them to later atrocities. Police and civilian violence against blacks and other minorities is an old, thousand-times-told American story. But the pandemic and the economic paralysis forced the public to focus on these crimes, turning them into widely recognized injustices. Street protests ensued, and support rose as never before for redress of ancient wrongs visited on nonwhite Americans.

After Trump's well-earned defeat at the hands of Joe Biden in November 2020, Trump fired up his cult followers with his Big Lie. On January 6, 2021, a date that will live alongside September 11, 2001, in historic infamy, a large mob of Trump supporters attacked the Capitol Building in a riot that killed five people, including a police officer, and injured dozens. This mob intended to execute officials they deemed guilty of stealing the 2020 presidential election from Donald Trump and to use force and violence to reinstate Trump as president. This fourth calamity was watched all around the world and watched with satisfaction by Trump, who did nothing to contain the violence. This insurrection put an appropriate exclamation point at the end of the Trump presidency. But still, while Donald Trump was the indispensable actor, I don't blame him exclusively for this riot. The commentators rightly pointed out that he agitated the mob, but the mob members were ready to be radicalized. Those who listened to Trump's lies are just as culpable for the mayhem as he is.

These four crises did not touch me personally, since I had retired a few years before. As to COVID-19, its main effect on my life was to put a hold on my world travels for a couple of years. I resolved to avoid being part of the COVID-19 problem. I always wore a mask inside public buildings, and I was always careful to maintain distance from other people. I got my vaccinations when my number was called. Since my need for social gatherings is rather spare, I felt little dislocation as a result of my physical isolation, with Frances's company and long telephone talks with my adopted daughter Gwen (see chapter 1) and others in my family satisfying my social requirements.

Since I had familiarized myself with African American history, the racial-injustice protests did not teach me much that I did not already know, but they brought the issue into sharper focus for me.

4. Heroes and Villains

An era like the Trump age naturally delineates people's character in vivid detail. In smoother times, people of deficient character and personal liberty can appear as worthy as their betters, since no real tests are being administered. But not so in the Trump era; if one was disgraceful, it showed. If one was sublime, it showed. The heroes who served our country well during these crises deserve to be remembered and emulated. The villains who disgraced and damaged our country should be rebuked. I have added a few dishonorable mentions for those who did not make a bad situation worse but declined to make it better.

Heroes: African American voters, especially women. These voters got Joe Biden's nomination back on the road after white voters tried to drive it into the ditch. These and other minority voters then overruled white voters in the general election and elected Joe Biden. I credit black voters with saving our country.

Heroes: Three million white male voters who defected from Trump in 2016 to Biden in 2020.[8] This was a large fraction of Biden's popular-vote-victory margin. White men were the only gender and ethnic cohort who voted at a lower percentage for Trump in 2020 than in 2016. While 58 percent of them still voted for Trump in 2020—hardly a heroic portion—the 5 percent drop was significant since it happened with such a large part of the electorate. Much is made of the greater absolute number of minority voters turning out in 2020 to give Biden the edge, but I believe that if these three million unsung heroes had not crossed over, Biden's electoral college prospects would have been much shakier.

Villain: Donald Trump himself. Enough is said elsewhere.

Villains: Trump's base of cult supporters. These sad people are the clan members described above, who loved Donald Trump because he provided them with relief from their personal hells. They intimidated Republican lawmakers by supporting Trump-inspired primary challengers; believed and spread Trump's lies; attacked the American Capitol on January 6, 2021; attacked minority American citizens; and committed numerous other crimes on Trump's behalf during his presidency.

Dishonorable mentions: The mainstream, noncult 2020 Trump voters. Since these voters did not bring about four more years of a Donald Trump presidency, they are not villains. But in considering how to cast their votes, they could have and should have taken note of the damage Donald Trump had already inflicted our country. Two types of these voters come to mind. First, there were voters who were perfectly aware of Trump's shortcomings but so laser-focused on personal pet issues that they counted on Trump to address—such as banning abortions, restricting minority rights, or blocking supposedly Socialist Democratic policies— that they ignored the peril and damage caused by Trump. Second, there were citizens who voted straight-ticket for the Republican Party label without much thought, simply because they had always so voted. "Party loyalty," they called this behavior, and they imagined it to be responsible and respectable civic engagement. But what is *party loyalty* but a fancy name for passivity, a weak will, a closed mind, and a wish for others to think for one on Election Day?

Heroes: The health-care workers who worked themselves to skeletons in saving people from COVID-19 death and disability. These selfless people deserve lionizing from everybody, and they undoubtedly lowered the COVID-19 death and long-term disability rates.

Villains: Willful violators of COVID-19 health guidelines, including rejecters of vaccinations and antimask "freedom fighters," who imagined that recklessly ignoring safety was a mark of freedom from tyranny. As self-absorbed as Donald Trump himself, they spared not a thought for the people they would infect, the hospitals and health-care workers they would overburden, or the people needing emergency surgery that they would crowd out of hospitals. These miscreants serve as a reservoir that enables the COVID-19 virus to mutate and form new strains, complicating immunization efforts around the world. This is not personal liberty at all; it is merely insolent swagger or solipsism that does not accept other people's existence. These people are bereft of any thought, word, or deed that would disturb the repose of a despot.

Heroes: The scientists who selflessly went into overdrive to develop COVID-19 vaccines to tamp down this pandemic and the scientists employed by the Trump administration who tried, in most frustrating circumstances, to inform the public about this disease.

Villains: Trump administration officials who spread disinformation about the COVID-19 pandemic and muzzled those who wished to tell the truth to the public.

Heroes: Law enforcement officers who put themselves at risk and sometimes got themselves harmed or killed to protect lawmakers and clear the Capitol Building during the January 6, 2021, riot. Also heroes are law enforcement officers who did their best, with no bias, to keep rival demonstrators apart and peaceful.

Villains: Law enforcement officers who wounded and murdered African Americans—long before and during Trump's tenure.

Dishonorable mentions: The cops and court officials who reinforced our double justice system by coming down hard on Black Lives Matter protestors but treating the January 6, 2021, Capitol Hill rioters with unbecoming and unprofessional gentleness.

Heroes: Black Lives Matter protesters who called the public's attention to ongoing injustices perpetrated against African American and other minority citizens.

Villains: Trump-supporting counterprotesters who got violent at protests—in some cases, to discredit the Black Lives Matter protests.

Dishonorable mentions: Violent Black Lives Matter protesters and violent hangers-on looking for a rumble. These individuals validated widespread prejudices concerning protestors generally.

Heroes: Legislators who repeatedly and vainly attempted to bring Donald Trump to account for his many crimes in office. Especially meritorious are the Republican legislators who defied their party leaders and voted on the side of truth and justice.

Villains: Republican legislators who blocked attempts to rein in Trump's criminal and treasonable behavior— mostly because they imagined they could use Trump and his manic cult followers to further their own careers at the expense of their country.

Heroes: Officials and legislators who ignored Trump's threats and blandishments and followed the law, counting state popular votes and electoral votes according to the law, not according to Trump, and certifying Joe Biden's election to the presidency. Other officials turned aside other Trump dictatorial demands, such as using government agencies to overturn the 2020 presidential election, prosecuting anti-Trump comedians, and shooting Black Lives Matter protestors. It is a sad day when doing what is expected or required makes one a hero, but given the overheated atmosphere endured by these officials, I have no doubt they served our country well.

Villains: Officials and legislators who took part in "voter fraud" legislative charades and frivolous legal actions,

the third- and fourth-rate attorneys who stayed rich
and busy by backing these actions, and the officials who
cooperated with Trump in his attempts to overturn the
2020 presidential election results.[9]

Heroes: Generals and retired defense secretaries—
including two Trump secretaries—who emphatically
disavowed military involvement in our political process,
thereby warning Trump away from any attempt to use
them for extraconstitutional means to preserve his
unholy administration.

Villains: Lieutenant General Michael Flynn, who
suggested that Trump declare martial law to clamp
down on "disputed" states in the 2020 presidential
election and force a change in the voting results. Also
villainous are the active and retired military personnel
who participated in the sacking of Capitol Hill on
January 6, 2021.

Heroes: Reputable, conscientious news outlets who fact-
checked themselves constantly and kept our orientation
true by keeping us posted on factual news.

Villains: So-called news outlets and individual
commentators who prostituted themselves to
Donald Trump and tried to gaslight the public with
disinformation.

Heroes: Nongovernmental organizations, such as the
American Civil Liberties Union, Common Cause,
the Southern Poverty Law Center, and more, who
channeled opposition to Trump's policies and sued to
block his actions.

Villains: White supremacist and conspiracy-theory
organizations, such as Proud Boys, QAnon, Oath

Keepers, and Three-Percenters, who worked independently or in tandem with each other to further Trump's illegal power plays and to prolong his incumbency.

Heroes: Teachers, law enforcement, fire fighters, food handlers, sanitation workers, and transportation workers who risked their own safety to keep the country going during the COVID-19 pandemic.

5. Historical Perspectives

Though the Trump administration is but a short time past, I believe that several historical conclusions can now be drawn.

During the first three years of Trump's single term, I debated with myself over where Trump should rank among presidents. That he would be very low I never doubted. His touted successes—the economy prior to 2020, the new confrontation with China, and the order to produce COVID-19 vaccines at record speed—appeared to me to be merely the orchestra conductor waving his baton in time to the music. These policies would have been implemented regardless of who was in office, and they required nothing but assent to what would have happened anyway. These were the attributes of a mediocre president. Trump's failures vastly overshadowed these small accomplishments.

The hundreds of thousands of lives lost because of his bungled COVID-19 response, his persistent and multipronged effort to reverse the 2020 election, and his encouragement of bigotry and dictatorship have convinced me that he is more unfit for a position of authority in a free society than any of his predecessors. In order to fact-check my analysis, I consulted the 2021 C-Span Presidential Historians Survey.[10] While I was in accord with this evaluation of Trump on most of the criteria, I take issue on a few of them.[11] I place Trump with or slightly below James Buchanan, at the bottom of the list.

For all our traditions of liberty and rule of law, I do not say, "Tyranny could never happen here." Authoritarianism did, in fact, happen here blatantly for minorities, especially blacks and Native Americans, for the first 350 years of our history. There is a large contingent of thoroughly disaffected Lost Cause Trump bitter-enders in our country. In many ways, they are reminiscent of the American Confederates after the Civil War and the Germans in the Weimar Republic after the Great War. Fed on lies and propaganda throughout their respective conflicts, rejecting all news sources that did not validate their illusions, all three groups "knew" for four years that their victory was inevitable and divinely ordained. Wholly unprepared for their defeat; attributing it to "unlawful" subterfuge by their opponents; thoroughly estranged from their own people and their own countries, whose new norms and moralities they could not digest; and pining for a mythical Edenic national past, all three groups employed violent terrorists in attempts to overthrow governments and regain ascendancy. They mired their lives in hatred, violence, revanchism, and Big Lies about stolen victories.

I have seen several instances of law enforcement openly sympathizing with the Trump-supporting bitter-ender terrorists. I feel the same uneasiness about this coddling of American right-wing extremists as I felt in Israel upon witnessing the way ultraorthodox Jews were allowed to manhandle the police at the Temple Mount (see chapter 11). This same right-wing bias in law enforcement was one of the main roads to the undoing of the German Weimar Republic.

But in an odd way, I feel that the Trump administration, for all the damage it caused, will have certain salutary effects on our country. The egregious bigotry, corruption, and injustice that characterized Trump's policies aroused resistance among the American general public—resistance that would not have materialized under a more subtle or benign administration. Conveniently coupled with the mass use of social media, which converted every injustice into nationwide headlines, and the COVID-19 pandemic, which cleared the air of everyday activities and focused public attention onto these headlines, this resistance significantly raised general awareness of the damage that a bad presidency can inflict on our country.

The vital role played by minorities, particularly African Americans, in the demise of this presidency made those minorities much more aware of their power and much more jealous of maintaining it. Having been treated recently to a Jim Crow president, they are much less likely to behave with cynicism or fatalism in future elections. They have been rendered more patriotic by this misadventure, which called their attention to the stake they have in the continued well-being of our country. By being allowed to participate actively in our civic life on an equal footing with everyone else, they can get the country to "love us back," as Doc Rivers, coach of the Philadelphia 76ers, put it. The country certainly owes them that much at least after what they did to save us all from another four-year Trump disaster.

Many people were made aware of the fact that real freedom is hard work. Our liberties require constant vigilance and active defense for their maintenance against would-be tyrants and against those who dislike effort and would rather coast through life as servants of a despot. Liberty and rule of law are never to be taken for granted; a dictatorship could steal upon us unless we stay informed about the issues and act vigorously in pursuing our freedoms. Simply remaining free of lies and moral degeneration, which are essential to tyrants, is a major undertaking. It is important to contact legislators and get civically involved. Voting intelligently in all elections is necessary for the preservation of our democracy.

We have gone through a bumpy ride over the last several years, and more bumpy years await us before we arrive at a smoother road. But I still have cautious hope. Though the Weimar German parallels and warnings are clear and ominous, there are many differences. Our population is ethnically and culturally much more heterogeneous than was Weimar Germany's and is much less apt to unite in support of a dictator who hails from one demographic group. The Weimar German right dominated all the significant power structures—businesses, churches, the police, the judiciary, the army, and universities. The Weimar German right brazenly murdered—often with impunity—"November criminals" who signed the Treaty of Versailles. The American right dominates only the Republican Party, though it has infiltrated other American institutions. But the American right lacks the political clout to murder "January criminals" who certified Joe Biden as president. The majority of the American public is accustomed to living under a liberal and democratic order; the Germans in the 1920s were neither practiced nor enthusiastic in exercising liberties. Around the United States, there arose a spirited resistance to the American right—coalescing into political action groups and nongovernmental organizations dedicated to the preservation of democracy and rule of law. This resistance contrasts favorably with the dispirited and divided resistance to the right in Weimar Germany by the centrist and leftist elements in their society. I have observed much intellectual and moral vitality among younger people, Democrats, and minority populations in America. These people are largely inhospitable to authoritarianism and bigotry. Over time, I believe they will have the strength and stamina to overcome the reactionary forces in our country, as their counterparts in Weimar Germany unfortunately did not. Thus, I am somewhat hopeful that at the end of these trials, we will be a better and stronger country for having passed this moral test. "The arc of the moral universe is long but it bends toward justice."[12]

CHAPTER 13

ENDINGS AND REFLECTIONS

Here I have arrived, and for all the hills and vales I have traversed, I can say that life has been worth living. Reflecting on my past, on my travels, and on the state of our society today, I am struck by how advantaged I have been. As a middle-class white American male, I have had to dig and delve on my own behalf many times, and I have been slapped down many times, but on the whole, I have thrived, largely due to opportunities that would have arrived much more tardily and reluctantly had I been another race, nationality, or gender. For this reason, I dare not grow too haughty over my achievements or overly confident of my character and personal liberty.

I have often reflected on the fact that I never raised a family. Perhaps I was too independent to be happy in such a situation. At any rate, I have somewhat compensated by trying to be a good person in the biblical sense and to avoid as much as possible the purposeless drift I have observed in many lifelong singles.

I have recently become a more involved "parent." During a trip that Frances and I took to Africa a couple of years ago, we visited the Lesedi School in Zimbabwe, which is privately financed since the governments of most African countries, including Zimbabwe, feel no obligation to serve their citizenry, for reasons cited in chapter 11. This school is near Victoria Falls, and we were given the option of donating money for its operation. I contribute to the educations of three children in this school:

Thandolwenkosi Zikhali (girl), Sibusiso Ndlevu (boy), and Monique Mudhliwevhu (girl). They are in elementary school, and I exchange messages with them for holidays, birthdays, and other occasions. I must confess a certain feeling of maladroitness in communicating with young children, but the British sponsor of my efforts reassures me I am doing just fine. I derive satisfaction from reading the letters and watching the intellectual growth of these children.

I don't know whether I will ever meet my children personally, as it is difficult to travel to a rural corner of a third-world country. Road Scholar, which brought me there in the first place, will be visiting different schools over the years in an effort to spread around the benefits of tourist compassion.

I will continue to fight for our country and its values because I believe they are worth defending. Our experiment consists in the construction, under a single government, of a society of laws and liberty that encompasses a wide variety of peoples diverse in race, national origin, religion, and many other attributes. Under normal historical circumstances, many of these groups would be at each other's throats, and some have little or no experience in representative, accountable government or rule of law. This is what is remarkable, and fragile, about our experiment. Nobody has done anything quite like this in the past, though some European countries are starting this experiment perforce as they accumulate refugees and immigrants from various parts of the world. The Roman Empire attempted this sort of a mix but failed; their liberty and rule of law did not survive.

This experiment has sparked resistance from the reactionary, closed-minded people in all countries so affected. But diversity and tolerance are our chief strengths; we all must move away from the obsolete blood-and-soil so-called patriotism that was responsible for the endless wars, death, and suffering during the last century. This tribal chauvinism defines what a great nation is not; it forces despotism, dependency, and degradation on all societies who embrace it.

My vision for a great nation is a harmonious conglomeration of variegated people working to provide maximum opportunity for each individual to realize his own potential however he wishes. But status must be achieved in the sweat of one's brow rather than in the stamps on one's birth certificate. Nations based on caste squander many of their resources in maintaining the caste system, and they are wary of change and innovation, for fear those might disrupt the castes. Nations that use all their human potential to the best advantage of the nation while allowing each individual to maximize his fulfillment will inevitably thrive. But in order for this equality of opportunity among different individuals to persist, there must be an overarching government to make sure everyone plays the game fairly. In the absence of such a supervisor, equality among groups is an unstable equilibrium: one group, unwittingly or wittingly, will come upon an excess of resources, making it stronger vis-à-vis the other groups. This same group will use its new strength to gather still more resources, continuing in a positive feedback loop until all other groups have been squeezed out of any resources at all. The result is yet another caste system. This is exactly what happened in our country with Americans of European ancestry prior to voting rights acts and other fair-play laws. This is exactly what happens with dominant tribes under African dictatorships today. To preserve stable relationships among groups, laws and society should strive to minimize the impact on policy of the inevitable forever-with-us bigots.

There are limits to my tolerance; while I advocate maximum freedom for all sorts of cultures, I hold that care must be taken to bar the importation of tendencies that would undermine our liberty and rule of law. Kinship-based practices, such as forced marriages, child brides, honor killings, mutilation of women and the barring of women from education, and collectivist group rights and morality, must be suppressed. Immigrant groups with a history of mutual enmity must be assiduously discouraged from continuing their old-country hostilities after arriving on our shores; this imported tribal warfare has marred our history all too often. A central task of the government is to prevent these tendencies from undermining our stability and our WEIRD political philosophy, which are essential to individual liberties and rule of law. Individual welfare and liberties should be top priority; each individual should be allowed to develop himself as long as he harms no one else.

One sign of national greatness is the willingness to evolve with changing times and to admit and try to correct past errors. This willingness to face change is especially vital in variegated, rapidly changing societies, such as ours. My patriotism is fortified by this willingness in the United States. Most Americans are by now secure enough to accept our warts along with our monuments. This willingness is reflected partly in the displays in the National Museum of the American Indian and the National Museum of African American History and Culture in Washington, DC. In both of these museums, revered Founding Father Thomas Jefferson is depicted as a thoroughgoing scoundrel—which, from the standpoint of red and black history, he most assuredly was. I am also gratified by the availability of literature that gives our country's history from minority perspectives. These books provide a complement to the standard-issue histories of our struggles and triumphs in the Civil War and the World Wars, as well as in the Depression and the periods of peace. By examining this literature,[1] I have upgraded my own perception of our history from the two-dimensional stage prop presented to me in grade school and high school to a fully developed three-dimensional history that values truth and portrays our entire nation. Admittedly, this literature is supremely painful to read—not because of any nationalistic insult I feel but because of the distress I derive from the atrocities committed against individual human beings simply because of their complexion, religion, national origin, or sexual identity. My motivation for this study springs partly from my natural curiosity, partly from my abhorrence of Donald Trump and his wish to reinstate the conditions that enabled these crimes, and partly from my long association with African American women, to whom I wish to do justice. This process is a necessary part of my education and maturation; that this material can be presented to the American public without arousing widespread anger and opposition is encouraging.

Unfortunately, there still exist pockets of resistance in America to this largeness of spirit. Some people still cling to the infantile notion that all faults must be hidden, as if any mention of them is an insult to the entire country and must be suppressed. These oppositionists are Americans shocked by the future, throwbacks to the 1920s (see chapter 10) who are not inclined to address any of the multitude of problems confronting our country, including COVID-19, climate change, firearms violence, systemic racism, wealth imbalance, and more. In fact, many of them are not disposed even to concede that these problems exist. Mulish, closed-minded unwillingness to leave comfort zones undoubtedly motivates the majority of them. But the white supremacist component of these oppositionists has recently been aroused into more than usual activity by the present ongoing repurposing of our country. Heretofore defined as a white, Christian, European-descent country, we have recently been transforming into a multiracial and multicultural society with room for all races, national origins, religions, genders, and sexual orientations. White supremacists, driven to fury by these demographic changes, constitute an especially toxic ingredient to this mix, inclined as they are to violence, hobbled as they are by failure to live well, and driven as they are by resentment, self-pity, and excuses.[2]

These oppositionists have recently been taking active steps to pervert our search for national renewal. While attempting to create political divisions to further their own careers, white supremacists and the Republicans who court their political support hypocritically decry serious study of our great national sins—slavery and the slaughter of Native Americans—as "too divisive." They even try to put legal restrictions on teaching and discussing our country's injustices past and present, labeling such studies as cancel culture or critical race theory to be assiduously avoided! *The 1776 Report*, pushed by the Trump administration,[3] was a feeble and laughable attempt to reinstate 1950s history classes, but it serves as a warning that we must be vigilant about maintaining the integrity of our educational system. This Republican effort to censor our education and our political dialogue is especially distressing to me; if we erase our past and cover it with kitschy tales like those taught to me in school and expressed in *The 1776 Report*, we erase ourselves. We lose sight of who we are, what made us that way, and how we can best move forward. We cease to be informed citizens and become feckless, credulous subjects incapable of thinking critically, participating effectively in our civic life, exercising our liberties under law, and devising solutions to our problems and vulnerable to disinformation and propaganda that make us ripe for exploitation by despots.

We can gain instruction and warning from watching what is happening in countries where people are taught censored history. Prominent among these countries is Turkey, which adamantly and shrilly refuses to admit the 1915 massacre of Armenians and to atone and correct for that monstrous injustice. Another country with this failing is Russia, which will not process the crimes of Joseph Stalin.[4] Needless to say, Turkey and Russia are not noted for internal freedom, enlightened public opinion, or moral leadership in the world.

It seems to me that the demographic repurposing mentioned above, which our nation and some other nations are now undergoing, constitute a Second Enlightenment. This is a necessary process, like the seventeenth- and eighteenth-century First Enlightenment. In both Enlightenments, old superstitions and prejudices were discarded, and a world view more compatible with modern reality was adopted. The First Enlightenment—born of the horrors of the religion-spawned Thirty Years' War (1618–1648); the musings of philosophers in that era; and the spread of commerce, literacy, and WEIRD psychology over Europe—broke the authority of clergy and princes and, over the centuries, gave rise to science, technology, and widespread literacy and popular, transparent, and accountable government. Less beholden to the church, people became more tolerant and less inclined to persecute one another over religious differences. This Enlightenment proceeded at different paces and at different times in different countries and reached varying degrees of completion. Indeed, in some countries, it barely occurred at all. But overall, it left the human race in a more advanced political and social state.

The severity of suffering during the long twentieth-century war from 1912 to 1994 resulted largely from perverted applications of First Enlightenment thought. Scientific Socialism on the left and scientific racism on the right, which had nothing to do with either science or Descartes's *Discourse on Scientific Method*, culminated in Stalin's millions of dead and Hitler's Holocaust, respectively. These so-called sciences merely added a veneer of First Enlightenment terminology to human tribal instincts that have been with us since the Pleistocene Age. The Second Enlightenment—which has arisen from the horrors of the long twentieth-century war, mass communication, social media, mass world travel, and the mixing in close proximity of people with varying backgrounds and ethnicity—is necessary to break people's thrall to ancient tribalism. In the United States, this Second Enlightenment is already well underway: today we regularly see newscasters on television, city administration officials, and corporate leaders who vary widely in gender, race, national origin, religion, and sexual identity. During my early life, this diversity would have been the occasion for angry calls to the station, and boycotts of sponsors. But the continued progress of our Second Enlightenment is by no means assured; there are plenty of headwinds already described. As our country, our neighborhoods, and our workplaces grow steadily more diverse, the success of this Second Enlightenment grows steadily more vital to our national survival; we cannot function as a society in the presence of constant intergroup hostility. It is all the more necessary that we be vigilant and active against those who want to restore the authority of the old caste clergy by denying our social problems and whitewashing our history.

I have recounted a life that could not have taken place in a society featuring masters and slaves, ignorance and caste, pride and prejudice. Though I have stumbled in spots, I hope this life has been a successful growth process. I have related my tours of the wreckage left by the Holocaust, the Cambodian massacre, the Vietnam War and the Communist experiment generally, the Armenian genocide, the two World Wars, and the American and South African apartheids. These man-made hells—which flourished in the absence of liberty; the suppression of character; and the ascendancy of lies, ignorance, and bigotry—underscore the importance of the success of the Second Enlightenment. This success will leave us a better and stronger nation.

My goal will be to aid and abet this Second Enlightenment as far as it is in my power to do so—in the United States and elsewhere in the world. In this way, I will be not only working to preserve liberties wherever I can but also doing my little bit to lend a helping hand to those who have always had to struggle harder than I did to achieve goals similar to mine. I must work out lingering bigotry in myself, given my belief that bigotry is in everyone's bones as a maladaptive leftover from ancient times. Overcoming one's own bigotry is not an accomplishment but a process, like becoming good or wise. Like the Second Enlightenment, it must be worked as a project over a lifetime, and it will never be totally completed.

NOTES

Introduction

1 For a beautiful illustration of the behavior of people lacking personal liberty but cursed by imposed freedom, see *The Future Is History: How Totalitarianism Reclaimed Russia* by Masha Gessen, published by Riverhead Books in 2017. This book outlines the lamentable tale of the Russian people's stumbling and fumbling journey from glasnost to Vladimir Putin.

2 There are dozens of Bible verses on this topic. I will cite a few of them: Ephesians 4:2, 1 Corinthians 13:4–8, Colossians 3:8, and Psalms 34:13.

3 An entertaining fictional account (no doubt based in fact) of Soviet dictator Josef Stalin's use of and attitude toward the corrupt, self-seeking Viktor Abakumov, head of counterintelligence in the Soviet Defense Ministry, can be found in chapter 20 of *The First Circle* by Aleksandr Solzhenitsyn, published by Bantam Books in 1969: "Give Us Back Capital Punishment, Josef Vissarionovich." Stalin's first act upon attaining the Communist Party general secretary title was to get personal control of the party's physical resources so he could decide who received rewards. His extensive use and rewarding of thieves and various other criminals are well documented in many Stalin biographies.

4 The relationships of cult leaders, such as Sun Myung Moon, Jim Jones, and Donald Trump, with their followers illustrate this method of control perfectly.

5 Examples of this phenomenon abound in history: the destruction of the Roman Republic by Julius Caesar and Caesar Augustus between 50 BC and 25 BC; the destruction of the German Weimar Republic by Adolf Hitler in 1933; and the destruction of Russian liberties by Vladimir Putin in the years from 2005 to 2015, to name just a few. These dictatorships were not forced upon the people; the overwhelming majority accepted the tyranny with relief. One could truly say these despotisms were established in response to disorders and incompetence. But I would rejoin that the scarcity of good

character and personal liberty among the people induced them to respond to their new freedom by acting to destroy that freedom. Lacking the personal liberty necessary to utilize their freedoms effectively and the good character necessary to conduct their personal lives passably without close supervision, did they not themselves create the chaos they deplored in excusing their new dictatorship?

6 Rick Shenkman, *Political Animals: How Our Stone-Age Brain Gets in the Way of Smart Politics* (Basic Books, 2016).

7 Joseph Henrich, *The WEIRDest People in the World: How the West Became Psychologically Peculiar and Particularly Prosperous* (New York: Farrar, Straus, and Giroux, 2020).

8 Jonathan F. Schulz, Duman Bahrami-Rad, Jonathan P. Beauchamp, and Joseph Henrich, "The Church, Intensive Kinship, and Global Psychological Variation," *Science* 366, no. 6466 (November 8, 2019): eeau5141, http://dx.doi.org/10.1126/science.aau5141. This article's analysis of different parts of the world suggests that Africa and the Middle East are the world's weakest areas for WEIRD thinking and strongest areas for kinship-based psychology. In my opinion, this correlates with massive amounts of what WEIRD people would call *corruption* in these parts of the world but what kinship-oriented people would regard as "serving one's family" (meritorious even when at the expense of the public good—see my musings in chapter 11).

9 For a detailed analysis of the relationship between racism and caste in the United States, see Isabel Wilkerson, *Caste: The Origins of Our Discontent* (New York: Random House, 2020).

Chapter 1

1 Isaiah 58:7, Matthew 25:35, and Matthew 25:36.

2 See Luke 21:1–4.

3 The White Rose Society, led by Hans and Sophie Scholl, is much too unsung now. The story of these incredibly brave and principled people is well told in *A Noble Treason: The Story of Sophie Scholl and the White Rose Revolt against Hitler* by Richard Hanser, published by Ignatius Press in 2012.

4 Sergei Magnitsky was a Russian lawyer who uncovered and investigated the plundering of the Russian government in a tax-fraud scheme by Russian dictator Vladimir Putin and other oligarchs. He was atrociously murdered by Putin's henchmen for his honesty and courage. His sad tale is recounted in *Red Notice: A True Story of High Finance, Murder, and One Man's Fight for Justice* by Bill Browder, published by Simon and Schuster Paperbacks in 2015.

5   Senator John McCain, a moral giant of our time, always put country first. Captured and imprisoned during the Vietnam War, he refused to leave his torture chamber until all his fellow prisoners were released. In his memoir, *The Restless Wave: Good Times, Just Causes, Great Fights, and Other Appreciations*, written with Mark Salter and published by Simon and Schuster in 2018, he recounts his political life, wherein he behaved heroically on other occasions: he lost a state primary election because he insisted on telling the truth to voters who preferred lies; he defended his political opponent, African American president Barak Obama, from conservative lies and slander; and he voted to retain health care for poor Americans, against the wishes of his party's hierarchs—an act of compassion for which Donald Trump never forgave him.

6   Russian dictator Vladimir Putin's criminal career is capably outlined in *The Man without a Face: The Unlikely Rise of Vladimir Putin* by Masha Gessen, published by Riverhead Books in 2014.

Chapter 2

1   Edith Sheffer, Asperger's Children: The Origins of Autism in Nazi Vienna (W. W. Norton and Company, 2018). Sheffer traces the evolution of the meaning of autism from the late nineteenth century onward and points out that its meaning shifted over time, not only due to scientific advances but also due to changes in public opinion of what was socially acceptable behavior.

2   Dennis Normile, "China's Childhood Experiment," *Science* 357, no. 6357 (September 22, 2017): 1227, citing Linda Richter, University of Witwatersrand, Johannesburg, South Africa.

3   Dennis Normile, "China's Childhood Experiment," *Science* 357, no. 6357 (September 22, 2017): 1228–9, citing Scott Rozelle, Stanford University, Palo Alto, California.

4   "The Wild Duck," *Four Great Plays by Henrik Ibsen*, trans. R. Farquharson Sharp (Bantam Dell, 1959), 253–358.

5   Dennis Normile, "China's Childhood Experiment," *Science* 357, no. 6357 (September 22, 2017): 1228–9, citing Scott Rozelle, Stanford University, Palo Alto, California.

6   J. D. Vance, *Hillbilly Elegy: A Memoir of a Family and Culture in Crisis* (Harper Collins, 2016).

Chapter 3

1 Capwell Wyckoff, The Mercer Boys in the Ghost Patrol (World Publishing Co., 1951).

2 Roy Chapman Andrews, *All about Dinosaurs* (Random House, 1956).

3 Frederick Pough, *All about Volcanoes and Earthquakes* (Random House, 1953).

4 Howard Pease, *The Jinx Ship* (Garden City, NY: Doubleday, 1947).

5 Lucy Fitch Perkins, *The Dutch Twins Primer* (Houghton, 1917).

6 Jane Porter, *Thaddeus of Warsaw* (1803). The Third Partition of Poland, the backdrop for this story, erased Poland from the map of Europe in 1795 as Poland was divided among the three great powers: Austria, Prussia, and Russia.

7 Sloan Wilson, "Crisis in Education," *Life* 44, no. 12 (March 24, 1958): 26–38. This is the first in a series of articles about this topic.

8 Glenn Wagner, "Gismo the Great," *Boys' Life* 46, no. 11 (November 1956): 74–5.

9 José Schorr, "You Be the Judge," *Saturday Evening Post* 230, no. 20 (November 16, 1957): 140. My search for this episode in this magazine turned up other misogynistic judicial rulings, such as a ruling that women could be barred from a golf course until evening because their slow, clumsy golfing would impede the male golfers or that single women could be barred from serving at a tavern because they did not have husbands to protect them from the perils of the job. But the ruling I cited wins first prize for chutzpah.

10 I suspect this well-known male behavior is a hangover from an earlier evolutionary state when physical beauty was associated with a healthy female organism who would provide the male with healthy offspring to continue his genetic line. Scars and other imperfections indicated a less healthy woman—a less propitious vessel for his genes. But after several thousand years of large, sedentary aggregates of humans, necessitating the acquisition of the traits defining good character, this male approach is neither morally appropriate nor efficacious.

Chapter 4

1 John Updike, Rabbit, Run (Random House, 1960); John Updike, Rabbit Redux (Alfred A. Knopf, 1971); John Updike, Rabbit Is Rich (Alfred A. Knopf, 1981); John Updike, Rabbit at Rest (Alfred A. Knopf, 1990).

2 Electrolytes are compounds that exist as dissociated positively and negatively charged ions, such as sodium chloride (table salt, $Na+$ $Cl-$). I varied the concentrations of the electrolytes in water solutions and plotted the electrical

resistance as a function of concentration. The results were as expected: electrical resistance rose as concentration diminished, since fewer charged ionic electrical current carriers were available in dilute solutions. Electrical resistance was higher for solutions of weak electrolytes, such as acetic acid (vinegar, CH_3COOH, which remains mostly as neutral molecules when dissolved in water), than for strong electrolytes, such as sodium chloride. This happens because of the greater concentration of electrical current carriers (ions) produced by strong electrolytes.

3   Simply put, the Hall effect is a voltage difference occurring across a strip of conducting material when an electrical current is run lengthwise through the strip and a magnetic field is applied to the strip, perpendicularly to the plane containing the strip. This is due to the fact that the magnetic field applies a force (Lorenz force) on the moving current carriers (electrons) in the strip. This Lorenz force is perpendicular to the motion of the electrons, pulling them to one side of the strip. This sideways force increases with the speed of the electrons and the intensity of the magnetic field. The excess of electrons on one side of the strip and the resulting deficiency of electrons on the other side cause the voltage difference across the strip; a galvanometer attached across the strip will detect a small electrical current.

I verified that the Hall effect occurred with copper and other metallic strips. Mr. Schump informed me of the anomalous Hall effect that would arise with strips of iron and other ferromagnetic materials. The anomalous Hall effect means the Hall voltage across an iron strip is in the opposite direction from the Hall voltages in other metal strips, with all other experimental conditions being the same. I verified and displayed this effect also in my exhibit.

For the chemical solutions, I measured the Hall effect voltage for varying concentrations of salt in water. Based on erroneous reasoning, I posited a Hall effect starting at zero for pure water, rising and topping out at a maximum and then decreasing as salt concentration increased. My data seemingly verified this dubious conclusion, but three factors corrupted my experiment. First, confirmation bias induced me to gather data that verified my ideas— an all-too-common mischief among scientists. Second, I often operated the tangent galvanometer improperly with the salt solutions; this compromised some of my data. Third, the fact that I was doing Hall effect measurements on a liquid strip of salt solution at all introduced a phenomenon I should have noted but did not. This phenomenon became apparent from the behavior of several dust motes floating on the surface of a few of my salt solutions. When the required current was applied to the solution and the required magnetic field appeared, the dust motes traveled circularly. I failed to understand that this circular motion was a perfect illustration of a magnetic field exerting a Lorenz sideways force on moving charged particles. Moving electrons and salt ions pulled sideways will travel in a circle, like swinging a ball on a string in a circle. The electrons and salt ions stirred the salt solution circularly, which in turn pushed the dust motes in circular paths. Thus, a whirlpool formed in the solution, pulling charged particles away from where they were pushed by the magnetic field and disrupting the Hall effect charged particle distribution that showed up so neatly in strips of solid metals. As salt concentration increased, so did the number of salt ions available to enlarge the whirlpool and so did the power of the whirlpool to counteract the Hall effect—possibly explaining the observed decrease in Hall current with added salt concentration. Contrary to Mr. Schump's standing advice, I did not note this dust mote behavior in my experimental results, and I did push ahead with my preordained theory. This is not the way to conduct science! Had I been more mature and knowledgeable, I would have noted this dust mote activity, figured out what was happening, and remarked on it in my display. But this complex whirlpool mechanism is extremely difficult to verify and quantify. This is probably why my subsequent searches of scientific literature for studies of the Hall effect on liquid conductive strips turned up nothing.

4 Naoto Nagaosa, Jairo Sinova, Shigeki Onoda, A. H. MacDonald, and N. P. Ong, "Anomalous Hall Effect," *Review of Modern Physics* 82 (May 13, 2010): 1539. This very extensive article points out that the anomalous Hall effect is anomalous not only in the direction of the current generated by the application of the perpendicular magnetic field but also in the intensity of the current and its behavior as the intensity of the magnetic field is varied. The article narrates the history of the controversy among proponents of various models used to explain the anomalous Hall effect. This controversy ran from the 1970s to the 2000s, but experimental work has been in progress for more than a century. The article summarizes the various theories advanced to explain this effect and the theoretical and experimental studies performed on different materials. Finally, the authors draw their own conclusions and suggest future experimental exploration paths for further understanding of the anomalous Hall effect.

5 William L. Shirer, *The Rise and Fall of the Third Reich* (Simon and Schuster, 1960).

6 J. D. Vance, *Hillbilly Elegy: A Memoir of a Family and Culture in Crisis* (Harper Collins, 2016).

7 People who harbor have-nots' revenge can bear their own hardships and failures stoically enough if they can manufacture sufficient excuses and scapegoats. But under no circumstances can they endure for one moment another person's success. Confronted with a successful individual, they expend all their energy not on bettering their own condition but on attempting to destroy the other person.

It is natural to feel envy and even occasional resentment toward people who outstrip us, even if we recognize the reasons. But I have spent some time pondering and researching the origin of the destructive acting out—the expending of energy and status to bring down a successful individual, coupled with unwillingness to help oneself. If this mindset is indeed envy, it is certainly a malignant form of it. Envy is usually mollified upon the attainment of the desired object, while have-nots' revenge usually cares not at all about this attainment. Have-nots' revenge is not about acquisition but about revenge—stopping at nothing short of divesting the other individual of his possession or status and sometimes going beyond that.

I see the following commonality in individuals afflicted with have-nots' revenge. These people are victims themselves—denizens of static, corrupt, oppressive caste societies that offer neither opportunity for betterment nor moral role models. People who behave this way have usually lived on the lower rungs of such societies for generations, more or less miserably—long enough that the very concepts of social, economic, and even physical mobility have disappeared. Being demeaned for so long, they have learned to feel dependent, hopeless, helpless, and insignificant in the face of life's challenges and vicissitudes. So foreign are striving and achievement to these people that instead of attributing someone's rise to hard work, they see shady dealings and violations of norms long established by the caste system. Having formed social bonds based on shared oppression and fatalism, members of low castes see their upwardly mobile colleague as a betrayer fracturing those bonds. An upwardly mobile member of an even lower caste is seen as a gate-crasher usurping scarce resources and status. Either scenario constitutes a violation of caste rules; fear, hatred, and resentment are likely to result. In her book *Caste: The Origins of Our Discontent*, published by Random House in 2020, Isabel Wilkerson notes a connection between caste life and this poisonous brand of envy. See chapter 16, "Last Place Anxiety: Trapped in a Flooded Basement," 238–44.

People of this psychology are particularly toxic to liberty and particularly congenial to tyranny since they share with the tyrant the desire to destroy people with personal liberty and character. An informal, and most likely subconscious, unholy alliance can thus form between the oppressors and the oppressed. The motivations for the ruin of good people are different for the tyrant and for his subjects who harbor have-nots' revenge, but the result is the same: the elimination of all those who could serve as pillars and exemplars for a free, dynamic society.

8 Alfred Lubrano, *Limbo: Blue-Collar Roots, White-Collar Dreams* (John Wiley and Sons, 2004).

Chapter 5

1   Dr. Marcia McNutt, head of the National Academy of Sciences and an accomplished geophysicist, recounted her university challenges in a recent article: Ellen Ruppel Shell, "Hurdling Obstacles," Science 353, no. 6295 (July 8, 2016): 116–9. Dr. McNutt described being brushed off by a physics professor, Dr. William H. Wright, who told her baldly that women come and go in the physics curriculum, but none ever finish. Later on, Dr. McNutt declined to write a testimonial honoring Dr. Wright upon his retirement. This story resonated with me. Dr. McNutt finished her undergraduate work in 1974, which put her several years behind me in school but still back far enough that she experienced the inequities of those dark ages before women's liberation took hold. During that era, she would have had to be an exceptional woman indeed to grind through a physics curriculum while withstanding the pressure from family and fellow students to find a husband and settle down to Ozzie and Harriet heaven in the suburbs. Clearly, Dr. McNutt has always been blessed with a copious amount of personal liberty, and she can serve as an example for women in this and all other eras.

   While my hat is off to Dr. McNutt, I would be interested to know more about Dr. Wright's background. If he came in prejudiced at the outset, then Dr. McNutt's action at his retirement was justified. But what if Dr. Wright had had sad experiences with unliberated female students back in the day? Did he commit time and effort to trying to mentor female physics majors only to have them leave physics after a year or two to drop out and get married or to study education or home economics while hunting for a man? If I had mentored several aspiring female physics students and seen my efforts wasted thus, I would have been just as cynical as Dr. Wright when yet another woman, a total stranger to me, showed up in my office to consult about majoring in physics.

   At Montana State University, I knew a physics student more familiar to Dr. Wright. She made sure we all understood she was a physics major, but before her junior year was out, she was married and had dropped out of school. Many years later, the Montana State University newsletter told the story of a female physics major who graduated with a 4.00 cumulative—president's list permanently. She was from a small Montana town appropriately called Wisdom. Her escape from the airless wife-and-mother orthodoxy was gratifying to me; I hope she has had a fulfilling career as a physicist.

2   *Paint Your Wagon* is a Broadway musical with book and lyrics by Alan J. Lerner and music by Frederick Loewe. Productions were performed on Broadway in 1951 and the West End in 1953.

3   Bernard B. Fall, *Viet-Nam Witness 1953–1966* (Praeger, 1966).

4   Saba Valadkhan, "Construction of a Minimal, Protein-Free Spliceosome,"
     Science 307, no. 5711 (February 11, 2005): 864.

Chapter 6

1   Harper Lee, To Kill a Mockingbird (J. B. Lippincott and Co., 1960).
2   William H. Whyte, *The Organization Man* (Simon and Schuster, 1956).
3   John 4:1–42.
4   See Tim Madigan, *The Burning: Massacre, Destruction, and the Tulsa Race Riot of 1921* (St. Martin's Press, 2001).
5   See David Grann, *Killers of the Flower Moon: The Osage Murders and the Birth of the FBI* (Doubleday, 2017).
6   See Victor Luckerson, "The Promise of Oklahoma: How the Push for Statehood Led a Beacon of Racial Progress to Oppression and Violence," *Smithsonian* 52, no. 1 (April 2021): 26–35. It probably didn't help that Oklahoma abutted on three Confederate-sympathizing states, making it convenient for segregationist whites to populate Oklahoma. Furthermore, Oklahoma became a state during the period around the turn of the twentieth century when southerners were feeling frisky in Congress and in the country at large. They more or less dominated policy in Congress, where southern Democrats held most of the committee chairs by virtue of seniority, and they were erecting statues all over the South commemorating their fallen Civil War "heroes"—statues that have become moral eyesores in the twenty-first century. The last vestiges of legal and social consideration for African Americans left over from Reconstruction were being extinguished everywhere at that time.
     Not many years after achieving statehood, Oklahoma became one of the source states from which African Americans fled during the Great Migration. See Isabel Wilkerson, *The Warmth of Other Suns: The Epic Story of America's Great Migration* (New York: Vintage Books, 2010).
7   Alan I. Leshner, "Student-Centered, Modernized Graduate STEM Education," *Science* 360, no. 6392 (June 1, 2018): 969–70.

Chapter 7

1   For one of myriads of articles deploring this sentiment, see Massimiano Bucchi and Federico Neresini, "Why Are People Hostile to Biotechnologies?" Science 304, no. 5678 (June 18, 2004): 1749.

2   For example, see the "Working Life" entry by Yumeng Mao, "What Industry Can Teach Academia," *Science* 365, no. 6459 (September 20, 2019): 1342. Mao describes some university science faculty members he encountered as imagining that they are the acme of their professions and that their positions are coveted by all worthwhile people. All industrial scientists supposedly wish they could enter academe but cannot pass muster at a university and have to settle for the second string: private industry careers. I sympathize with Mao, and I fully subscribe to his message, congruent as it is with my own adventures.

3   My proposal consisted of an experimental verification of a seafloor sedimentation rate model proposed by a couple of Dr. Van Andel's colleagues: W. H. Berger and G. R. Heath, "Vertical Mixing in Pelagic Sediments," *Journal of Marine Research* 26 (1968): 134–43.

4   This educational concept was promulgated by Carl Rogers at the Center for Studies of the Person in La Jolla, California, in 1969. His goal was to depart from the traditional schoolmaster approach of drilling students with rote memorization and instead stimulate their curiosity and get them to enjoy learning information deemed relevant. Rote learning was to be abolished or severely curtailed. Instruction was to be "child-centered," whatever that means. But aren't some memorizations necessary, such as multiplication tables, the alphabet, and word meanings?

Chapter 8

1   Ralph F. Keeling, "Recording Earth's Vital Signs," Science 319, no. 5871 (March 28, 2008): 1771–2.

2   David W. Griffith, Charles D. Keeling, J. Alexander Adams Jr., Peter R. Guenther, and Robert B. Bacastow, "Calculations of Carrier Gas Effects in Non-dispersive Infrared Analyzers. II. Comparisons with Experiment," *Tellus* 34, no. 4 (August 1982): 385–97.

3   Charles D. Keeling, J. Alexander Adams Jr., Carl A. Ekdahl Jr., and Peter R. Guenther, "Atmospheric Carbon Dioxide Variations at the South Pole," *Tellus* 28, no. 6 (December 1976): 552–64.

4   Robert B. Bacastow, Charles D. Keeling, J. Alexander Adams Jr., C. S. Wong, Tim P. Whorf, and David J. Moss, "Atmospheric Carbon Dioxide, the Southern Oscillation, and the Weak 1975 El Niño," *Science* 210, no. 4465 (October 13, 1980): 66–8.

5   Florian M. Schwandner, Michael R. Gunson, Charles E. Miller, Simon A. Carn, Annmarie Eldering, Thomas Krings, Kristal R. Verhulst, David S. Schimel, Hai M. Nguyen, David Crisp, Christopher W. O'Dell, Gregory

B. Osterman, Laura T. Iraci, and James R. Podolske, "Spaceborne Detection of Localized Carbon Dioxide Sources," *Science* 358, no. 6360 (October 13, 2017): 192.

6   This pressure may have diminished in most American workplaces since those far-off times, as foreign competition forced American firms to adopt more competitive and pragmatic practices.

Chapter 9

1   A death march in computer software development is a frantic all-out effort to complete an assignment in a seemingly impossible time frame. Day-and-night panic characterizes this work, and all other work is shoved aside to allow every available human body to participate fully. It can arise from external circumstances, such as the Gulf War, cited in the text; poor management that fails to plan for delivery deadlines; underestimation of an effort and subsequent commitment to a brazenly aggressive schedule; or other causes. Everybody is usually totally spent at the end. An excellent text describing the origins and traumas of death marches is Edward Yourdon, Death March: The Complete Software Developer's Guide (Prentice Hall, 2004).

Chapter 10

1   Inaugural address delivered to the University of St. Andrews on February 1, 1867.

2   Andrei Amalrik, *Will the Soviet Union Survive until 1984?* (Harper and Row, 1970).

3   One day God called down to Dmitri and said, "Dmitri, you have been a good man, so I would like to reward you. I will grant you one wish for anything you want."

Dmitri thought for a few seconds and then said, "All right, give me a cow."

Immediately, a cow appeared in Dmitri's barn. Then God called down to Sergei, Dmitri's neighbor, and said, "Sergei, you have been a good man like Dmitri, so I would like to grant you a wish also."

Without skipping a beat, Sergei exclaimed, "Kill Dmitri's cow!"

The moral and psychological pathology is plain. One would normally expect Sergei to say, "Give me a cow," "Give me two cows," or "Give me a houseboat" or whatever he feels would elevate his status satisfactorily. Instead, Sergei, lacking the concept of self-betterment and resentful of violators of his caste rules, forgoes the opportunity to ameliorate his own situation in order to bring down Dmitri. The cow itself is not at issue; what galls Sergei is Dmitri's intolerable behavior.

4   Dee Brown, *Bury My Heart at Wounded Knee: An Indian History of the American West* (Holt, Rinehart, and Winston, 1971).

5   Dorothy Rabinowitz, "A Darkness in Massachusetts," *Wall Street Journal*, January 30, 1995. A subsequent series of *Wall Street Journal* stories by Rabinowitz flesh out this gruesome tale. Also see "The Amirault Tragedy: Fort Hill Design" by Bob Chatelle.

6   The False Memory Syndrome Foundation is a Philadelphia-based nonprofit organization founded in 1992 by Peter and Pamela Freyd, who were traumatized by their daughter's false allegations of sexual abuse by them during her childhood. This organization has sponsored and enabled research about memory and its reliability. These people have done much to debunk the pop psychological concepts concerning traumatic memories and have led the way in exonerating those caught up in the childhood sexual abuse fad of the late twentieth century. I have invested in their cause over the years.

7   Aleksandr Solzhenitsyn, "Repentance and Self-Limitation in the Life of Nations," an essay in *From Under the Rubble* (Little, Brown, 1973).

8   An excellent account of this fiasco can be found in Margaret MacMillan, *Paris 1919: Six Months That Changed the World* (London: J. Murray, 2001).

9   The passage of this law was decades in the making via a determined, persistent, and resourceful set of people of low character waging political warfare against everyone not hailing from northwestern Europe. Not all were equally hard-line on this issue, and many were otherwise *progressive* in the sense of that word at the time: prolabor, pro–black rights, proenvironment, and so on. An excellent history of the various anti-immigration pressure groups and the symbiotic relationship of these groups with the bogus "science" of eugenics can be found in Daniel Okrent, *The Guarded Gate: Bigotry, Eugenics, and the Law That Kept Two Generations of Jews, Italians, and Other Immigrants out of America* (Scribner, 2019). The "scientific" basis for this law was later adapted by the Nazis as justification for their exterminations of Jews, Romany, Slavs, homosexuals, and others. Indeed, in his book *Mein Kampf,* Hitler approvingly cites this American policy as a model to be duplicated. Isabel Wilkerson's *Caste: The Origins of Our Discontent*, published by Random House in 2020, goes into more detail about how the Nazis used American racial practices as models for their 1935 Nuremberg Laws, which codified their racist policies.

   Okrent's book is also an excellent portrayal of the immature level of biological science from 1880 to 1924. The lack of good data, and the paucity of people trained to think rigorously in this area, left a space that was filled by an array of quacks and scribblers who passed themselves off as scientists. Some eugenics "scientists" simply advertised their own prejudices as scientific conclusions, forcing inconvenient facts into conformity with their preconceptions (an error repeated by many people today). Others knew they had to gather data and analyze it in order for their conclusions to qualify as scientific, but their data were improperly gathered, and their reasoning was shoddy. Still others rejected eugenics out of hand but lacked rigorous data sets to bolster their positions. The eugenics publications, which would never see print in a reputable modern scientific journal, were received enthusiastically in the 1920s by many intelligent and prominent people, who eventually used the "scientific" cachet as partial justification for the Johnson-Reed Act.

Scientists in later generations actually gathered good data, analyzed it, and concluded that the entire concept of eugenics was bogus, relying as it did on the discredited notion of a human racial hierarchy and on the erroneous idea that single genes determine such diffuse traits as willpower, criminal behavior, and intelligence.

10   A thorough account of the Greenwood massacre can be found in Tim Madigan, *The Burning: Massacre, Destruction, and the Tulsa Race Riot of 1921* (St. Martin's Press, 2001). This riot, often described at the end of the twentieth century as "America's Kristallnacht" (recalling the German-government-sponsored November 1938 riot against Jews), was intensified by the fact that many of the blacks were Great War veterans who had kept their weapons and, of course, their training. This black resistance resulted in many white casualties and, naturally, greatly increased white rage and ferocity. The Rosewood riot of 1923 was smaller in scale but just as deadly to the victims. Both towns had been quiet, predominantly black settlements; Greenwood even had a prosperous urban infrastructure consisting of doctors, lawyers, and a business district. Both riots were sparked by women of dubious character pointing at black males and charging, "Rape!" Both towns were destroyed during the riots. (I suspect that have-nots' revenge drove much of the violence in Greenwood, particularly among lower-caste whites. Tulsa was said to be a tinderbox just before the massacre, and I can think of no other source for such fury. Successful blacks have always been intolerable to less-than-successful whites, because these blacks have violated life's rules by leaving their designated caste. We see the same behavior today when working-class white male policemen harass and arrest blacks simply for owning a house or car that the cops deem too luxurious to be appropriate for the caste to which they have assigned blacks.)

I single out the Greenwood massacre as a defining moment for this era because it was the worst single white-on-black atrocity in US history, approximating in slaughter the sum total of the entire Red Summer of 1919.

11 The story of the Osage oil swindles and their aftermath is told in David Grann, *Killers of the Flower Moon: The Osage Murders and the Birth of the FBI* (Doubleday, 2017).

12 This embarrassing ceremony is recounted in Harold Holzer, "For the People," *Civil War Times* 58, no. 5 (October 2019): 38–45.

13 A fascinating irony regarding the race riots of the 1920s can be noted by contrasting these riots with the story of the 1903 Kishinev (then in the Russian Empire) pogrom against the Jews. See Steven J. Zipperstein, *Pogrom: Kishinev and the Tilt of History* (New York: Liverwright Publishing Corporation, 2018). This riot gave rise to a crescendo of outrage that washed around the world and was particularly intense in the United States.

The Kishinev story resonated for years, amplified by a gut-kicking poem by H. N. Bialik called "In the City of Slaughter." This affair moved a few Americans to draw parallels between Russian Jews and African Americans. According to Zipperstein, the National Association for the Advancement of Colored People was started by a couple of sympathetic Jews, Anna Strunsky and William Walling, at that time. And yet the irony! Situated halfway between the 1903 Kishinev pogrom and the 1938 German Kristallnacht anti-Jewish riots (which also drew worldwide condemnation and even some grumbling within Germany itself), the 1921 race riot that destroyed Greenwood was just as senseless as the Kishinev riot; the Greenwood casualty list was longer; and the Greenwood property destruction was greater. But not a line of poetry or a ripple of outrage proceeded from Greenwood for generations to come—only a few feeble local expressions of regret over the next few weeks, followed by decades of silence. This default is made clear by Tim Madigan at the end of his book—and please note the 2001 copyright date. Why this dereliction? Probably several causes gave rise to it. Only in recent decades have we Americans acquired the character to confess and redress the crimes of our own country with the same earnestness as we confess and redress the crimes of other countries. In the United States around that time, white atrocities against blacks were so commonplace that perhaps Greenwood was not considered newsworthy, even though it was one of the worst riots of its kind, consuming whites along with blacks. The menace of the Ku Klux Klan was undoubtedly sufficient to cow into silence those few who even heard of this atrocity, thus suppressing the story at its source. Besides, in the 1920s, it was generally accepted that Jews were more human and more deserving of consideration than African Americans. Finally, the exhausted moral numbness of the 1920s, brought on by the traumas of the Great War and the 1918–1921 influenza epidemic, cast a leaden blanket of indifference over public reaction to atrocities everywhere. Whatever the reasons for the contrast between the reaction to Greenwood and the reaction to Kishinev, this bestial Greenwood combination of murderous ethnic cleansing and an apathetic public served as an apt opening for this sordid interwar age and a grim preview of the Holocaust not far down the road.

14 An excellent account of this moral default is in Gordon Thomas and Max Morgan-Witts, *Voyage of the Damned: A Shocking True Story of Hope, Betrayal, and Nazi Terror* (New York: Stein and Day, 1974).

15 Marc Wortman, *1941: Fighting the Shadow War—a Divided America in a World at War* (Grove Atlantic, 2016).

16 An excellent account of the incompetence, silliness, and jumpiness leading up to the Great War is given in Christopher Clark's *The Sleepwalkers: How Europe Went to War in 1914*, published by Harper Perennial in 2014. For those who wonder about Clark's pro-Austrian and anti-Serbian tilt, there are many other competent histories of this period written in the last thirty years.

17 Thomas Pakenham's *The Scramble for Africa: The White Man's Conquest of the Dark Continent from 1876 to 1912*, published by Random House in 1991, offers a thorough and horrifying tale of the behavior of the Europeans in Africa in the decades leading up to the Great War. The psychology of Europeans at the time, and the effect of each African kerfuffle on European official and public opinion, is well documented, and it is easy to see how this ignoble steeplechase added to the European mutual rage as the years passed.

This scramble, in fact, was a dress rehearsal for the long war of the next century. The behavior of the Europeans toward African blacks constituted practice runs for the horrors the Europeans would later visit upon one another: forced-march displacement and extermination of entire populations, slave labor spiced with torture and starvation, economic pillage, and a hue and cry about "master races."

18 Columbia University professor William Archibald Dunning (1857–1922) led and personified the Southern usurpation of this history.

19 Eric Foner, *The Fiery Trial: Abraham Lincoln and American Slavery* (New York: W. W. Norton and Company, 2010). This book provides an excellent account of Lincoln's education, political evolution, and thoughts on the American Civil War.

20 Stephen Budiansky, "Dark Days in the Southland," *Civil War Times* 47, no. 6 (December 2008): 46–53. This is an account of John Richard Bennett's tour of the American South in 1865—well before the radical Republicans had the opportunity to "antagonize" the Southerners.

21 Ron Chernow, *Grant* (New York: Penguin Books, 2017).

22 Louis W. Koenig, "The Election That Got Away," *American Heritage* 11, no. 6 (October 1960).

23 In his work *The Souls of Black Folk*, W. E. B. DuBois cites white hostility to successful blacks in order to refute the argument that blacks can succeed

entirely unassisted. The extinction of Greenwood, Oklahoma, in 1921 entirely destroys this argument (see note 10).

Chapter 11

1   For the curious: Armenia, Australia, Austria, Azerbaijan, Bermuda, Botswana, Bulgaria, Cambodia, Canada, Chile, Czech Republic, Denmark, Estonia, Finland, France, Georgia, Germany, Greece, Hungary, Iceland, Ireland, Israel, Jordan, Kiribati, Laos, Latvia, Lithuania, Mexico, Myanmar (Burma), Netherlands, New Zealand, Norway, Palestinian Territories, Poland, Romania, Russia, Serbia, Slovakia, South Africa, Sweden, Thailand, United Kingdom, United States, Vietnam, Zambia, and Zimbabwe.

2   The British colonials in Africa were no lovers of liberty, but their behavior there, at least according to Thomas Pakenham, showed them to be the least bad of a host of bad actors. See *The Scramble for Africa: The White Man's Conquest of the Dark Continent from 1876 to 1912* by Thomas Pakenham, published by Random House in 1991. The bias of a British author is apparent here, but from all my sources, I can think of nothing the British did in Africa or elsewhere that remotely approaches the atrocious Belgian policy in the Belgian Congo, which resulted in millions of deaths and mutilations. This toll would be classed today as a genocide, and King Leopold II of Belgium, who had all the markings of a psychopath, would be regarded as a top-flight war criminal. This horror is recounted in more detail by Adam Hochschild in his book *King Leopold's Ghost: A Story of Greed, Terror, and Heroism in Colonial Africa*, published by Mariner Books in 1999. A fictional account of Belgian Congo's crimes is available in Joseph Conrad's classic novelette *Heart of Darkness*, which arrived on the scene a century prior to Hochschild's study. Both of these works give a true picture of the pith-helmeted European colonialists, which was unfortunately omitted from my sanitized school studies.

There were people with high character and personal liberty who took up the cause of the suffering black Congolese and who should inspire people everywhere and at all times. There were people of low character who supported King Leopold and permitted the "Great Forgetting" (Hochschild's phrase), which erased Congolese suffering from memory. Hochschild graphically lays out the struggle between these sets of characters. The Great Forgetting led to the utter failure of my history lessons in grade school and high school to mention the mass murders and slave labor in Africa, and to kitschy tracts about so-called benevolent European colonialists bringing "civilization" and

"Christian salvation" to the "savage" Africans. How many Americans still believe this bosh, never having been introduced to corrective accounts?

The Belgians were not alone; the almost equally depraved French behavior in the French Congo, the German massacre of the Herero in Southwest Africa, and wanton slaughter by Carl Peters in German East Africa also outdid the British in criminality. British crimes there were all right, but the British government rose above all this at times.

3   An excellent history of the ideologically driven slaughter in the Baltic states, Poland, Ukraine, Belarus, and Russia during the 1930s and 1940s is found in Timothy D. Snyder's *Bloodlands: Europe Between Hitler and Stalin*, published by Basic Books in 2010.

4   A good general primer on the modern phase of this history (since the 1967 Six-Day War) is Michael Oren's *Six Days of War: June 1967 and the Making of the Modern Middle East*, published by Oxford University Press in 2002.

5   *Wikipedia* informed me about the sad details of Hans Goslar's background and fate.

6   Freedom House is a US-government-funded nongovernmental organization that researches the state of democracy, political freedom, and human rights all around the world. It publishes an annual report on the level of political rights and individual liberties in each country in the world, rating each of these two parameters on a scale of 1 (most free) to 7 (least free).

7   See Tariq Dana, "Corruption in Palestine: A Self-Enforcing System," Al-Shabaka, the Palestinian Policy Network, August 18, 2015. Dana calls the Palestinian approach to government "patron-clientelism," which sounds exactly like an old-fashioned crony system. Also see Jonathan F. Schulz, Duman Bahrami-Rad, Jonathan P. Beauchamp, and Joseph Henrich, "The Church, Intensive Kinship, and Global Psychological Variation," *Science* 366, no. 6466 (November 8, 2019): eeau5141. This article states that kinship psychology is strong throughout the Middle East. Perhaps some of the rampant Palestinian corruption stems from this psychology—serving one's relatives and tribe at the expense of all else.

8   A definitive account of the first conflict between Azerbaijan and Armenia can be found in Thomas de Waal's *Black Garden: Armenia and Azerbaijan through Peace and War*, published by New York University Press in 2013. *Wikipedia* supplied me with the account of the second Azerbaijan-Armenia war.

9   See the telegram from Ho Chi Minh to President Harry Truman on February 28, 1946.

10 See the telegram from Jefferson Caffery, US ambassador to France, to Secretary of State Edward R. Stettinius on March 13, 1945. From Office of the Historian, *Foreign Relations of the United States: Diplomatic Papers, 1945, the British Commonwealth, the Far East*, vol. 6, document 175. De Gaulle

could not understand American policy, so he said. The Russians were moving apace into Europe, perhaps to occupy western Germany and then France. If the French public realized the Americans opposed the French in Indochina, the French public would be terrifically disappointed, and where would that lead? Did the Americans really want France to become part of the Russian Empire? "We do not want to become Communist," said de Gaulle, "and we hope you do not push us there."

This lecture does not hold together, either logically or militarily. If the Russians had pushed too far west into Europe in 1945, the remedy would have been to move US troops into Europe to counter that threat directly, not to involve ourselves in a fantastic Far East adventure to prop up a dead empire. Would the French really have permitted the Russians to occupy their soil and dictate their policy just because we allowed their obsolete empire to die a timely death? Had we answered this French appeal properly—with a derisive snort—we would have saved ourselves much trouble in Southeast Asia in future decades!

11 The egregious folly of racism as a guide to foreign policy is well described in Margaret MacMillan, *Paris 1919: Six Months That Changed the World* (London: J. Murray, 2001). MacMillan posits that the refusal of the European powers to treat the Japanese on an equal footing with themselves, due to racial prejudice, was the beginning of the journey to the Japanese attack on Pearl Harbor in 1941. Likewise, our high-handed treatment of the Vietnamese in the late 1940s was a first step toward our humiliation there a generation later.

12 See Michael Keen, "Lost Opportunities for Peace: Vietnam 1945–1950," Senior Division Historical Paper, United States Army Center of Military History.

13 See Elizabeth Becker, *Bophana: Love in the Time of the Khmer Rouge* (Cambodian Daily Press, 2010). Bophana's story was reconstructed by Elizabeth Becker from records recovered at Tuol Sleng. *Wikipedia* has supplemented my material on this topic.

14 For a good account of Cambodia's tortured twentieth-century history, see Philip Short, *Pol Pot: The History of a Nightmare* (London: John Murray, 2004).

15 Abby Seiff, "At a Cambodian Lake, a Crisis Unfolds," *New York Times*, September 30, 2019.

16 "The Vietnamese plant the rice, the Cambodians watch the rice grow, the Lao listen to the rice grow" is a well-known French comment on the differences among the three countries as to pace of life and attitude toward hard work. This remark jibes with my personal observations and stories I have heard about the laid-back Laotians and Cambodians as opposed to the industrious

Vietnamese. This is admittedly a generalization, but it is based on data I possess at present.

17 See Thomas Pakenham, *The Scramble for Africa: The White Man's Conquest of the Dark Continent from 1876 to 1912* (Random House, 1991). The crusade against slavery became more and more hypocritical as the nineteenth century wore on, and European colonial powers found that their rivalries, and the extraction of minerals, crops, and ivory from Africa, left little room for moral striving as to slavery. With a few notable and noble exceptions, the Europeans continued to pay mere lip service to the ending of the slave traffic—lip service intended mainly as a club with which to beat their economic rivals, the Middle Eastern slave traffickers. European actions against the Middle Easterners were mainly designed to prevent their disruption of European colonial enterprises and not to provide succor to African slaves.

18 See Thomas Pakenham, *The Scramble for Africa: The White Man's Conquest of the Dark Continent from 1876 to 1912* (Random House, 1991), 579.

19 Jonathan F. Schulz, Duman Bahrami-Rad, Jonathan P. Beauchamp, and Joseph Henrich, "The Church, Intensive Kinship, and Global Psychological Variation," *Science* 366, no. 6466 (November 8, 2019): eeau5141, http://dx.doi.org/10.1126/science.aau5141. This article delves into the psychology of kinship-based societies, such as those found extensively in Africa. The authors assert that service to family and tribe, and the subordination of all else to this service, dominates the ethical perceptions of African officialdom. I feel this ethic contributes much to the nepotism, theft of public resources, merchandising of office positions, and other corrupt practices that cause so much grief in Africa.

Chapter 12

1 The books I have read about Trump voters and how Trump came into his undeserved position include Tim Alberta, American Carnage: On the Front Lines of the Republican Civil War and the Rise of President Donald Trump (New York: HarperCollins, 2019); Jonathan M. Metzl, Dying of Whiteness: How the Politics of Racial Resentment Is Killing America's Heartland (New York: Basic Books, Hachette Book Group, 2019); Timothy P. Carney, Alienated America: Why Some Places Thrive While Others Collapse (New York: HarperCollins, 2019); Alfred Lubrano, Limbo: Blue-Collar Roots, White-Collar Dreams (John Wiley and Sons, 2004); and J. D. Vance, Hillbilly Elegy: A Memoir of a Family and Culture in Crisis (HarperCollins, 2016). I also heard and read numerous news articles online, in newspapers, and in television throughout 2016 and beyond.

2 See the following personal memoirs: Mary L. Trump, PhD, *Too Much and Never Enough: How My Family Created the World's Most Dangerous Man* (New York: Simon and Schuster, 2020); and Michael Cohen, *Disloyal: The True Story of the Personal Attorney to President Donald J. Trump* (Skyhorse Publishing, 2020). While it is true that Cohen was dishonest and has been prosecuted for it, I can credit his account because it is corroborated by other sources and because his devotion to his family clearly made his loved ones influential in persuading him to come clean and start a new life. Of particular note is his father, Maurice Cohen, a Holocaust survivor, who played a conspicuous role in the reform of his son.

3 The statistics relevant to the devolution of the Republican Party are summarized in Chris Cillizza, "The Republican Party Isn't Who You Think It Is," *The Point*, CNN Politics, June 5, 2019. According to this article, the demographic shift in the Republican Party from primarily college-educated white-collar suburban whites who identify with Reagans, McCains, Bushes, and Romneys to primarily semieducated white voters who embrace Donald Trump was well underway by 2010. Also see Stuart Stevens, *It Was All a Lie: How the Republican Party Became Donald Trump* (Knopf, 2020).

4 This great paradox—Americans using their votes to sabotage their own best interests in order to vent their cultural grievances—is discussed in many books. On this topic, I have read Jonathan M. Metzl, *Dying of Whiteness: How the Politics of Racial Resentment Is Killing America's Heartland* (New York: Basic Books, Hachette Book Group, 2019); and Timothy P. Carney, *Alienated America: Why Some Places Thrive While Others Collapse* (New York: HarperCollins, 2019).

5 Joseph Henrich, *The WEIRDest People in the World: How the West Became Psychologically Peculiar and Particularly Prosperous* (New York: Farrar, Straus, and Giroux, 2020); and Jonathan F. Schulz, Duman Bahrami-Rad, Jonathan P. Beauchamp, and Joseph Henrich, "The Church, Intensive Kinship, and Global Psychological Variation," *Science* 366, no. 6466 (November 8, 2019): eeau5141, http://dx.doi.org/10.1126/science.aau5141.

6 See Timothy P. Carney, *Alienated America: Why Some Places Thrive While Others Collapse* (New York: HarperCollins, 2019). Also see Isabel Wilkerson, *Caste: The Origins of Our Discontent* (New York: Random House, 2020).

7 See Timothy P. Carney, *Alienated America: Why Some Places Thrive While Others Collapse* (New York: HarperCollins, 2019). J. D. Vance's *Hillbilly Elegy: A Memoir of a Family and Culture in Crisis*, published by Harper Collins in 2016, gives a good practical overview of a life background that can produce these lost souls.

8   Fabiola Cineas and Anna North, "We Need to Talk about the White People Who Voted for Donald Trump," *Vox*, November 7, 2020. While I admit that misogyny may have driven many of these men to vote against Hillary Clinton and for Donald Trump in 2016, I will give them the benefit of the doubt, because anything that spared us a second Trump term was urgently needed.

9   Books outlining the history of the attempt to steal the 2020 presidential election include Carol Leonnig and Philip Rucker, *I Alone Can Fix It: Donald J. Trump's Catastrophic Final Year* (New York: Penguin Press, 2021); Michael Wolff, *Landslide: The Final Days of the Trump Presidency* (New York: Henry Holt and Company, 2021); and Michael C. Bender, *Frankly, We Did Win This Election: The Inside Story of How Trump Lost* (New York: Grand Central Publishing, Hachette Book Group, 2021). As we speak, more tales of this criminality are being revealed in the testimony of witnesses before various investigating bodies.

10   Online address is https://www.c-span.org/presidentsurvey2021.

11   Trump was fourth from the bottom in this analysis—virtually tied with Franklin Pierce and ahead of Andrew Johnson and James Buchanan. The C-Span historians gave Trump his highest marks in the categories of "Economic Management," "Public Persuasion," and "Vision/Setting an Agenda." I believe those were indeed Trump's strongest suits, and his economic management was rightly graded as mediocre. But I felt the other two were wide of the mark. Trump certainly was a persuader and a setter of an agenda, but some weight must be given to the direction of the persuasion and the contents of the agenda. Hitler and Stalin were both world-class in these categories, but this hardly makes them positive historical figures.

12   Dr. Martin Luther King Jr., "Remaining Awake through a Great Revolution," speech given at the National Cathedral, March 31, 1968.

Chapter 13

1   A few examples of my readings include Dee Brown, Bury My Heart at Wounded Knee: An Indian History of the American West (Holt, Rinehart, and Winston, 1971); Tim Madigan, The Burning: Massacre, Destruction, and the Tulsa Race Riot of 1921 (St. Martin's Press, 2001); David Grann, Killers of the Flower Moon: The Osage Murders and the Birth of the FBI (Doubleday, 2017); W. E. B. DuBois, The Souls of Black Folk (1903); David Zucchino, Wilmington's Lie: The Murderous Coup of 1898 the Rise of White Supremacy (New York: Atlantic Monthly Press, 2020); and Isabel

Wilkerson, The Warmth of Other Suns: The Epic Story of America's Great Migration (New York: Vintage Books, 2010).

2   The white "master race" has always been an important refuge for a wide variety of failed people, and it is no coincidence that white supremacists draw their adherents mainly from the less-than-wildly-successful elements of society. However, the white supremacist mob that sacked the US Capitol on January 6, 2021, contained, in addition to the usual futile rabble bemoaned in many of my source books, a few ostensibly successful people: CEOs, military veterans, lawyers, police officers, and more. But I maintain that all of them still must have had egregious failings. It simply does not make sense to me that a prosperous, psychologically robust individual with everything to lose would jeopardize his future—or his life—by participating in such a destructive and quixotic mission.

An article by Patrick Tucker in *Defense One*, "Why Do People Join ISIS? Here's What They Say When You Ask Them" (December 8, 2015), lists nine motivations that can drive ISIS fighters. I believe this research could be profitably conducted on the Capitol Hill rioters and on white supremacists generally. The specific pathology that I believe animates these rioters—fear and loathing of the increasing potency and potential of Americans who are not white, Christian, and heterosexual—could translate into at least six of these nine motivations. And certainly, many of these motivations are indifferent to socioeconomic status; they can afflict lawyers and realtors along with alienated dropouts.

3   Recently scotched by Joe Biden, this report recommends so-called patriotic education as a replacement for substantive and educational history. This patriotic-education treatise reads just like the old history texts I endured sixty years ago—apotheosizing the Founding Fathers, accepting the discredited Southern-imposed Dunning school of our Civil War and Reconstruction, omitting all mention of blemishes on US history, glossing over the roles played by nonwhites, and painting a rosy picture of unending progress. It would be a terrible tragedy for us to go back to that mindless and mind-numbing history course material that was so long on propaganda and so short on training for critical, mature thinking. This report does call for the careful study of the high-minded principles that serve as national goals, if not guides for actions—a vital component of any study of US history.

4   In chapter 11, I mentioned the shameful discouragement of Armenian memorials in Washington, DC, in the past by the US government in order to appease our authoritarian Turkish allies.

In Anne Applebaum's book *Gulag: A History*, published by Doubleday in 2003, one of her last chapters, "Memory," relates her travels in Russia, where she canvassed ordinary Russians concerning Stalin's brutality. Only a small minority showed interest in drawing lessons from the Stalin era. The largest segment of the interviewees simply shrugged and offered no thoughts on the matter. Others replied, "Stay out of our internal affairs!" or "That is too long ago. We have different problems now."

Printed in the United States
by Baker & Taylor Publisher Services